HEAR THAT LONESOME
WHISTLE BLOW

Dee Brown spent the early part of his life in the lumber
camps and oil fields of the American South West. He
has worked as a printer, a journalist and a librarian,
and has published numerous books, mostly non-
fiction, dealing with the history of the American West.

ALSO BY DEE BROWN

Non-Fiction

The Westerners
Bury My Heart at Wounded Knee
The Year of the Century: 1876
The Gentle Tamers
Grierson's Raid
The Galvanized Yankees
Fort Phil Kearny
The Bold Cavaliers
Pawnee, Blackfoot, and Cheyenne
Tales of the Warrior Ants
Wondrous Times on the Frontier
The American West

Fiction

Action at Beecher Island
The Girl from Fort Wicked
Yellowhorse
Cavalry Scout
Showdown at Little Bighorn
They Went Thataway
Killdeer Mountain
The Way to Bright Star
Wave High the Banner

With Martin F. Schmitt

The Fighting Indians of the West
Trail Driving Days
The Settler's West

Dee Brown

HEAR THAT LONESOME WHISTLE BLOW

Railroads in the West

VINTAGE

Published by Vintage 2002

1 3 5 7 9 10 8 6 4 2

First published in Great Britain in 1978 by
Chatto & Windus

Vintage
Random House, 20 Vauxhall Bridge Road,
London SW1V 2SA

Random House Australia (Pty) Limited
20 Alfred Street, Milsons Point, Sydney,
New South Wales 2061, Australia

Random House New Zealand Limited
18 Poland Road, Glenfield,
Auckland 10, New Zealand

Random House (Pty) Limited
Endulini, 5a Jubilee Road, Parktown 2193, South Africa

The Random House Group Limited Reg. No. 954009
www.randomhouse.co.uk

A CIP catalogue record for this book
is available from the British Library

ISBN 0 09 944074 1

Papers used by Random House are natural, recyclable
products made from wood grown in sustainable forests.
The manufacturing processes conform to the environmental
regulations of the country of origin.

Printed and bound in Great Britain by
Cox & Wyman Ltd, Reading, Berkshire

···❦ **CONTENTS** ❦···

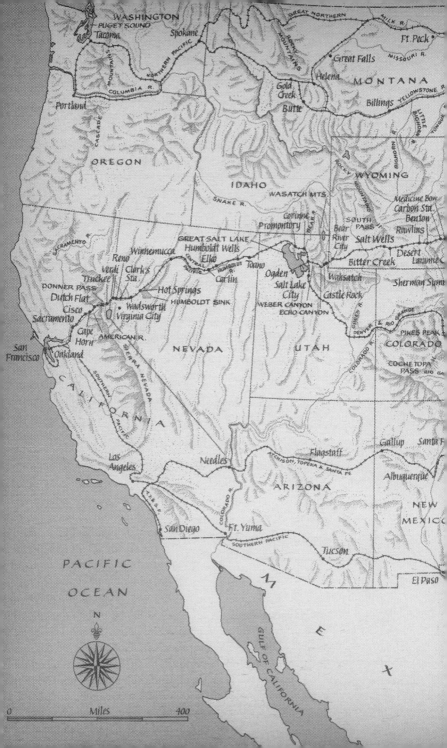

TRANSCONTINENTAL RAILROADS

We do not ride on the railroad; it rides upon us. Did you ever think what those sleepers are that underlie the railroad? Each one is a man, an Irishman, or a Yankee man.

—THOREAU

·◄❧ CHAPTER 1 ❧►·

The Iron Horse Comes to the Waters
of the Mighty Mississippi

"**A**MID THE ACCLAMATIONS of a multitude that no man could number, and the roar of artillery, making the very heavens tremble, punctual to the moment, the Iron Horse appeared in sight, rolling with a slow yet mighty motion to the depot. After him followed a train of six passenger cars crammed to the utmost with proud and joyful guests, with waving flags and handkerchiefs, and whose glad voices re-echoed back the roar of greeting with which they were received. Then came another locomotive and train of five passenger cars, equally crowded and decorated. This splendid pageant came to a stop in front of the depot, and the united cheers of the whole proclaimed to the world that the end was attained, and the Chicago & Rock Island Railroad was opened through for travel and business."

In 1854 many Americans were alive who had been born in the lifetime of George Washington, and celebrations of his birthday were still occasions of patriotic rejoicing and respect. That was why the builders of the first railroad from the East to reach the Mississippi River seized upon February 22 as the day to celebrate the "nuptial feast of the great Atlantic Ocean to the mighty Father of Waters." The track layers worked overtime to complete the final link, and the last rail was spiked to the ties only an hour before the Chicago & Rock Island's Locomotive No. 10, decorated with wreaths, garlands, and patriotic bunting, came whistling into view of the great river.

Rock Island, Illinois, was a town of between four and five thousand, a rival of Davenport across on the Iowa bank. The towns lived off steamboating, and numerous citizens of both communities hated railroads because of their threat to the thriving steamboat monopoly that dominated the Missis-

1

sippi and its tributaries. It had been the same back in the East—rivermen, canalers, and wagoners all feared and hated the railroads that kept moving westward. And now at Rock Island the iron tracks had reached the river heart of the republic. The Iron Horse was the marvel of the age, a metal monster panting as though energized with the forces of life, exhaling steam and smoke, its centered oil headlight reminding some observers of the one-eyed cannibal giants of Homer—the Cyclopes. To those more familiar with biblical references, the engine was Behemoth, its bones strong pieces of brass and bars of iron, and it could draw up the Mississippi into its mouth.

The presence of Locomotive No. 10 on the bank of the great river that day portended more than any man or woman there could have dreamed of. Its Cyclopean eye faced westward to the undulating land that flowed into a grassed horizon and curved over the limitless expanse of the Great Plains a thousand miles to a harsh upthrust of Shining Mountains, the Rockies, and then down to the Western Sea—that goal of European wanderers and seekers across North America for three centuries, the great ocean that Ferdinand Magellan named the Pacific.

Since the coming of the Europeans, the pioneers pushing always westward had been bound by waterways; the settlements they built were strung along the water routes like successive beads. Beyond the Mississippi, the Missouri River was the way West. Since Lewis and Clark, traders had marked overland trails to Santa Fe for trade with the Spaniards, to Oregon for furs, and to California for gold. Yet, compared to river commerce, the overland wagon caravans were insignificant. Away from the rivers few towns flourished. The American West was a vast and virginal land, awesome, beautiful, unbounded, and filled with immeasurable riches above and below the ground. Its ecosystem was a delicate balance of animals, grasses, shrubs, trees, and streams, with several dozen native civilizations—the American Indian tribes—blending into the whole. Even as late as the middle of the nineteenth century, the white invaders had brought no more change to the Western land than might have been accomplished by a handful of ants. Their puny wagon trains and

On Washington's Birthday 1854, Americans celebrated the arrival of this Rock Island passenger train at the banks of the Mississippi River. (Illinois State Historical Library)

their steamboats struggling against the Missouri currents left but slight traces of their passage. Even in the California goldfields, the seekers of wealth were as pygmies in a giant's land, building and abandoning camps in their restless searches, the wounded earth healing itself behind them.

Only the demonic power of the Iron Horse and its bands of iron track could conquer the West, and on this cold sunlit February day in 1854, Locomotive No. 10 stood on the edge of the frontier, softly breathing smoke and steam while its load of rejoicing passengers detrained to celebrate. An awaiting group of musicians struck up "Hail, Columbia," and the local dignitaries and those who had come from the East pushed into the spacious new depot where banquet tables awaited them.

The speakers that day were well aware that the occasion they celebrated was epochal. The human race had moved itself another notch forward in its long quest for the Western Sea. "If the roar of artillery and the scream of the Iron Horse which are now awakening the echoes of the Mississippi

Valley," said one, "could alone awaken the spirits of departed pioneers, what would they now behold! In the place of the immigrant wagon, conveying his single family, he would witness a vehicle conveying a family of cities, and drawn by an agent more powerful than Behemoth himself. He would be told that where he took months to perform his journey it was now done in a less number of days." Numerous references were made to the "iron steed" following the Star of Empire, to bands of iron binding ocean to river, and to the marking of an era in the history of the world's progress. One speaker compared the event to Venice's annual espousal with the Adriatic in celebration of that city's commercial prosperity.

As was the custom of the times, toasts were offered to everybody from George Washington down to the lowliest local politician. They toasted "the Press, the Telegraph and the Steam Engine, the three levers which move the world of modern civilization." The governor of Illinois toasted his state and eulogized the West, predicting that "the child is now living who will see this continent inhabited by four hundred millions of people, three hundred millions of which will be found in the Mississippi Valley." Fortunately, the governor was wrong; otherwise, his descendants in the late twentieth century would be living under population conditions similar to those of Asia. For years, however, the opening of new railroads would inspire politicians to orate upon the glories of unlimited growth.

After each toast, a man stationed near the depot entrance would signal the engineer on the Iron Horse outside to applaud with an ear-splitting blast from the whistle. And then the lively brass band would follow with a few bars from its favorite new march tune, "The Railroad Quickstep."

Excepting the long-winded and now long-forgotten politicians, the hero of the day was Henry Farnam, a forty-nine-year-old Easterner who had brought the first railroad into Chicago two years earlier and who was largely responsible for the building of the Chicago & Rock Island. A descendant of New England pioneers, Farnam was an earnest, strong-jawed, clear-eyed man who believed in honesty and hard work. Like the youthful Abraham Lincoln, he had read and

Henry Farnam
(Illinois State Historical Library)

*Thomas Clark Durant, skillful pro-
moter of Western railroad stocks and
bonds (Leonard Railroad Collection,
University of Iowa Libraries)*

*Samuel Benedict Reed, railroad construction engineer
(Photo by A. J. Russell, The Oakland Museum)*

studied by the dancing light of an open fireplace. After teaching himself mathematics he became a surveyor, got into canal building, and then foresaw the future and switched to railroads.

In the Rock Island depot that evening when Farnam was called upon to speak, he responded briefly, giving his associates most of the credit for completion of the railroad and expressing mild amazement over the rapidity with which the Iron Horse had crossed half the continent. Among his associates were four men whose names would become well known to most Americans during the next decade, when the building of the first transcontinental railroad attracted national attention. They were Thomas Clark Durant, skillful promoter of stocks and bonds; Peter Anthony Dey, surveyor and locating engineer; Grenville Mellen Dodge, who was Dey's assistant; and Samuel Benedict Reed, construction engineer. They all were vigorous young men, their ages ranging from the early twenties to middle thirties, and like Farnam they were Easterners from New England and New York State. Together they possessed a store of hard experience at canal and railroad building and financing. Dey and Dodge were already in Iowa, surveying a line westward, and Durant was negotiating for stock sales and land grants to construct a railroad from Davenport on the Mississippi to Council Bluffs on the Missouri. Soon they would change the name of the Chicago & Rock Island to the Chicago, Rock Island & *Pacific* Railroad. The C.R.I. & P. would never reach that Western Sea on its own tracks, but many of the men who built the Rock Island would be in the forefront of the great transcontinental railroad race.

After the banquet was ended that evening, Henry Farnam and his friends walked along the streets of Rock Island town. The dwellings and public houses were brilliantly illuminated to honor the great occasion, and across the dark river the lights of Davenport were equally bright. It was toward the West that the railroad builders' thoughts were inclined to run. None of them realized that they had fixed the destiny of Chicago as the railroad center of the continent and had guaranteed that the port city of New York would now become the commercial center of the young republic. The citizens of

New Orleans had yearned for that power, built upon water traffic, and St. Louisans had dreamed of creating a Queen City of rivers and railroads extending to lakes and oceans and gulf. But in Council Bluffs, the friends and associates of the firm of Farnam & Durant were already arranging for establishment of an incorporated town directly across the Missouri River in Nebraska Territory. Out of a rude collection of ramshackle dwellings, livery stables, fur-trading posts, and grog shops, they created a town to ensure that the railroad from the East would be logically impelled to cross the Missouri at that point and continue toward the Western Sea. On land taken from the ten clans of the Omaha nation of Indians, the new town was named for that dispossessed tribe, a precedent in railroad building that would continue across the West for another generation. Farnam and Durant were now ready to extend their railroad across Iowa. At the same time, they had to construct a connecting bridge, the first such structure to span the broad Mississippi.

It was mainly because of the island—Rock Island—in the middle of the river that Farnam and his locating engineers had chosen the town of that name to be the river terminus of their railroad. A bridge there, they reasoned, would be easier and less costly to construct and should offer a minimum hazard to steamboat navigation. Yet, before construction could begin, loud outcries arose from steamboat owners in St. Louis who saw the railroad as a threat to their booming freight monopoly. They charged that the bridge was "unconstitutional, an obstruction to navigation, dangerous, and it was the duty of every western state, river city, and town to take immediate action to prevent the erection of such a structure." As soon as Farnam's Railroad Bridge Company began construction of piers and the first superstructure, a stronger opposition came from Southern sectionalists, who for a decade had been fighting to ensure that the first transcontinental railroad would originate in the slave-holding South and cross the southern half of the country. Leader of this opposition was none other than Jefferson Davis, who seven years later, at the beginning of the Civil War, would become President of the seceding Confederate States of America. In 1854, Davis was in a strategic position to block the bridge; he was Secretary of War, and because the island in the Mississippi had once been used as a military reservation he informed Farnam's railroad company that Rock Island could not be used in construction of a river bridge.

Encouraged by this official contravention, the steamboat interests late in 1854 secured a federal injunction that charged the bridge builders with illegal trespassing, destruction of government property, and obstruction of steamboat navigation. When the case was brought to court in July 1855, however, the judge ruled for the Railroad Bridge Company, declaring that the bridge was not an obstruction to navigation and that "railroads had become highways in something the same sense as rivers; neither could be suffered to become a permanent obstruction to the other, but each must yield something to the other according to the demands of the public convenience and necessities of commerce."

Nine months later, Farnam's 1,535-foot-long bridge was completed, and on April 22, 1856, he was one of the passengers on the first train approaching it from the East. A newspaper correspondent described the crossing:

Swiftly we sped along the iron track—Rock Island appeared in sight—the whistle sounded and the conductor cried out: *"Passengers for Iowa keep their seats."* There was a pause—a hush, as it were, preparatory to the fierceness of a tornado. The cars moved on—the bridge was reached—"We're on the bridge—see the mighty Mississippi rolling on beneath"—and all eyes were fastened on the mighty parapets of the magnificent bridge, over which we glided in solemn silence. A few minutes and the suspended breath was let loose. "We're over," was the cry. "We have crossed the Mississippi in a railroad car." "This is glory enough for one day," said a passenger, as he hustled his carpet bag and himself out of the car. We followed, to view the mighty structure.

In Davenport and Rock Island, church bells began ringing and crowds that had gathered along both banks of the river broke into enthusiastic cheers. Telegraphers flashed the news back to cities in the East, where it created much excitement. "Civilization took a railroad trip across the Mississippi," declared the *Philadelphia Bulletin.* "The great bridge over the great river . . . was completed and a train of cars passed over it, carrying a load of passengers—commonplace passengers enough, perhaps, but passengers who will always look back exultingly and toast to their children and grandchildren that they were in the first train of cars that ever crossed the Mississippi." Like most Americans, the Philadelphia editor had his eye on the Western Sea: "Now that civilization has got safely over the Mississippi by steam, we see no reason why we may not live to see her take a first class ticket in a lightning train for the shores of the Pacific." He ended by predicting that "twenty years hence" railroad men would be tunneling the Rocky Mountains. His estimate was conservative; in less than ten years track crews would be blasting tunnels through the Rockies.

If Farnam and Durant believed their troubles with the Mississippi rivermen were behind them, they must have suffered a sharp jolt a few days later. Early on the morning of May 6, a persistent blowing of steamboat whistles and ringing of alarm bells brought the townspeople of Rock Island and Davenport out of their houses. Black smoke was boiling skyward from the new bridge. Just after dawn, the packet boat *Effie Afton*, out of New Orleans, had collided broadside against the bridge, the crash knocking down her chimneys and overturning her stoves, which set the vessel afire. Within minutes the blaze spread to a wooden section of the bridge, and while crowds watched from the bridge ends, one flaming span fell into the river. Both boat and bridge span went floating away with the current.

Up and down the Mississippi that morning, steamboat captains blew triumphant blasts on their whistles, arousing railroad partisans' suspicions that the collision had been intentional, that the *Effie Afton* had been sacrificed for the purpose of destroying the bridge. And they must have been convinced of a plot by the rivermen when the steamboat *Hamburg* raised a large banner that read: MISSISSIPPI BRIDGE DESTROYED. LET ALL REJOICE.

Believing that they now had the railroad company on the run, the steamboat interests opened a barrage of public attacks upon Farnam's Railroad Bridge Company. In St. Louis, rivermen and businessmen passed a joint resolution to take all necessary legal steps to have the bridge removed. A committee of steamboat pilots and captains inspected the bridge and solemnly reported that the structure was "a great and serious obstacle to navigation." And then the owner of the *Effie Afton* brought a heavy damage suit against the bridge company, charging that, among other things, the presence of the piers created a swift river current that had swept the packet boat out of control.

Farnam and his associates immediately sought out a first-rate lawyer, one who had a reputation for winning most of his cases. They found him in Springfield, Illinois, and his name was Abraham Lincoln.

Meanwhile, the railroad owners ignored the attacks upon their bridge and began rebuilding the burned section, putting it back into service in September. They also investigated the reasons for the *Effie Afton*'s presence at Rock Island; the boat's usual run was between New Orleans and Louisville and there was no explanation for her being in the upper Mississippi. Had the packet boat been rerouted purposely to destroy the bridge? Was the vessel loaded with inflammable materials? Nothing could be proved.

The case was long delayed in coming to court. On September 1, 1857, Abraham Lincoln visited Rock Island and made a personal inspection of the scene of the collision. He questioned the bridge master and several steamboat pilots and river engineers, and then after gathering all the information he could in this way, he walked out onto the bridge and sat on one of its stringers for an hour or so, studying the currents. With the assistance of a teen-aged boy named Ben Brayton, he determined the speed and direction of the currents by timing with his silver watch the movement of logs and brush that young Brayton dropped into the stream.

A week later, what was to become known as the landmark Rock Island Bridge Case opened sessions in the Saloon Building at Clark and Lake streets in Chicago. It soon became evident to spectators that what they were watching was a struggle between the economic forces of the North and those of the South. A victory for the steamboat interests would mean that the corn and wheat, the pork and timber —all the abundance of the burgeoning Midwest—would continue to move southward along the rivers. St. Louis, Memphis, and New Orleans would become the national cen-

Abraham Lincoln at the time he defended the railroads in the Rock Island Bridge Case of 1857 (Illinois State Historical Library)

ters of trade. On the other hand, a victory for the railroads would mean that commerce could move east and west in a steadily growing volume and thereby assure the destinies of Chicago and New York.

As the trial proceeded, a parade of boat owners, pilots, engineers, and bridge builders passed through the courtroom to be questioned and cross-questioned. During the first days, Lincoln spent much of his time sitting on a bench whittling, but when he did rise to challenge a witness he displayed an enormous fund of information about the measurements of the bridge, the exact lengths of spans, the water's depth, and the dimensions of the *Effie Afton*. At that time he was in his early forties; he wore a dark bush of hair and was clean-shaven. His control of the defense, "his clear statements and choice logic," and his frontier humor, which seemed so incongruous with his solemn and preoccupied appearance, won him a considerable amount of attention in the Chicago press and among men of power who two years later would push him into the race for President of the United States.

In his closing argument to the jury, Lincoln's knowledge of the river currents—gained with the help of young Ben

Brayton—enabled him to demolish one of the principal points of the plaintiffs. Using models of the *Effie Afton* and the bridge, he demonstrated that the starboard wheel of the steamboat could not have been operating at the time of the accident. "The fact is undisputed that she did not move one inch ahead while she was moving thirty-one feet sideways. There is evidence proving that the current there is *only five miles an hour*, and the only explanation is that her power was not all used—that only one wheel was working."

The theme that Lincoln emphasized repeatedly in his argument was that railroads had as much right to cross rivers as steamboats had to travel up and down them, and that travel between the East and the West was as important as between the North and the South. "Mr. Lincoln in addressing the court," said one observer, "claimed that rivers were to be crossed and that it was the manifest destiny of the people to move westward and surround themselves with everything connected with modern civilization."

Although the jurors failed to reach a decision and were dismissed, the railway people knew they had won a great victory. Steamboat supporters who had traveled from St. Louis, New Orleans, and other river cities went home disappointed and embittered, but were determined to continue their fight against the Rock Island bridge and any like it. In 1858 they tried—and failed—to secure congressional passage of a law forbidding bridges over navigable rivers. Later in that same year they finally won a battle in an Iowa court, the judge declaring the Rock Island bridge "a common and public nuisance" and ordering removal of "the three piers and their superstructure which lie within the State of Iowa."

The Chicago & Rock Island appealed to the Supreme Court, where at last the right of railroads to bridge rivers was settled legally forever. For some years afterward, however, whenever a new railroad bridge was built across a navigable river, mysterious accidents often occurred. And at least one more attempt was made to destroy the Rock Island bridge. On the night of June 5, 1859, a watchman making his rounds of inspection found in the middle of the bridge a collection of gunpowder, tar, oakum, and brimstone, heaped up and ready to be set on fire.

In the meantime, out upon the rolling plains of Iowa, Peter Dey and his young assistant, Grenville Dodge, had been making preliminary surveys for a railroad to run between Davenport on the Mississippi and Council Bluffs on the Missouri. Although this railroad across Iowa was to be built, owned, and operated by the same men who controlled the Chicago & Rock Island, they established the new company as a separate organization and named it the Mississippi & Missouri Railroad.

This was done mainly for financial reasons, and in the mind of Thomas Durant the making of money was the only reason why a man should spend his time and energies at railroad building. Pride of accomplishment, the excitement of opening new frontiers, and fulfilling society's need for transportation meant nothing to him. A photograph taken of Durant at about this time shows him seated at a table, happily totaling up figures on a long scroll of paper. Although he had graduated with honors from a medical college, he had become bored with medicine and had turned to making fortunes by speculating in grain futures and railroad stocks. Yet he still liked to be called "Doctor" Durant.

None of the officers of the M. & M. was more pleased than Durant that General John Adams Dix had agreed to serve as president of the company. Dix had been a U.S. senator, knew his way around the founts of political power in the East, and had managed to establish an image as an honest politician, which was as much of a rarity then as now. Dix's main function was to help the company in its efforts to secure federal land grants, and he was therefore only a nominal president. Henry Farnam, under the title of "chief engineer," performed most of the presidential duties in Iowa while Dix lobbied in Washington. As for Durant, his self-chosen task was to negotiate securities in New York and to direct field agents in efforts to persuade Iowa counties and towns to issue bonds and subscribe to stock.

To start the roadbed grading, Farnam assembled at Davenport six hundred laborers—mostly Irish immigrants—and in June 1855 they began laying tracks. "British iron," Farnam called these first rails, which had been shipped all the way from iron foundries in Great Britain. A month later, the M. &

M.'s first locomotive arrived. As the Rock Island bridge was not then completed, the Iron Horse had to be floated over on a flatboat ingeniously rigged with a temporary track from which the locomotive could be rolled onto a spur line and then up to the Davenport station.

The first locomotive was named "Antoine Le Claire" in honor of the son of a French fur trader and a Potawatomi princess. Le Claire was one of the founders of Davenport—a booster for the railroad—and had donated his townhouse for conversion into a luxurious railroad station. In the 1850s, new locomotives were as gaily painted and decorated as new stagecoaches, and the resplendent "Antoine Le Claire" also bore upon its side panels two bronze bas-relief statues of the man for whom it was named.

While a large crowd was gathering to admire the new locomotive, the engineer and fireman filled its boiler with water and its firebox with scrap lumber from a nearby sawmill. When the monster came to steaming life, the engineer invited spectators to climb aboard for the trial run. Among those who responded with delight was a group of Antoine Le Claire's Indian relatives and friends whose blankets were as brilliantly colored as the Iron Horse that had intruded upon

Antoine Le Claire (Iowa State Historical Society)

their lost land. "They swarmed upon and over her, a score of them," reported an observer, "and so, with all the passengers, red and white, that could be stuck on the tender and the cab, the first run in this section of the United States was made."

Iowans now bestowed upon Henry Farnam the title of "Farnam the Railroad King." Almost every day he was out with his workmen, driving them until they completed at least half a mile of track each day. At the same time, his partner Durant was busily converting the local excitement into money. As the rails moved westward, a surefire money-making device was to lay out town lots adjacent to the approaching railroad line and then auction them off to settlers pouring into the empty land. (Half a million people followed the railroads into Iowa during the 1850s.)

Land only a few miles distant from the line survey was so much cheaper than land adjoining it that the sly money-maker, Dr. Durant, bought up sections of distant acreage and then persuaded Farnam to abandon the original survey and shift the railroad northward so as to strike his holdings. He named a town site after himself, and funneled the lucrative receipts from lot sales back to his accounts in New York. It

The locomotive "Antoine Le Claire," first to run on the Mississippi & Missouri Railroad (Iowa State Historical Society)

was a typical Durant maneuver; he had no further interest in the town, which 120 years later had attracted less than fifteen hundred inhabitants.

Meanwhile, thirty miles to the west, the citizens of Iowa City, apparently fearful that the M. & M. might veer off in some other direction, hurriedly raised fifty thousand dollars which they promised the railroad as a prize if it could bring an Iron Horse into their town before January 1, 1856. In 1855, fifty thousand dollars was a fortune, and Farnam accepted the challenge. Although rain and cold weather slowed his track layers, he was within three miles of Iowa City on Christmas Day. Temperatures of zero and below, however, threatened to defeat him. Ice formed in locomotive boilers, and the workmen complained of frostbite.

On New Year's Eve, with the deadline only a few hours away, the end of the track was still several hundred feet from the Iowa City depot. Farnam ordered huge bonfires built along the right-of-way to furnish warmth and light, and he employed every man in Iowa City who was willing to work. The locomotive crawled to within two hundred feet of the station and then its boiler froze. Farnam set his trainmen to using pinch bars, and inch by inch they propelled the Iron Horse forward until it stood at track's end beside the station platform. A few minutes afterward, church bells began ringing to signal the new year of 1856. Three days later, with the temperature still well below zero, the first regularly scheduled passenger train rolled in from Davenport. Aboard was a huge shipment of fresh oysters, the first ever to arrive in the heart of Iowa. That evening Henry Farnam spent a considerable part of his fifty-thousand-dollar prize on a feast for all the people of Iowa City, serving them hot coffee, cake, and oysters "till broad daylight in the morning."

During the following year, Dr. Durant increased his efforts to persuade the villages and counties between Iowa City and the Missouri River to pledge more railroad bonds. He was aided in this campaign by Northern antislavery forces who were aroused over passage of the Kansas-Nebraska Act. This law, which created the new territories of Kansas and Nebraska, included a provision for settlers of the territories to decide for themselves whether they would allow slavery within their borders. A fierce immigration race had already begun between proslavery settlers from the South and antislavery settlers from the North, thus putting in motion a series of events that would soon lead to the first violent clashes of the oncoming Civil War.

"We advocate the building of this railroad earnestly as a peace measure," argued a Chicago newspaper editor. "The very announcement that the stock was subscribed and that the road was to be finished by the 4th of July, 1858, would at once settle this question." He predicted that antislavery immigrants would pour into the territories on the new railroad and the freedom of Kansas and Nebraska would be assured. Moreover, the railroad's stock was an excellent investment, paying perhaps twelve percent dividends.

None of this sectional rivalry was lost upon the railroad operators. After the Rock Island bridge was completed, they began advertising their two routes as "the great national road to Kansas and Nebraska." In that same year, the lobbying efforts of General John Dix in Washington paid off when Congress voted an Iowa land-grant act that guaranteed thousands of acres to the railroad builders. This was what Durant had hungered for, and as soon as the M. & M. had 400,000 acres of rich Iowa soil in its grab bag, he deliberately schemed to slow the building of the road. The land-grant act generously allowed ten years for the road's completion, and there were special taxation privileges. The longer the road was delayed, the more valuable the land grants would become, and the more eager the settlers to the West would be to increase the size of their stock and bond commitments in hopes of bringing the Iron Horse to their towns.

Although he did not fully understand what his partner was doing, honest Henry Farnam began to distrust Durant's policies and manipulations. "Durant," he said afterward, "unfortunately yielded to the general spirit of speculation which had taken possession of so many railroad men of that time." Farnam believed it was his duty to build the railroad as quickly and efficiently as possible. When Durant squeezed down on funds for road construction, Farnam recklessly spent some of his own money to buy materials and meet payrolls. In August 1857, a financial crisis in the East gave Durant and his New York associates an opportunity to order Farnam to cease all work on the M. & M. By this time, Farnam's distaste for Durant's business ethics reached the point where he could no longer continue in partnership with him. The firm of Farnam & Durant was dissolved, Farnam retaining his post as president of the Rock Island Railroad until Durant's power reached the point where he could force him out of that office and replace him with his brother, Charles Durant.

Thomas Durant scorned men who built railroads for the joy of building and whose moral principles got in the way of their profits. After he was rid of Henry Farnam, Durant enjoyed himself manipulating the farmers and villagers of Iowa, threatening to bypass towns or counties that did not buy more bonds, generating rumors that he would run his railroad north of Council Bluffs, bridge the Missouri at another location, and create a rival city to Omaha. As a result, many towns and counties voted bonds out of all proportion to their ability to pay, saddling their people with heavy debts for years into the future. For this, Durant offered no guarantees, and was not even liable for defaults if he failed to build tracks along original surveys.

When another railroad, the Chicago & Northwestern, began crossing Iowa through a tier of counties north of the M. & M., Durant did not respond with a track-laying race. The C. & N. reached Council Bluffs two years before the plodding M. & M. (which by then had been combined into the Chicago, Rock Island & Pacific Railroad), and one of Durant's employees, surveyor Grenville Dodge, was the principal speaker at the banquet arranged to welcome the builders of the supposed "rival" railroad. Few people knew, or cared, that the president of the Chicago & Northwestern was also vice-president of the Mississippi & Missouri, or that Dr. Durant had exploited the latter road almost into bankruptcy, sold his stock at a profit, and reinvested in the C. & N.

The whole affair, of course, was but a rehearsal for that "Grandest Enterprise Under God," the building of the first transcontinental railroad, the route to the Indies by way of the Western Sea.

CHAPTER 2

"With the Wings of the Wind"

"LESS THAN A QUARTER of a century ago," said Henry
Farnam, "the first locomotive was introduced into the United
States. Now, more than fourteen thousand miles of iron rails
are traversed by the Iron Horse with almost lightning speed."
Farnam was responding to a toast given at the celebration
that united the Atlantic with the Mississippi at Rock Island,
Illinois, on Washington's birthday, 1854. The first Iron
Horse had arrived in America almost exactly a quarter of a
century earlier, in May 1829. In August of the same year it
was given a trial run on a track near Honesdale, Pennsylvania. During that brief span of years (1829–54) the development of locomotives and the building of tracks for them to run
upon had been amazingly swift, even more so than was to be
the development of automobiles and paved highways in the
twentieth century.

In the first years of the nineteenth century, many Americans were keenly interested in reports from England that told
of astounding progress in the use of steam-propelled engines.
These were used mainly to replace horses, which for years
had been drawing wagons loaded with coal over railways that
ran from colliery pit-heads to shipping ports. In 1813, Americans heard about William Hedley's "Puffing Billy," which
could haul ten coal wagons at five miles per hour. In 1825,
they marveled over George Stephenson's "Locomotion,"
which reached a speed of sixteen miles per hour on the new
Stockton and Darlington railway. Four years later, Stephenson and his son perfected the "Rocket," with its multi-
tube boiler and improved system of exhausting steam, which
created a strong draft in the firebox. The "Rocket" was the
first true, breathing, pure-bred Iron Horse, and could travel
twenty-nine miles in one hour.

During this same period in America a number of imaginative people were planning railways—from New York to Philadelphia, from Baltimore to the West, from Albany to Lake Erie, from Charleston, South Carolina, to the West. In most cases, the planning did not include the use of steam power; the cars would be pulled by horses, as was done on the short lines that ran from coal mines to canals or rivers. In 1825, Colonel John Stevens demonstrated a one-cylinder steam-powered locomotive on a circular track on the grounds of his estate in Hoboken, New Jersey, but the public viewed it as an amusing toy. Not until 1828 did a trained engineer travel to England to examine the marvelous Iron Horse at work.

Horatio Allen was his name, and he was sent on his mission by John B. Jervis of the Delaware & Hudson Canal Company. (Less than a quarter of a century later, Jervis was serving as the first president of his friend Henry Farnam's Chicago & Rock Island Railroad.) Jervis authorized the twenty-five-year-old Allen to buy iron to replace wooden rails on the canal's horse-powered railways. In addition to the rails, if Allen discovered that the much-publicized English locomotives were as practical as they were said to be, he was to buy four of them.

Much impressed by what he saw, young Allen placed orders for four Iron Horses, and on May 13, 1829, the first English locomotive arrived in New York City. According to one observer, it resembled a mammoth grasshopper. "Its driving wheels were of oak-wood, banded with a heavy wrought-iron tire, and the front was ornamented with a large, fierce-looking face of a lion, in bold relief, and it bore the name of 'Stourbridge Lion.'" It was a four-wheeled engine with a cylindrical boiler, and had been built by Foster, Rastrick & Company at Stourbridge, England. Allen arranged to have the "Lion" blocked up in a New York foundry yard and there he brought it to life with steam, and "it became the object of curiosity to thousands who visited the works from day to day, to see the curious 'critter' go through the motions only, as there was no road for it about the premises."

In July, Allen shipped the locomotive by river and canal to Honesdale, Pennsylvania, and there on August 8 a fire was kindled under the boiler, and the "Stourbridge Lion" was readied for its first test. The railway that ran to the coal mines at Carbondale was made of hemlock timber that had cracked and warped from exposure, and after a straight section of five hundred feet it crossed Lackawaxen Creek on a curved trestlework about thirty feet high.

"The impression was very general," Horatio Allen recalled afterward, "that the iron monster would either break down the road or that it would leave the track at the curve and plunge into the creek. My reply to such apprehension was, that it was too late to consider the probability of such occurrences; that there was no other course but to have the trial made of the strange animal which had been brought here at such great expense, but that it was not necessary that more than one should be involved in its fate; that I would take the first ride alone, and that the time would come when I should look back to this incident with great interest. As I placed my hand on the throttle-valve handle I was undecided whether I would move slowly or with a fair degree of speed; but believing that the road would prove safe, and preferring, if we did go down, to go down handsomely and without any evidence

The "Stourbridge Lion," first locomotive imported from England, was given its trial run by Horatio Allen on August 8, 1829. (Smithsonian Institution)

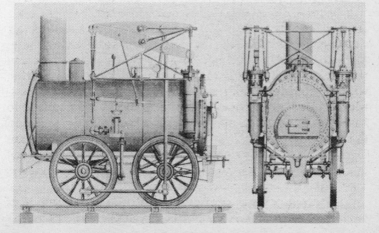

A contemporary artist's conception of the celebrated race between Peter Cooper's "Tom Thumb" and a horse-drawn rail car, August 28, 1830 (The New-York Historical Society)

of timidity, I started with considerable velocity, passed the curve over the creek safely, and was soon out of hearing of the cheers of the large assemblage present. At the end of two or three miles, I reversed the valves and returned without accident to the place of starting, having thus made the first railroad trip by locomotive on the Western Hemisphere."

Only a year later, Peter Cooper took the first locomotive built in America out for a trial run on the Baltimore & Ohio's recently completed thirteen miles of track between Baltimore and Ellicott's Mills in Maryland. Appropriately named "Tom Thumb," the locomotive was built by Cooper as a working model meant to convert the railroad's directors from their hidebound preference for horse-power over steam-power. On August 28, 1830, Cooper attached "Tom Thumb" to a car that resembled an open boat. It was crowded with beaver-hatted directors and their friends. Thus began the first journey by steam in America aboard an American-built locomotive. On the run to Ellicott's Mills, Cooper's passengers were delighted when he easily maintained speeds of fifteen to eighteen miles per hour, but on the return trip a horse-drawn car was waiting to challenge him at Relay House, from which point parallel tracks ran to Baltimore. Stockton & Stokes, stagecoach operators and advocates of horse-drawn rail cars, insisted that "Tom Thumb" engage in a race, and Cooper accepted. The horse leaped away into the lead, but "Tom Thumb" quickly overtook the animal and passed it with a burst of speed. A few minutes later, just as the driver of the horse was about to abandon the contest, the blower belt slipped from "Tom Thumb's" drum.

"The safety-valve ceased to scream," reported one of the passengers, "and the engine for want of breath began to wheeze and pant. In vain Mr. Cooper, who was his own engineer and fireman, lacerated his hand in attempting to replace the band upon the wheel; in vain he tried to urge the fire with light wood. The horse gained on the machine and passed it, and, although the band was presently replaced, and steam again did its best, the horse was too far ahead to be overtaken, and came in the winner of the race." Although Peter Cooper lost the race, he won his battle for steam-power. "Tom Thumb's" performance convinced the directors of the Baltimore & Ohio that they should bet their money on the Iron Horse. They announced a contest for a locomotive especially designed for their steeply graded and sharply curved railroad that was to be built through the Allegheny Mountains.

In the meantime, Horatio Allen—that dauntless driver of the "Stourbridge Lion"—had transferred his engineering skills to a new railroad that was being built westward from Charleston, South Carolina. Collaborating with one of the road's directors, he helped design a new locomotive, which was named "Best Friend of Charleston." The leading citizens of Charleston were determined that their city should become America's greatest seaport, and to achieve this aim they envisioned a railroad with many branches bringing into their harbor the rich produce of the South and the West. "Best Friend of Charleston," which had a vertical boiler shaped like a wine bottle, was America's first regularly scheduled passenger-train locomotive and it operated over what was then the longest railroad in the world. Unfortunately, on June 17, 1831, the "Best Friend's" fireman—who evidently underestimated the power of steam—became annoyed by the hissing of the safety valve and tied down the lever. The result was another "first" for "Best Friend." It was the first locomotive to explode, an accident that killed the fireman and badly scalded the engineer. Horatio Allen's mechanics managed to rebuild what was left of the locomotive, and it was appropriately rechristened "Phoenix." To restore the confidence of passengers on the Charleston & Hamburg Railroad, a flatcar heaped high with protective cotton bales was thereafter placed between the locomotive and its passenger cars—a practice that was continued for many years.

In the 1830s it seemed that every blacksmith, tinker, and ironworker, every wagonwright, carriagesmith, and boiler-maker—all the craftsmen of America—wanted to build a better locomotive. Among those drawn to the romance of the Iron Horse was a Philadelphia jeweler and bookbinder, Matthias William Baldwin. In 1831 he built a miniature

"Old Ironsides," the first of thousands of locomotives built by Matthias W. Baldwin (Smithsonian Institution)

steam locomotive for the Philadelphia Museum, and its efficiency so impressed the owners of the newly founded Philadelphia, Germantown & Norristown Railroad that they commissioned him to build a full-sized Iron Horse for a promised payment of four thousand dollars.

Before beginning work, Baldwin visited Colonel John Stevens's Camden & Amboy Railroad and made a thorough examination of the "John Bull," a recent import from the famed Stephensons' works in Newcastle, England. On November 23, 1832, Baldwin's "Old Ironsides" was ready for a test run. After correcting some imperfections, Baldwin turned the locomotive over to the railroad, expecting to receive the four thousand dollars. The company, however, complained that "Old Ironsides" did not meet their expectations. It could be used when the weather was fair, they said, but horses had to be substituted when the weather was poor. They finally settled for thirty-five hundred dollars; and the disgusted Matthias Baldwin told his mechanics: "That is our last locomotive."

The lure of the Iron Horse was too great, however, and Baldwin was soon at work on the "E. L. Miller" for the Charleston & Hamburg Railroad. Before he died in 1866 he personally supervised the building of fifteen hundred locomotives, and the company that bore his name built fifty-nine thousand Iron Horses before it was absorbed into a corporate conglomerate of the twentieth century.

By the 1840s, Baldwin and other locomotive builders of America and Britain had transformed the original crude machine into the powerful Behemoth that would change the face of the earth. The vertical wine-bottle boiler became horizontal; flanges were placed on the wheels instead of on the tracks; flexible beam trucks were designed to prevent binding or derailment when the engine rounded curves; a pilot or cowcatcher was placed on the prow; a weatherproof cab sheltered the engineer and fireman from the elements; flared spark-arresting smokestacks shaped like balloons, sunflowers, and cabbage heads replaced the straight stacks; boxed oil headlamps embellished with elaborate designs made night travel possible; brass-capped domes filled with sand to give traction to spinning wheels appeared behind the smokestacks; mellow-toned bells and melodious whistles added both safety and charm.

It was no wonder that when Americans were swept up in their national drive toward the Western Sea—their mania for Manifest Destiny—they looked upon the Iron Horse as "the wings of the wind," which would take them where they desired to go. In 1846, that Year of Decision when Americans moved to seize California, Oregon Territory, and much of the Southwest, locomotives and the recently invented telegraph figured largely in much of the bombastic oratory. For example, Congressman Charles W. Cathcart of Indiana, speaking on the floor of the House of Representatives, February 6, 1846: "The Iron Horse [the steamcar] with the wings of the wind, his nostrils distended with flame, salamander-like vomiting fire and smoke, trembling with power, but submissive to the steel curb imposed upon him by the hand of man, flies from one end of the continent to the other in less time than our ancestry required to visit a neighboring city; while by the magnetic telegraph the lightning of heaven is made subservient to the will of man in annihilating space. In storm and darkness, in the heat of a torrid sun or the chilling blasts of a Siberian winter, this mystical symbol of man's intelligence speeds its onward way. Truly it may be said, that with the social influence of these two great inventions, all the people of this continent may be moulded to one mind."

There were exceptions to this view, of course. Another orator predicted that railroads would "leave the land despoiled, ruined, a desert where only sable buzzards shall wing their loathsome way to feed upon the carrion accomplished by the iron monster of the locomotive engine." Few Americans, however, were exempt from the enchantment with the Iron Horse, not even Henry David Thoreau, the philosophic naturalist and recluse of Walden Pond, who abhorred expansionism and the war with Mexico, but who could say of the locomotives that passed on the Fitchburg Railroad: "When I hear the Iron Horse make the hills echo with his snort like thunder, shaking the earth with his feet, and breathing fire and smoke from his nostrils (what kind of winged horse or fiery dragon they will put into the new mythology I don't know) it seems as if the earth had sent a race now worthy to inhabit it." And Joaquin Miller, that wild and shaggy singer of the West, declared that there was more poetry in the rushing monster "than in all the gory story of burning Troy."

In the 1840s the locomotive reached its natural form, a configuration that would be refined through technology and expanded in size, yet was virtually the same machine that would dominate the rails for the next century. In that decade it seemed that every merchant, manufacturer, and visionary, every peddler, pitchman, and politician was planning or dreaming of a rail route to the Western Sea.

. Typical of the visionaries was John Plumbe, a Welshman who came to the United States in 1821 at the age of twelve and a few years later was working as a railroad surveyor in Pennsylvania. Always restless and ambitious, Plumbe moved on west to Iowa Territory, read law, and became a prosecuting attorney in the frontier county of Dubuque. There he spent much of his time organizing public meetings and corresponding with congressmen in a campaign to build a railroad to the Western Sea. He may have been the first advocate of

John Plumbe was ridiculed by U.S. Congressmen for proposing a transcontinental railroad. (The Library of Congress, taken from Palimpsest, Vol. 19, March 1938)

record for a transcontinental railroad, when in 1838 he sent a petition to Washington that brought ridicule from congressmen who said his proposal was as silly as asking the government "to build a railroad to the moon."

By the early 1840s, Plumbe was back in the East, where he somehow learned the new art of daguerreotypy. Four years before the great Mathew Brady entered the business, he opened a chain of studios from Boston to Washington. In Washington, Plumbe made the first photographs of the Capitol, the White House, and other buildings, and probably the first portraits of such famous Americans as Sam Houston, Henry Clay, John C. Calhoun, James K. Polk, and John Quincy Adams. Because only one copy could be made of a daguerreotype, he developed a method for reproducing lithographic copies on paper, a process that he called Plumbeotypy, but he never bothered to obtain a patent.

It was while he was in Washington that Plumbe became caught up in the transcontinental-railroad fever of the 1840s, and began traveling about the country trying to bring his dream to fruition. Because of his neglect, his daguerreotype studios went bankrupt, and he joined the California gold rush to recoup his fortune. John Plumbe found no gold; in fact, he spent most of his time in California trying to persuade the swarms of new residents there to join him in formulating plans for a railroad to link them with the Eastern states. By this time, the dream of the railroad had become an obsession he could not escape. In these later years of his life, Plumbe bore a curious resemblance to his contemporary Edgar Allan Poe—high forehead, down-curving mustache, brooding eyes. When he returned to Iowa in 1857 a defeated man, and found that others had stolen his dream and were bringing it to reality, he became so despondent that he committed suicide at the age of forty-six.

More practical than John Plumbe was Asa Whitney, a New England merchant whose resemblance to Napoleon Bonaparte was so marked that strangers often stared at him in amazement. Whitney conceived his plan for a transcontinental railroad while returning from a voyage to China in 1844. Five Chinese ports had recently (1843) been opened to trade, but Whitney was discouraged by the interminable sea distance from Boston or New York. A railroad across the North American continent seemed the best solution, and although rails had not then reached Chicago, Whitney began investigating possible routes from Lake Michigan to the Pacific Coast.

In 1845 Whitney addressed a memorial to Congress, recommending that a survey for a transcontinental railroad between the 42d and 45th parallels be authorized as soon as possible. He then went on a tour of the country, making speeches, visiting community leaders, and writing letters to newspapers in efforts to drum up support for the railroad. In the summer of that year he organized an expedition at his own expense to explore a rail route toward the Western Sea. Starting at Milwaukee, he and his party of young adventurers crossed the prairies to the Great Bend of the Missouri. At every opportunity Whitney sent back lengthy reports to newspapers, extolling the richness of the country through which his railroad would pass and urging the government to complete his survey from the Missouri to the Pacific Coast. After returning to the East, Whitney again entreated Congress to act. This time he presented them with specific geographical details for a transcontinental route, and offered to build the railroad himself in exchange for a land grant sixty miles wide from Lake Michigan to the Pacific. By selling off this land as the road was being built, Whitney said, he could raise sufficient funds to pay expenses for construction. He estimated that the great work could be accomplished in less than fifteen years, and that "the over-population of Europe must and will flock to it."

The main obstacle as he saw it was the occupancy of the Indians, their land titles not having been extinguished, but Whitney assured the Congress that the native Americans were "ready and willing to sell all that may be desirable for this object, and for a very small sum . . . and this road would produce a revolution in the situation of the red as well as the white man. The Sioux Indians occupy and claim nearly all the lands from above latitude of about 43° from the Mississippi to the Rocky Mountains. They are numerous, powerful, and entirely savage."

Whitney shrewdly pointed out that the building of the

railroad would drive the "savage" Sioux and their buffalo northward, "and we can then succeed in bringing the removed and small tribes to habits of industry and civilization, and their race may be preserved until mixed and blended with ours, and the Sioux must soon follow them."

The transcontinental railroad was a part of the nation's destiny, Whitney maintained, a destiny that could not be realized without it. "Now *only* is the time in which it can be

Senator Thomas Hart Benton (Culver Pictures)

John C. Frémont (Culver Pictures)

done . . . some one's whole efforts, energies, and life must be devoted to it." And if he, Asa Whitney, could be the instrument to accomplish this great work, that honor would be enough; he would ask no more.

By this time Whitney had aroused the suspicions of the South. That region's commercial interests wanted no part of a transcontinental railroad originating on the shore of Lake Michigan, and their political representatives in Washington began a drumfire of publicity against "the railroad schemes of Asa Whitney."

In the late 1840s, largely as the result of the efforts of Whitney and John Plumbe, a series of railroad conventions was held in various cities, every one of which yearned to become the originating point for the first transcontinental railway. At one of these meetings in Chicago in 1847, Whitney's plan was condemned, and during the following months an imposing number of opponents began offering rival proposals. Stephen A. Douglas, who was soon to achieve fame in his debates with Abraham Lincoln, represented the Chicago viewpoint and advocated a route to Council Bluffs that would later be followed by the Chicago & Rock Island Railroad. The arguments offered against Whitney's route were that it was too far to the north; the climate was harsh; there was no fuel for Iron Horses; the Indians were hostile; and the land would probably never be inhabited by white settlers. One opposition group called it "a scheme of gigantic robbery."

Another of Whitney's enemies was Senator Thomas Hart Benton of Missouri, a leader in the national movement to acquire more Western territory for the United States. Benton wanted St. Louis to be the terminus for the transcontinental route, and quoted his son-in-law, the five-foot-two-inch-tall explorer John C. Frémont, as advocating "a great central path" along the Santa Fe Trail to Bent's Fort and then through the Rockies at Cochetopa Pass. In one of his speeches Benton visualized an Iron Horse puffing alongside a Rocky Mountain peak transformed by a sculptor into a giant statue of Columbus, with one arm extended westward, the other holding an inscribed tablet: THERE LIES THE EAST! THERE LIES INDIA! As for Sam Houston of Texas, he of course wanted assurances that the road would pass through that recently annexed state.

Among the Southerners who opposed Whitney was John C. Calhoun, who had reached the melancholy conclusion that the South and the North were already acting as two nations. If there was to be a transcontinental railroad, he and his followers wanted the Charleston & Memphis road to be extended westward from the latter city. As for New Orleans, the port city, its leaders bitterly opposed all proposed routes across the continent and fought for a sea-and-land route that would use the narrow isthmus of Panama, or Tehuantepec as it was then called, for a short and inexpensive connecting railroad.

During the lively debates over all these various routes, no mention was ever made of the native Americans, the Indians who had lived for centuries on the lands into which the Iron Horses must intrude, puffing and steaming and trailing dark smoke plumes. The Indians were ignored as completely as if they held no more rights to the land than did the buffalo or the antelope. Only Asa Whitney remembered them, and his principal concern was to extinguish their land titles and then either force them to become like white men or drive them out of the way.

Despite all the opposition to Whitney, in July 1848 he managed to get a bill introduced in the Senate "to set apart and sell to Asa Whitney, of New York, a portion of the public lands, to enable him to construct a railroad from Lake Michigan to the Pacific Ocean." Senator Benton immediately led a fierce attack upon the bill and won the support of the majority, who felt that a thorough survey of all possible routes to the Pacific should be undertaken before Congress took further action.

A few months later, with the Mexican War ended and vast land spoils in the West awaiting division between partisans of the North and South, two significant railroad conventions were held in St. Louis and Memphis. Hundreds of representatives from all parts of the United States attended, but all they could agree upon was that the U.S. Army should make an extensive series of surveys to determine the best route for a railroad. Asa Whitney attended the conventions, and as he listened to the debates it must have been apparent to him that no compromise on the location of a transcontinental railroad would ever be reached. As John C. Calhoun had already realized, the United States was not one nation but two, and out of the bitter rivalries secession and war were all but inevitable.

In a last desperate attempt to secure financial backing for his railroad to the Western Sea, Whitney journeyed to England in 1851, but he found that the bankers there were involved in other varieties of exploitation. Typical of the attitudes he confronted was this comment by a London newspaper: "If our friends should really get from the Mississippi to Oregon, it will be a thousand pities that they should stop there. A tubular bridge across Behring's [sic] strait would literally put a girdle round the earth—and then the predilection of American citizens might be gratified by the establishment of a perpetual circulation."

After seven years of effort, Asa Whitney now abandoned his dream of the Iron Horse and the Western Sea. Retiring to his dairy farm at Locust Hill near Washington, he peddled milk in the nation's capital, enjoying life too much to destroy it by suicide as John Plumbe had done, and although he took no further part in the building of a transcontinental railroad, he did live to see his dream accomplished.

Meanwhile, in its usual ponderous manner, Congress got around to authorizing the Secretary of War, on March 1, 1853, to employ the Corps of Topographical Engineers to make surveys to ascertain the "most practical and economical route for a railroad from the Mississippi River to the Pacific Ocean." The Secretary of War was Jefferson Davis, and being a Southern leader he had already settled upon a rail route between the 32d and 35th parallels. Nevertheless, Davis quickly ordered engineering expeditions into the field to explore possible routes along parallels as far north as the Canadian border. One reason for the Secretary's haste was that Congress had granted him only ten months to complete the surveys, an almost impossible task considering the state of transportation at that time and the difficulties of determining grades and finding suitable passes through the Rocky Mountains.

Throughout its history, the Army Corps of Engineers has had a covert and often corrupt relationship with politicians, and the episode of the Pacific railway surveys was no exception. Soon after the surveys began, a company that called itself the Atlantic & Pacific Railroad was founded in New York. It proposed to build a transcontinental railroad from a Southern terminus across Texas between the 32d and 35th parallels to what was then the village of San Diego, California. The president of the Atlantic & Pacific was one Robert J. Walker, a former senator who had been involved in land scandals, bond repudiations, and other high-finance confidence schemes in Mississippi. Jefferson Davis owed a considerable political debt to Walker, whose influence and sponsorship had made possible the rise to power of the future President of the Confederacy.

Furthermore, Walker was the brother-in-law of Major William Helmsley Emory, a haughty red-bearded Maryland aristocrat, a West Point graduate, and one of the most influential officers of the Army's Topographical Engineers. Emory had accompanied General Stephen Watts Kearny's Army of the West on its triumphal conquest of New Mexico and California in 1846, and he and a number of fellow officers had acquired large holding of real estate for modest sums around the village of San Diego. A transcontinental railroad with a western terminus at San Diego would make them all very rich. Furthermore, the commander of the Corps of Topographical Engineers, Colonel John James Abert of Virginia, was so interested in the Southern route that even before the Pacific railroad surveys were authorized, he sent Lieutenant-Colonel Joseph E. Johnston (later an important Confederate general) to Texas to find a rail route by way of El Paso to San Diego.

Outside the closed orbit of the Corps of Engineers were others with private gains to be promoted. Senator Thomas Hart Benton was so determined that St. Louis (which lies between the 38th and 39th parallels) should be the terminus, and he so distrusted the Corps of Engineers, that he dispatched his own surveying party, complete with a press agent, to find a route westward along the 38th parallel. And then Benton's son-in-law, John C. Frémont, followed up with still another survey along the 38th to make certain that the most favorable route would end not in San Diego but in northern California, where Frémont himself claimed sizable land holdings. Another proponent of the St. Louis terminus was Pierre Chouteau, who had grown wealthy in the fur trade. As the fur trade was declining, Chouteau put his money into a St. Louis factory to make iron rails and went to Washington to lobby for the 38th parallel route.

A former officer of the Corps of Engineers, Isaac Stevens, was equally determined to convince the government that Asa Whitney's long-promoted route between the 47th and 49th parallels was far superior to the others. Not long before the surveys were authorized, the politically inclined Stevens had resigned his commission in the Engineers to become governor of Washington Territory. In this vast and unexploited land he hoped to build his political and economic fortunes, and he needed the transcontinental railroad to ensure fulfillment of his dream. Although he was now a civilian, Stevens persuaded Jefferson Davis to let him direct the military personnel of this Northern survey party. Among the officers was

Captain George B. McClellan, later to become commander of the Union Army and a candidate for President of the United States.

Stephen A. Douglas, another ambitious politician, owned enough strategically located land in Chicago to become a millionaire if his favored route westward through Council Bluffs and Omaha was chosen, but being a shrewd businessman he hedged on his bets by buying up the site of a proposed terminus on Lake Superior after he learned that Isaac Stevens's survey might be shortened to that point. As for Douglas's rival, Abraham Lincoln, the future President evidently agreed with his debating partner that the route through Council Bluffs–Omaha and South Pass was the most practical. Lincoln acquired land interests at Council Bluffs.

Insofar as facilitating the selection of a railroad route across the West, the surveys of the Corps of Engineers accomplished nothing. As the reports were published, Southern partisans exaggerated the advantages of the 32d parallel and the disadvantages of the 48th. Northern partisans took the opposite position, and in the highly charged atmosphere of the 1850s neither side was willing to accept a compromise route. The government spent more than a million dollars in publishing over a period of five years the thirteen quarto volumes of explorations and surveys for a Pacific railroad, and although they contained little information that would have assisted a field surveyor in marking out a railway line, they were filled with an extraordinary amount of detail relating to geology, geography, land forms, American Indians, weather, trails, botanical specimens, birds, mammals, reptiles, and fish. Hundreds of illustrations, many of them tinted, accompanied the text; an artist was attached to each surveying party, and most of the pictures were drawn in the field. Today, the reports stand not as a guide for the routing of railroads but as a priceless compendium of the virgin West immediately before its despoilation by the Iron Horse.

Surprisingly, the route along which the first transcontinental railway eventually was built was not surveyed by any of the exploring parties of the Corps of Engineers. Its various sections were already well known of course to fur traders, Oregon-bound emigrants, and California goldseek-ers. It lay between the 40th and 45th parallels, a band across the continent that has long fascinated meteorologists and geographers because it is the track of America's most intense climatic storms, a broad swath of highly charged energy that apparently is transferable to its human inhabitants. The great centers of production in America are within this belt. It is worth noting that several members of the Pacific rail-road survey parties compared the routes they were survey-ing with this well-known South Pass route, and that they usually favored the latter, which lies directly across the 42d parallel.

Soon after the railroad survey expeditions were sent into the field, another curiously related series of governmental ac-tions began to take place. In August 1853, the President of the United States, Franklin Pierce, ordered the Commis-sioner of Indian Affairs, George W. Manypenny, "to visit the Indian country to confer with the various tribes, as a prelimi-nary measure, looking to negotiation with them for the pur-pose of procuring their assent to a territorial government and the extinguishment of their title, in whole or in part, to the lands owned by them."

Manypenny did not visit tribes of the far Southwest or the Northwest; he went nowhere near the parallels favored for transcontinental railroad routes by partisans of the South or North. Instead, he visited the Omaha, Oto, and Missouri, the Sauk and Fox, the Kickapoo, Delaware, and Shawnee—mostly tribes that only a few years earlier had been driven across the Mississippi to new lands that they had been prom-ised were theirs "as long as the grass shall grow or the waters run." With these tribes Commissioner Manypenny made treaties from 1854 through 1857, taking from the Indians vast areas of land for the government of the United States.

For instance, on May 6, 1854, Manypenny persuaded the Delawares to cede to the United States all their land except eighty acres to be reserved for each tribal allottee, and con-vinced them that the value of these remaining holdings would be greatly enhanced by a railroad through their country. (Eventually the Delawares were forced to surrender all their land and retreat to Indian territory, where they completely vanished as a tribe.) On May 17, four representatives of the Sauk and Fox tribes were invited to visit Washington, and while there they ceded four hundred square miles of land. When the series of treaties was completed, these Indians had surrendered title to 18 million of their 19,342,000 acres, most of which lay along or was adjacent to the belt bound by the 40th and 45th parallels. Evidently there was some spoken or unspoken consensus within the government that the rail route to the Western Sea would follow the parallels of the lower forties, and so the lands were made ready, titles duly legitimized, for transfer to the exploiters of the first trans-continental railroad.

CHAPTER 3

War Slows the March to
the Western Sea

DURING THE 1840s when Mark Twain was participating in various escapades around Hannibal, Missouri, with his fellow teen-ager Tom Blankenship (whom he later immortalized as Huckleberry Finn), the town was astir with rumors of a railroad. Hannibal was a riverboat town on the Mississippi and mainly Southern in its attitudes, but railroad fever was everywhere. Anybody who owned a map could see that a railroad running west from Hannibal to the Missouri River would cut several hundred miles off the long haul down to St. Louis and then up the Missouri to its big bend where Kansas and Nebraska began. When the town's businessmen gathered to discuss the railroad, they often met in the office of Hannibal's justice of the peace, John Clemens, who was Mark Twain's father.

For their Missouri River terminus, the Hannibal railroad enthusiasts came to favor St. Joseph, which had been a prosperous fur-trading post for half a century, and in 1849, after the discovery of gold in California, quickly turned into a boom town. As many as twenty steamboats a day stopped at St. Joe to unload hordes of emigrants and goldseekers bound west from there on wagon trains. To supply this migration, food, tools, clothing, wagons, and horses also had to be brought up the river. "St. Joseph is quite a village and doing quite a great deal of business at this time," one westbound traveler recorded, "but the way they fleece the California emigrants is worth noticing."

Hannibal's merchants and bankers had taken notice and were eager to share in this Western money flow. Some envisioned their railroad as pausing only temporarily at St. Joseph before bridging the Missouri and plunging on across the continent to the Western Sea. Raising money to build a railroad was a slow process, however, and before the dreams and talk were translated to action John Clemens died, leaving young Samuel (Mark Twain) Clemens an orphan.

Not until the autumn of 1850 did the charter holders of the Hannibal & St. Joseph Railroad suddenly discover a way in which they could finance their project. In September of that year, the Congress established a precedent in government aid by granting more than two million acres of public land to the Illinois Central Company to be used in raising money for construction of a railroad from Chicago straight southward to the town of Cairo at the confluence of the Ohio and Mississippi rivers. With this example before them, representatives of the Hannibal & St. Joseph hastened to Washington and demanded the same kind of grant—six sections of land for each mile of completed track—and they got it. With millions of dollars worth of Missouri farmland under its control, the Hannibal & St. Joseph soon found itself being wooed by financial giants from the East.

Setting another pattern that would be followed in construction of the first transcontinental railroad, the directors of the Hannibal & St. Joseph built simultaneously from the eastern and western ends of their survey. In this way, the railroad reached the Missouri River long before any of its rivals. On February 13, 1859, Joseph Robidoux, the old Mountain Man who founded St. Joseph for the American Fur Company, drove a golden spike at Cream Ridge near Chillicothe, and the Hannibal & St. Joseph was completed. As Rock Island had done exactly five years earlier, the town of St. Joe postponed its celebration until Washington's Birthday. To mark the great occasion, a jug of water from the Mississippi was hauled overland by the railroad to St. Joe, and there with appropriate oratory the contents were mingled with the waters of the muddy Missouri. In that year, Mark Twain was earning his living as a steersman on a Mississippi River steamboat.

Other events significant to Western railroads occurred during 1859. At about the same time that the first Iron Horse came steaming into St. Joe, a young Pennsylvanian who had emigrated westward to seek his fortune was persuading the Kansas territorial legislature to grant him a railroad charter.

He was muttonchop-whiskered Cyrus K. Holliday, one of the founders and the first mayor of the capital city of Topeka. His railroad vision was a track running from the Missouri River to Topeka and then westward along the old Santa Fe Trail—the Atchison, Topeka & Santa Fe. With the help of two powerful senators, Holliday was soon beseeching the federal government for a land grant, but it was March 3, 1863, before President Lincoln signed the act that gave the paper railroad 2,928,928 acres of the people's land in Kansas, and eventually millions more in states farther west.

In August 1859, Abraham Lincoln, whose signature was to make effective three immense railroad grants during his later presidency, was in Council Bluffs, Iowa. He was there to inquire into realty holdings that he had taken as security for a debt and also a homestead allotment due him for militia service in the Black Hawk War. At the hotel where Lincoln was staying he met a sturdy, dark-bearded young man of twenty-eight who had just returned from a journey up the Platte Valley. The young man was Grenville Dodge, and he had been making a preliminary survey along the 42d parallel for his employer, Henry Farnam of the Rock Island and Mississippi & Missouri railroads. "We sat down on the bench on the porch of the Pacific House," Dodge said afterward, "and he [Lincoln] proceeded to find out all about the country we had been through, and all about our railroad surveys . . . in fact, he extracted from me the information I had gathered for my employers, and virtually shelled my woods most thoroughly."

Whether Lincoln was impressed by young Dodge's arguments for a Council Bluffs–Omaha terminus for a transcontinental railroad is difficult to determine. In later life Dodge proved himself to be such an accomplished twister of the truth that all his statements must be carefully examined. Years afterward, Dodge claimed that Lincoln summoned him to a meeting in the White House during the spring of 1863 and that their discussion led to the President's using his authority to designate Council Bluffs as the starting point of the Union Pacific Railroad. The record shows, however, that Dodge was nowhere near Washington in the spring of 1863 and that Lincoln made his decision several months later, after

*Theodore Judah (de Grummond Collection,
University of Southern Mississippi Library)*

meeting with Thomas Durant and Peter Dey. It is likewise
difficult to determine what influence Dodge may have had
upon Durant, or what significance there may be in the fact
that both Dodge and Lincoln owned land in the Council
Bluffs area.

It was also during 1859 that a thirty-three-year-old Connecticut Yankee devoted his days to persuading assembly-
men in Sacramento, capital of the new state of California,
that they should take the initiative in building a railroad to
the East, from whence most of them had come. He was Theodore Judah, a civil engineer who had journeyed there to help
build a short-line railroad from Sacramento to the gold mines
east of the town. Before the road was completed, Judah became infected with the same fanaticism that had driven John
Plumbe and Asa Whitney in their fruitless efforts to promote
a transcontinental railway.

Although his humorless persistence won him the name
"Crazy Judah," he managed to assemble a number of delegates in October 1859 at San Francisco for an official California railroad convention. Representatives of stagecoach and

steamboat interests ridiculed Judah's belief that a railroad could be built across the rugged Sierras, but he persuaded the delegates to endorse a route eastward by way of the California overland trail which after passing through the Rockies followed the Platte Valley to Omaha and Council Bluffs. Perhaps as much to be rid of him as to support him, the delegates then voted to send Judah to Washington to lobby for his transcontinental railroad. Unlike his visionary predecessors, Theodore Dehone Judah was a trained engineer and a bulldog; the world would soon hear more of him.

In 1859, however, the Hannibal & St. Joseph Railroad seemed to be the most likely candidate for extension across the continent. It was the only completed rail route to the overland staging towns along the Missouri, and its passenger and freight traffic was heavy and profitable. In the spring of the following year, the road's hopes were boosted even more when Pony Express mail service to California was inaugurated at St. Joseph.

At about noon on April 3, 1860, a special messenger carrying mail from New York, Washington, and other Eastern cities crossed the Mississippi by ferry and boarded a special train on the Hannibal & St. Joseph. That day the engineer set a record that was not beaten for fifty years, by bringing the messenger into St. Joe in less than five hours, just in time to transfer the mail to the saddlebags of Johnny Frey, the first Pony Express rider. Flags were flying, bands were playing, and crowds were cheering orators who predicted that the Hannibal & St. Joe would soon extend its tracks "upon which a tireless Iron Horse will start his overland journey." A cannon boomed and jockey-sized Johnny Frey leaped into his saddle and galloped for the ferry that would take him across the Missouri to begin the long 1,966-mile run to California. "Hardly will the cloud of dust which envelops the rider die away," said St. Joseph's mayor Jeff Thompson, "before the puff of steam will be seen upon the horizon." So certain were the directors of the railroad that they would soon be hauling mail all the way to California, they ordered construction of a post-office car, the first of its kind, upon which mail could be sorted and bagged.

In that summer of 1860, however, the madness of oncoming war was spreading across the nation, and before another year passed, the diminutive Johnny Frey exchanged his Pony Express buckskins for the blue uniform of the Union Army. He marched off toward the South to die at the hands of the Arkansas Rangers. Mayor Jeff Thompson chose the gray uniform of the Confederacy and was soon leading guerrilla cavalry raids against the railroad he had so much praised and admired, the Hannibal & St. Joseph. As for Mark Twain, he became an unemployed steamboat pilot when war closed the Mississippi River to commercial steamboat traffic. He returned to pro-Southern Hannibal and drilled briefly with a group of young men he had known since boyhood. They called themselves the Hannibal Confederate Militia, but after a few days they became bored with drilling in the woods and disbanded. Not long afterward, Mark and his brother Orion (who had campaigned for Abraham Lincoln and been rewarded with a lucrative government appointment in Nevada Territory) arrived in St. Joseph. There they boarded a stagecoach bound west for the land of the future, leaving the Civil War behind them.

In the meantime, "Crazy Ted" Judah, having had little success as a lobbyist for his Pacific railroad, left Washington to return to California. He was still determined to build a transcontinental road. His new plan was to form a railroad company and sell enough stock to public-spirited Californians to get construction started. Being a practical engineer, he knew that he could not extract funds from practical businessmen until he proved to them that Iron Horses could cross the formidable Sierras. Discarding the impractical survey made in 1854 by Lieutenant Edward G. Beckwith for the Corps of Engineers, Judah went into the Sierras and made his own survey. An investor in a railroad, he reasoned, "does not care to be informed that there are 999 different varieties and species of plants and herbs, or that grass is abundant at that point; or buffalo scarce at that. His inquiries are somewhat more to the point. He wishes to know the length of your road. He says, let me see your map and profile, that I may judge of its alignment and grades. . . . Have you any tunnels, and what are their circumstances? . . . How many bridges, river

crossings . . . how about timber and fuel? Where is the estimate of the cost of your road, and let me see its detail."

And so while Civil War battles raged in the East, Judah
spent the summer mapping out a route through the Sierras
that was more than a hundred miles shorter than the Corps of
Engineers' survey. It would run from Dutch Flat through
Donner Pass and the Truckee River canyon, and then down
to the Washoe gold country of Nevada. It was the recent discovery of gold and silver, the fabulous Comstock Lode, in
Nevada that helped more than anything else to attract Sacramento's business leaders to Judah's railroad dream. The California gold rush, which had made them wealthy, was declining, and they were eager to extend their money-making
enterprises into Nevada. Judah's railroad might never be
completed, but his plan required a wagon road for hauling
supplies, and whoever owned that highway would control
commerce into and out of the booming Nevada mining towns.

Several of Sacramento's leading merchants, therefore,
decided to join "Crazy Judah" in his railroad scheme. Leland
Stanford operated a wholesale grocery business and was
planning to run for governor as a candidate of Abraham Lincoln's new political party, the Republicans. Collis P. Huntington and Mark Hopkins had started a miners' supply store
in a small tent in Sacramento and had built it into the largest
hardware enterprise on the Pacific Coast. Charles Crocker
owned a dry-goods store. Others were jewelers, owners of
mines, traders of various sorts. But it was Stanford, Huntington, Hopkins, and Crocker—the Big Four—who would
dominate the railroad that they incorporated on June 28,
1861, as the Central Pacific Railroad of California. Stanford
was president, Huntington vice-president, Hopkins treasurer, and Judah the chief engineer. On October 9 the officers
approved Judah's final survey and ordered him to return to
Washington as an accredited agent of the Central Pacific "for
the purpose of procuring appropriations of land and U.S.
bonds from the government, to aid in the construction of this
road."

Soon after Judah arrived in Washington, the recently
completed telegraph line across the continent brought the

news that Leland Stanford had been elected governor of California. The chief engineer was delighted, of course; he had not yet discovered that he was involved with men who could be absolutely ruthless wherever money was concerned. He was in somewhat the same position as Henry Farnam, but Farnam had only Dr. Durant to contend with while Judah had four men possessed of the same rapacious qualities.

As he was beginning his campaign for government assistance, Judah discovered that other railroad forces were hard at work on Capitol Hill. Representatives of the Hannibal &

Officers of the Central Pacific, clockwise from top left: Charles Crocker, Collis P. Huntington, President Leland Stanford, Mark Hopkins
(Culver Pictures)

St. Joseph were there, of course, but the most energetic group was headed by James C. Stone, president of the Leavenworth, Pawnee & Western Railroad Company. Stone employed a professional lobbyist to manage his campaign, although the Leavenworth company like the Central Pacific was only a paper railroad. With the assistance of the U.S. Office of Indian Affairs, however, it had swindled the Potawatomies and Delawares out of exclusive rights to hundreds of thousands of acres of tribal land.

In reporting this transaction from Leavenworth, Indian agent Thomas B. Sykes described the land as "surplus" and valued it at $1.25 per acre, although similar land in the area was then selling for ten dollars per acre. "By this treaty fifty miles of railroad is secured to the Territory of Kansas, without one dollar being paid from the territorial treasury or by the general government. . . . This is the first and greatest link in the great Pacific railway, west of the State of Missouri. It is another step toward the Pacific shores. It is another link in the iron chain that is to bind the Atlantic to the Pacific."

Agent Sykes failed to mention that not one foot of track had yet been laid, nor did this fact seem to concern the Leavenworth lobbyists in Washington. They had a good supply of stock certificates and land titles, which they showered upon influential Washingtonians such as Senator J. F. Simmons, journalist Benjamin Perley Poore, and politicians Thaddeus Stevens and James G. Blaine. Chief engineer Judah of the Central Pacific soon found himself working in close alliance with the Leavenworth promoters, and duly received twelve hundred shares of Leavenworth stock. During the spring of 1862, while armies were locked in battle in nearby Virginia, Thomas Durant joined the lobbyists. His aim of course was to persuade Congress to designate a transcontinental route across Nebraska from Omaha–Council Bluffs, but he appeared willing to compromise provided that there was money in it for him. Not long afterward, Collis Huntington, the domineering, heavy-framed vice-president of the Central Pacific, arrived in Washington. Evidently he feared that chief engineer Judah was not aggressive enough to make certain that Congress would give the Central Pacific everything it wanted.

Had the Civil War not been in progress, the powerful lobby of the Leavenworth group and the demonstrated success of the Hannibal & St. Joe Railroad quite likely would have swung Congress to their choice as the first links in a transcontinental railroad. Unfortunately for these companies, however, the Confederates were raising hell with Missouri railroads, wrecking trains, blowing up bridges, and capturing trainmen. The Rebels went so far as to kidnap the president of the Hannibal & St. Joe, threatening to shoot him unless he ordered train service completely halted. As for the projected Leavenworth railroad, it also was in border territory, vulnerable to raids by William Quantrill, Sterling Price, and other Confederate cavalry leaders.

It was soon obvious to those preparing the "Act to Aid in the Construction of a Railroad and Telegraph Line from the Missouri River to the Pacific Ocean" that the road would have to be built farther north. In the act's final version, the railroad was given a name, Union Pacific Railroad Company, and it was authorized to construct "a single line of railroad and telegraph from a point on the western boundary of the State of Iowa to be fixed by the President of the United States." Upon completion of forty consecutive miles of any part of the railroad, the company would receive title to five alternate sections of land on each side of the line and "bonds of the United States of one thousand dollars each, payable in thirty years after date, bearing six per centum per annum interest . . . to the amount of sixteen said bonds per mile." In the same act, the Central Pacific was authorized to construct a railroad from the Pacific coast to the eastern boundary of California upon the same terms and conditions as the Union Pacific—which meant that both would receive enormous land grants.

To ease the disappointment of supporters of the Leavenworth, Pawnee & Western and the Hannibal & St. Joe, the act also offered generous grants to them, provided that they extended their tracks westward across Kansas and joined the main line of the Union Pacific at the 100th meridian. Then, almost as an afterthought, the authors of the act stated that the government "shall extinguish as rapidly as may be the Indian titles to all lands falling under the operation of this act," although they made no recommendation as to how this was to be accomplished. In recognition of the difficulties of building a railroad under wartime conditions, the Union Pacific Company was given until July 1, 1876, the centennial of the republic, to lay its tracks to the western boundary of Nevada Territory.

On July 1, 1862, the day that his Army of the Potomac began retreating in Virginia after the Battle of Malvern Hill, President Lincoln signed the act, creating the Union Pacific Railroad Company. Thus was assured the fortunes of a dynasty of American families, many of whose names appear in the document as "commissioners," 158 of them—Brewsters, Bushnells, Olcotts, Harkers, Harrisons, Trowbridges, Langworthys, Reids, Ogdens, Bradfords, Noyeses, Brooks, Cornells, and dozens of others, including Huntington and Judah and a handful of swaggering frontier buccaneers such as Ben Holladay, the stagecoach king of the West.

Huntington and Judah wasted no time in transferring their company's activities to New York, where they established credit and placed orders for rails and locomotives for shipment by sea to California. Competition for any sort of iron was intense because of wartime demands for guns and military rolling stock. They were also handicapped by a restrictive clause in the Union Pacific act, which had been added by that wily old congressman from Pennsylvania, Thaddeus Stevens. Although Stevens had received a block of Leavenworth stock in exchange for his vote, that was not sufficient to satisfy him. He had also demanded insertion of a clause requiring that "all iron used in the construction and equipment of said road to be American manufacture." In addition to being a congressman, Stevens was an iron manufacturer. Consequently, when Huntington and Judah found themselves faced with high prices and long delays in obtaining rails and other equipment, they were forbidden to buy British iron, which was readily available and comparatively inexpensive and could have been delivered by sea to California almost as quickly as from New York.

In spite of these difficulties, the energetic founders of the Central Pacific managed to assemble enough equipment in California by the end of the year to announce that groundbreaking ceremonies would be held in Sacramento on January 8, 1863. On that morning heavy rains muddied the streets, but before noon the sun was shining brightly and a procession of carriages decorated in patriotic bunting wound hub-deep through the mud to a temporary platform near the Front Street levee a short distance above K Street. Bales of hay had to be strewn around the platform so that spectators would not sink into the mire while listening to the oratory. Even then, most of the women refused to subject their long skirts to the muck and so made their way to the balcony of a nearby hotel where a local brass band had also taken refuge.

The ceremonies began with the band playing "Wait for the Wagon" while two flag-covered wagons rolled up before the rostrum. On one of them was a large banner depicting hands clasped across the continent and bearing an inscription: MAY THE BOND BE ETERNAL.

After an interminable invocation by the local minister, Charlie Crocker, the former dry-goods merchant who now called himself general superintendent of the Central Pacific Railroad, arose to start the speech-making. Crocker's face was deeply flushed above his chin beard; he weighed more than 250 pounds and could bellow like a bull. At high noon he introduced the president of the Central Pacific, who was also the governor of California, Leland Stanford. Dignified in his frock coat and high silk hat, Stanford promised that the Pacific and Atlantic coasts would soon be bound by iron bonds. On the agenda of the day, his next duty was to turn the first spadeful of earth that would start construction of the railroad. As this was an impossible feat to accomplish in the straw-covered mud, someone had thoughtfully loaded a tubful of dry dirt into one of the wagons, and Stanford gravely leaned from the platform and lifted out a spadeful. "Nine cheers!" shouted Charlie Crocker, and the crowd responded.

"Everybody felt happy," reported the *Sacramento Union*, "because after so many years of dreaming, scheming, talking and toiling, they saw with their own eyes the actual commencement of a Pacific railroad." Ironically, the man whose dreams and schemes had led to this happy celebration was not present on that day. He was in the East, on one of his periodic journeys by sea and isthmus, desperately trying to obtain enough credit and iron to get the railroad built. A few months later, as he was crossing through the Panama jungles, a mosquito bit him, and on November 2, 1863, Theodore Judah died of yellow fever. Now his railroad was completely in the hands of greedy exploiters—the Big Four—Stanford, Huntington, Crocker, and Hopkins.

Meanwhile in the East, the Union Pacific Railroad was off to a much slower start. The bitter Civil War was closer at hand (the orators in faraway Sacramento had scarcely mentioned that conflict). In addition, the Union Pacific's ownership was much more numerous and diffused than that of the Central Pacific. Several ambitious men were jockeying for control, but none had been successful. In September 1862, sixty-eight of the original "commissioners" assembled in Chicago to hold their first meeting. They passed various resolutions, recommended the opening of stock subscription books in all the principal cities of the Union, and assured one another that "the pressure of war should not discourage the friends of the work, nor deter them from entering vigorously upon its prosecution." About all that was accomplished was the election of William B. Ogden of Chicago as president and Henry V. Poor as secretary. Ogden was already well on the way toward establishing his family's fortune through railroad promotion, and Poor was editor of the *Railroad Journal* and an avid collector of statistics on the subject.

Although Dr. Thomas Durant was not one of the Union Pacific commissioners and did not attend the original meetings in Chicago, he spent a considerable amount of his time during 1863 in scheming to seize the seat of power in that yet amorphous organization. According to the act that created the transcontinental railroad, two million dollars in stock had to be sold before construction could begin, and no one person could subscribe to more than two hundred shares at a thousand dollars per share, ten percent down. Noting that stock sales were moving very slowly (only 150 shares had been subscribed by March 1863), Durant adroitly arranged to buy more than the required two million dollars in stock in the names of several friends. Dr. Durant himself paid the ten percent down payment for them. Not only was he now in a position to control the next election of officers, which was set for October 1863, he was also ready to unload some of his Mississippi & Missouri stock at a profit sufficient to recover the down payments he had made for his friends on the Union Pacific stock. Although construction of the Mississippi & Missouri Railroad was still stalled in the middle of Iowa, Durant slyly released stories to the press announcing that the M. & M. Railroad had been "selected as the commencement of the Pacific route." As usual, Durant's trick worked. The stock soared in price and he sold out at the high point, increasing his personal fortunes considerably.

And then on October 30, at the organizational meeting of the Union Pacific in New York, Durant, using his majority of stockholder votes, replaced Ogden as president with old John A. Dix, the powerful politician who had worked to secure the Iowa land grants for Durant's M. & M. Dix was an excellent choice to serve as front man for Durant. He had a reputation for honesty, and spent most of his time strutting about Washington in a general's uniform. Durant knew that Dix would never bother him. Henry Poor, the railroad statistician, remained as secretary. As for Durant himself, he chose the title "vice-president and general manager," and he was so elected.

During this period of intense manipulation, a new associate had moved into Dr. Durant's orbit. He was George Francis Train, an unpredictable eccentric who had made a fortune in shipping and railroads. Train had been dabbling in street railways in England when the Civil War brought him back to America to help save the Union. He was still in his early thirties, and when chance brought him in touch with Durant, the romance of the transcontinental railroad immediately aroused his enthusiasm. In their viewpoints, Train and Durant were opposites. Durant enjoyed the acquisition of money and he had the patience of a spider in weaving webs to snare it. Train had little regard for money other than to use it in the enjoyment of life; his zest for action kept him in a state of perpetual impatience.

Train could not understand why the Union Pacific was so slow in getting construction started at Omaha. After all, almost a year had passed since the Central Pacific had broken

*George Francis Train, impassioned orator at the Union Pacific
groundbreaking ceremonies, Omaha, December 2, 1863 (New York
Public Library Picture Collection)*

ground at Sacramento, and its contractors were already laying
track toward the Sierras. Shadows of competition were also
on the horizon. President Lincoln had awarded an enormous
land grant to Cyrus K. Holliday, and if the Atchison, Topeka
& Santa Fe started moving it might well win support for a
transcontinental route from a changeable Congress. An even
greater threat appeared in the person of John C. Frémont. His
father-in-law, Thomas Hart Benton, had died in 1858, but
their old dream of a route from St. Louis along the 38th parallel still persisted in Frémont's mind. Frémont had made a
fortune from gold discovered on his California holdings. In
1863 he used a good part of it to form a partnership with
Samuel Hallett and buy a controlling interest in the Leavenworth, Pawnee & Western. At Frémont's insistence, they
changed the name to Union Pacific Railway, Eastern Division. Frémont meant to take his railroad to the Western Sea.
In the summer of 1863, while Union armies were winning
great victories at Gettysburg and Vicksburg, he advertised for

four thousand tons of iron rails to be delivered at Leaven-worth.

The impatient George Francis Train therefore had little difficulty in persuading Durant that the Union Pacific must hold a ground-breaking ceremony at Omaha. On December 2, 1863, two miles south of the ferry landing at Council Bluffs, several hundred people including the governor of Ne-braska and two companies of artillery assembled to hear Train deliver one of his impassioned orations. "The great Pacific railway is commenced," he cried, "at the entrance of a garden 700 miles in length and twenty broad. The Pacific railroad is the nation and the nation is the Pacific railway. This is the grandest enterprise under God!"

In response to a telegram from Durant, engineer Peter Dey, who had run surveys for the westward-pointed railways across Illinois and Iowa, came over from Iowa City. After the governor had turned a spadeful of earth, Dey read messages from Durant and from President Lincoln, the crowd cheered, and the artillery companies fired salutes to the great occa-sion.

Train returned to New York, certain that the railroad would be under construction by spring. A few weeks later, Dey received a telegram informing him that he had been ap-pointed chief engineer of the Union Pacific. As soon as the Nebraska mud dried out in the spring, Dey assembled a small gang of workmen and graded a few miles straight westward from Omaha. In 1864, however, the war was going badly for the Union, the armies suffering their last great bloodbaths be-fore the end. Durant shut down on expenditures and went off to Washington to lobby for increased benefits for the Union Pacific. Train stormed about, impatient at the delay. He vis-ited Omaha from time to time, built a new hotel because he did not like the one that was there, and then casually bought some cheap Omaha real estate, which like everything else he touched rapidly turned into millions of dollars.

At last the war ended, and hordes of young soldiers found themselves cut loose in a changed America. Thousands of them were immigrants—Irish, Germans, Swedes; thou-sands were former slaves, wandering westward in their first odyssey of freedom; thousands were defeated Confederates

Omaha as it was when the Union Pacific began building westward (Photo by A. J. Russell, The Oakland Museum)

Because no railroad had reached the Missouri River at Omaha in 1865, construction materials for the Union Pacific had to be hauled on steamboats to the Omaha landing. (Nebraska State Historical Society)

whose homes had vanished in the cataclysm of war. They were sturdy, muscular young men accustomed to hardships and dangers, accustomed to taking orders.

Instead of sinking into a slow period of recuperation at the close of its bloodiest war, the nation seemed to pause only momentarily, much like a person taking a deep breath of relief, and then it plunged into a frenetic race to rebuild. The Americans were searching for something—riches and power, riches and greatness, riches and fame. Greed was in the air. The Gilded Age was beginning.

Late in 1865, only a few months after the war's end, steamboats as numerous as wild geese were pushing up the Missouri River toward Omaha. (The railroads in Iowa were still months away from reaching the Missouri.) Some of the boats were loaded with iron rails, locomotives, shovels, plows, spikes; others carried passengers, mostly young men heading westward, looking for work. They were all coming together at Omaha, turning the languid trading posts and grog shops into a boom town, a city that would be the nation's center until parallel rails of iron stretched across the continent.

·◄▄ CHAPTER 4 ▄►·

Drill, Ye Tarriers, Drill, While the Owners Take the Plunder

IN THE LATE AUTUMN OF 1864, while General William Te-cumseh Sherman was marching through Georgia and the Civil War seemed close to its end, a dandified Easterner arrived in Omaha to inspect the twenty-three miles of grading that had been completed by chief engineer Peter Dey. His name was Colonel Silas Seymour, and he wore fancy clothing, kept his close-clipped graying hair and goatee neatly brushed at all times, and contrived an aristocratic air. He informed Dey that Dr. Durant had appointed him "consulting engineer" of the Union Pacific and that he was ready to perform his duties.

As the honest Mr. Dey was soon to discover, Colonel Seymour's title was a cover for espionage. Durant distrusted Dey, who liked to believe that the managers of the railroad were "trustees of the bounty of Congress." Dey also claimed to admire men of "integrity, purity and singleness of purpose." The earnest engineer was too much like Henry Farnam to suit Durant's tastes; in fact, Dey made no secret of his wish to have Farnam serve as president of the Union Pacific.

During 1864, Durant had successfully accomplished two major maneuvers that made it possible for him and his close associates to enter upon a colossal looting of the people's treasury and plundering of national land resources, and he wanted no interference with his plans. The first objective he achieved was establishment of an organization known as the Credit Mobilier. In conversations with George Francis Train, Durant had discussed the practicalities of railroad building and ownership. From previous experience, both men knew that the big money was made by construction contractors rather than by the operators or stockholders. Train recalled a

57

financial organization he had encountered in France—the Société Générale de Crédit Mobilier, which operated as a holding company to siphon off profits from construction of public works. By using such an apparatus, Durant could make contracts with himself at any price per mile he chose to set for construction of the railroad across the continent. Acting as an agent for Durant, Train purchased the charter of an incorporated Pennsylvania fiscal agency and converted it to the Credit Mobilier of America. Durant admitted afterward that he had gained control of this super-money-making device for a personal expenditure of only five hundred dollars.

Durant's second triumph of the year was to secure passage of a more generous Pacific Railway Act, one that granted twice as much land per mile (12,800 acres instead of 6,400), gave all iron and coal deposits under the land to the railroad, and permitted it to sell first-mortgage bonds to the public. In this grand steal he had the help of that equally greedy lobbyist for the Central Pacific, Collis Huntington. Durant took $437,000 of Union Pacific funds to Washington for lobbying expenses, and although some of his associates later charged that he put most of the money in his own pocket, proof was found that he had spent $18,000 entertaining congressmen at Willard's Hotel. He also spent a great deal more than that distributing Union Pacific stock to congressmen in exchange for their votes. Even by present-day standards of governmental venality, the methods used by Durant and Huntington were exceptionally crude. Congressman Oakes Ames, who with his brother Oliver manufactured shovels in Massachusetts, became a loyal ally and helped to pressure the 1864 Pacific Railway Act through the war-corrupted Congress. The Union Pacific was thus guaranteed a magnificent land grant, 19,000 square miles, a domain larger than the states of Massachusetts, Rhode Island, and Vermont combined. In recognition of their services, Durant invited Oakes and Oliver Ames into the tight little circle of Credit Mobilier stockholders.

With all these arranged riches awaiting the taking, Durant was now ready to begin railroad construction, and his first move was to send one of his New York henchmen to Omaha to sound out Peter Dey. The chief engineer had already submitted estimates of construction costs per mile for the first hundred miles across the rolling prairie country of eastern Nebraska. Dey's estimates averaged between $20,000 and $30,000 per mile, and Durant knew that Dey's figures were close to the real costs. What Durant wanted was an inflated estimate, at least $50,000, which would pour $20,000 to $30,000 per mile of excess profits into the closely held Credit Mobilier. Durant therefore sent one of his couriers, John E. Henry, out to see Dey, and Henry informed the engineer that Durant wanted the estimate raised to $50,000 per mile. As Dey had no knowledge then of the Credit Mobilier scheme, he complied with the request but at the same time made it clear that he believed $30,000 per mile was sufficient to cover costs.

Durant's next move was to arrange for an accomplice named Herbert M. Hoxie to submit a contract bid for construction of the first one hundred miles of railroad at $50,000 per mile. Hoxie was a crafty Iowa politician who had arranged various deals for Durant during the building of the Mississippi & Missouri Railroad in that state. Not long after Durant accepted Hoxie's bid, Hoxie transferred his contract to Credit Mobilier, which was controlled of course by Durant. Later investigations indicated that for this simple piece of paperwork Hoxie received $10,000 in Union Pacific bonds.

In November, Dey received a copy of the transferred Hoxie contract, and immediately suspected Durant's scheme. When Colonel Seymour arrived with the announcement that he was the Union Pacific's "consulting engineer" and began suggesting changes in the surveyed route westward from Omaha, Dey bluntly refused to cooperate. With Durant's secret backing, however, Seymour then proposed a more circuitous route, one that would require nine more miles of track to reach the same point that Dey's twenty-three miles of preliminary grading reached in a direct line. Seymour's purpose was obvious to Dey: the circuitous route would provide an increased government subsidy during the first days of construction, would enable the Union Pacific to acquire more valuable land close to the developing city of Omaha, and would eliminate a few embankments and bridges. Being an engineer who believed that railroad routes should be shortened wherever possible, Dey could not accept Seymour's proposal for professional reasons. And being an honest man, neither could he accept the inflated Hoxie–Credit Mobilier contract. On December 8, he wrote his letter of resignation: "My reasons for this step are simply that I do not approve of the contract made with Mr. Hoxie for building the first hundred miles from Omaha west, and I do not care to have my name so connected with the railroad that I shall appear to indorse this contract."

Durant never bothered to acknowledge Dey's letter of resignation. He simply informed Colonel Seymour that he was now the acting chief engineer of the Union Pacific and should get on with building the circuitous route. (Forty years later, when the U.P. entered upon a program of shortening its lines out of Omaha, it abandoned Seymour's route and used Dey's original direct route.) Although Seymour had some experience as a consulting engineer for Eastern railroads, he actually knew very little about railroad construction; for instance, he still believed that parallel timbers made better supports for rails than did cross ties. When he was ordered to use cross ties, he bought cheap cottonwood ties instead of contracting for hardwood, and then after discovering that they rotted quickly he invested hundreds of thousands of dollars in a wood-preservation device. A steam-pressure process known as Burnetizing forced zinc into the cotton-wood, but time eventually proved it to be almost worthless.

Samuel B. Reed, who had worked with Dey and Farnam on the railroads out of Chicago, directed most of the surveying for the revised route, and he quickly recognized Seymour for the popinjay he was. Even the Pawnee Indians laughed at Seymour when he rode out on horseback to inspect the progress of the road; on these occasions he usually wore a black silk top hat and carried an umbrella to protect himself from the summer sun.

It was July 10, 1865, before Seymour's crew laid the first rail, and the best they could do across the level prairie was one mile of track per week. In October, when Durant visited Omaha with General William T. Sherman to try to speed up construction, only fifteen miles of track had been completed. Funds were running short, and more miles of track were needed in order to claim more money from the government. The invitation to Sherman was probably one of George Francis Train's promotion ideas, and Durant entered into it enthusiastically. Next to General Grant, Sherman received more attention from the press than did any other of the Civil War heroes, and the Union Pacific was in dire need of good publicity to spur sales of its stock.

To please Sherman they painted the general's name in gilt letters on Union Pacific Locomotive No. 1. As no passenger cars had yet been brought up the Missouri, they attached to the Iron Horse a platform car covered with upended nail kegs to which boards were fastened for seats. Sherman, Durant, Train, and the dozen or so other men in the party wrapped themselves in buffalo robes and rode the fifteen miles to end of track at Sailing's Grove, where they picnicked on roast duck and champagne. "The party was jolly in going out and hilarious in coming in," an Omaha newspaper reported. "Everybody was anxious for a speech from Sherman."

Sherman made no speech, but between drinks he told of how he had invested money in a proposed railroad while he was stationed in California before the war, and had lost all of his investment. "I might live to see the day," he said, "but can scarcely expect it at my age, when the two oceans will be connected by a complete Pacific railroad." As Sherman was only forty-five, he undoubtedly was taunting Durant and his associates for their slowness in building tracks across the easily spanned Nebraska plain. During that autumn, some Eastern newspapers had been even more critical, for instance the *New York Times*:

"With numerous plans and many subsidies from Congress, the parties who have been urging the project of a Pacific railroad have failed to carry them out. Their schemes are all broken to pieces, or they are used for speculative purposes, in bolstering up some sinking or perhaps bogus stock. . . . The people on the Pacific side, with their usual energy, commenced their end of the route some two years since, and, notwithstanding the war and the high price of gold, have ascended over half way from Sacramento City to the summit of the Sierra Nevada mountains."

Before Sherman departed Omaha, there must have been private conversations about this problem of slackness. Durant was becoming increasingly aware of a provision in the Pacific Railway Act that might cause the Union Pacific to lose its transcontinental subsidy entirely if one of the Kansas railroads should reach the 100th meridian first. That autumn, the old Leavenworth road, which had changed its name to Union Pacific, Eastern Division, completed sixty miles and its work crews were reported to be laying a mile of track each day. Durant made an effort to neutralize the Eastern Division through financial control from New York, but he failed in this and he knew that if the Kansas railroad reached the 100th meridian before the Union Pacific, the government might very well assign it the right to continue building to California.

It was soon obvious to Durant that although Colonel Seymour might be a loyal crony, he lacked the drive to win the now-developing 257-mile race to the 100th meridian. A new chief engineer had to be found, and Sherman highly recommended thirty-five-year-old Grenville Dodge, who had been one of his most dependable generals during the Georgia campaign. Durant remembered Dodge from his work in Illinois and Iowa before the war and was wary of him because of his former close association with Henry Farnam and Peter Dey. Yet he chose Dodge eventually, the young general agreeing to leave the Indian-fighting Army and report for duty in May 1866.

In the meantime, Durant also employed another former general, John S. Casement, who had commanded a division and was from Sherman's home state of Ohio. Before the war Casement had been a track hand in Michigan and then foreman of a track-building gang in Ohio. In the spring of 1866, after accepting the Union Pacific track-laying contract through Durant's Credit Mobilier, Jack Casement and his brother Daniel arrived in Omaha. Standing in his laced boots, Jack Casement reached only five feet four inches, and Dan was even shorter, "five feet nothing." They resembled a pair of bearded midgets, but those who might have been deceived by their appearance soon joined in the general opinion that they were "the biggest little men you ever saw." Adam

General John S. Casement (Photo by A. J. Russell, The Oakland Museum)

Dan Casement, standing left in doorway, with field headquarters associates (Photo by A. J. Russell, The Oakland Museum)

Schoup, employed by Jack Casement as his personal wag-
oner, said he "never saw a man you worked harder for. Many
times we drove 24 hours, changing horses, and when I played
out, Jack drove."

From the swarms of westward-bound men coming up the
Missouri, the Casements hired about a thousand of the stur-
diest. Although tradition holds that most of these men were
Irish, there was a goodly number of American-born veterans
of the Union and Confederate armies and several former
Negro slaves. To fill out the ranks, General Dodge made the
startling proposal that the contractors use captured Indians to
do the grading, with the Army furnishing "a guard to make
the Indians work, & to keep them from running away." He
was not taken up on this proposition to enslave red men; after
all, most of the workers building the railroad had just finished
four years of fighting a war to free four million black slaves.

To solve the problem of logistics in building a railroad
supplied by a single track pushing out across hundreds of
miles of uninhabited country, the Casement brothers invented the "work train." To an Iron Horse they attached
about a dozen cars, each one designed to serve a special purpose—a car filled with tools, one outfitted as a blacksmith
shop, another with rough dining tables and kitchen and commissary, others with built-in bunks, and at the end several
flatcars loaded with rails, spikes, fishplates, bolts, and other
road-building supplies. It was in fact a self-sufficient small
town on wheels.

With the arrival of General Dodge in May, the building
of the Union Pacific took on all the aspects of a military
operation. "The men who go ahead [surveyors and locators]
are the advance guard," noted one newspaper correspondent,
"and following them is the second line [the graders] cutting
through the gorges, grading the road and building the bridges.
Then comes the main body of the army, placing the ties, laying the track, spiking down the rails, perfecting the alignment, ballasting and dressing up and completing the road
for immediate use. Along the line of the completed road
are construction trains pushing 'to the front' with supplies.
The advance limit of the rails is occupied by a train of long

box-cars with bunks built within them, in which the men sleep at night and take their meals. Close behind this train come train loads of ties, rails, spikes, etc., which are thrown off to the side. A light car drawn by a single horse gallops up, is loaded with this material and then is off again to the front. Two men grasp the forward end of the rail and start ahead with it, the rest of the gang taking hold two by two, until it is clear of the car. At the word of command it is dropped into place, right side up, during which a similar operation has been going on with the rail from the other side—thirty seconds to the rail for each gang, four rails to the minute. As soon as a car is unloaded, it is tipped over to permit another to pass it to the front and then it is righted again and hustled back for another load.

"Close behind the track-layers comes the gaugers, then the spikers and bolters. Three strokes to the spike, ten spikes to the rail, four hundred rails to the mile. Quick work, you say—but the fellows on the Union Pacific are tremendously in earnest."

Jack and Dan Casement certainly were in earnest. They set a goal of one mile of track per day, offering each track layer a pound of tobacco if a mile of track was laid between sunup and sundown. When they reached that goal, the Casements offered three dollars per day instead of the regular two dollars if the men could lay a mile and a half. And then as the workmen sweated under the midsummer sun, the Casements offered four dollars for two miles a day.

It was at about this time that the iron-men laying the rails, the head spikers, the fishplate bolters, the track liners, and the back-iron men began to sing as they worked. Among the popular songs were "Whoops Along, Luiza Jane," "Pat Maloy," and "Brinon on the Moor." Off duty, they had harmonicas and jew's harps to accompany their voices, and one workman afterward recalled singing such gems as "How Are You Horace Greeley, Does Your Mother Know You're Out?" and "I'm a Rambling Rake of Poverty, the Son of a Gambolier."

Exactly when they created their own railroad worksongs is difficult to determine. A contemporary observer noted the peculiar rhythm of track laying, with the track boss commanding "Down," "Down," every thirty seconds to signal the dropping of the rails into place. "They were the pendulum beats of a mighty era; they marked the time of the march and its regulation step." The spike drivers also developed a grunting exhalation of breath to accompany the rhythmic ring of their sledgehammers, but the railroad ballads of the period seem ill fitted to this beat: "The great Pacific railway for California hail, Bring on the locomotive, lay down the iron rail," or "Poor Paddy he works on the railroad." More suited was "Drill, my Paddies, drill. Drill all day, No sugar in your tay, Workin' on the U.P. Railway." Not until twenty years later, however, was the chorus of that song—which is more closely associated with the building of the Union Pacific than is any other—set to music and published:

> Drill, ye tarriers, drill.
> Drill, ye tarriers, drill,
> Oh, it's work all day
> No sugar in your tay,
> Workin' on the U. Pay Ra-ailway!

As for Dr. Durant and his cronies, there is no record of what they sang as they collected the $16,000 per mile from the government for the track laid by the workmen, the $25,000 per mile of excess profits from Credit Mobilier, the 12,800 acres of land per mile, and whatever else they were able to divert from the sales of stocks and bonds. Instead of singing, they were always spending money to generate money, and there never seemed to be enough.

By August 1, the work train was 150 miles west of Omaha, and more laborers were added to the payroll. As the nights grew colder, Casement supplied the men with tents, and every night the tent city moved another mile or two across the plains of Nebraska.

Early in that summer of 1866, the employers of the Casement brothers were given another incentive to loosen their purse strings and speed construction. Congress unexpectedly lifted the Pacific Railway Act's restriction on the Central

Pacific, which forbade that railroad to build any farther than 150 miles east of the California-Nevada border. From now on, the meeting point of the two railroads would be determined by the rapidity with which each could lay tracks eastward and westward. The news came like a pistol shot signaling the start of a race across the continent. The Union Pacific responded by employing more graders and throwing them fifty to a hundred miles out ahead of the track layers. General Dodge packed his surveying instruments and with Sam Reed, who had been appointed superintendent of construction, headed for Wyoming to choose the final route through the Rockies.

After the Casement brothers easily won the 247-mile race to the 100th meridian on October 5, 1866, Durant, Train, and Seymour organized a grand excursion to that point on the Nebraska plain. They sent invitations to President Andrew Johnson and members of his cabinet, to all members of Congress and foreign ambassadors, and, more importantly from Durant's viewpoint, to numerous wealthy investors. "No railroad excursion of similar character and magnitude," boasted Colonel Seymour, "had ever been projected in this or any other country."

President Johnson did not accept; he was growing suspicious of what he called "the railroad aristocracy" and feared that its financial and political power was replacing the old slave-holding "oligarchy." By the time the various parties from the East joined at Omaha, however, the excursionists numbered more than two hundred of the nation's richest and most powerful men and women, with a corps of newspapermen and a photographer to record the events. Being a gourmet himself, Colonel Seymour arranged for elaborate bills of fare to accompany the receptions and balls at Omaha—boiled trout à la Normande, leg of mutton with caper sauce, quails on toast, buffalo tongue, escalloped oysters Louisiana style, antelope with sauce Bigarde, brazed bear in port wine sauce, grouse in Madeira sauce, and teal ducks à la royale.

For the rail journey from Omaha to the 100th meridian, the excursionists boarded four brand-new passenger coaches, and had the run of a saloon car outfitted with a bar, a mess car for meals, the U.P. directors' car, and Dr. Durant's private car, which had been Abraham Lincoln's official car during the war and had been acquired by Durant after it was used to transport the assassinated President's body from Washington to Springfield, Illinois. (The Lincoln car was said to have built inside its walls sheets of boiler plate strong enough to stop rifle bullets. After Durant exchanged it for one of George Pullman's special cars, his associates continued to use the Lincoln car when traveling across the plains where defiant Indians occasionally fired on passing trains. In its later years the ornate fittings were removed, crude wooden seats installed, and it was used to transport immigrants at bargain rates.)

Excursionists from the East at the 100th Meridian

At Columbus, Nebraska, they stopped for the night at a tent encampment luxuriously furnished with mattresses, buffalo robes, and blankets, and by the light of campfires and a harvest moon they watched a band of Pawnees perform a war dance. The next morning, the train rolled on to the fifteen-hundred-foot Loup–Fork bridge, where the Pawnees, mounted on horses, again entertained with a mock battle. After it was over, Dr. Durant paid off the actors with the usual baubles and gimcracks, a gesture meant to please his guests who were unaware that the Pawnees had forced Durant to pay a hundred dollars cash down before they would perform. The Pawnees had been dealing with white men going West for a long time, and had learned the emptiness of their promises and the value of their money.

(*New York Public Library Picture Collection*)

When the excursionists reached the 100th meridian, instead of finding track layers at work, there was only a wide arched sign bearing the inscription: 100TH MERIDIAN, 247 MILES FROM OMAHA. The Casement brothers and their "tarriers" had moved on another twenty-two miles west. Eager to show his guests how a railroad was built, Durant ordered the excursion continued to end of track, where they watched the sweating workmen until sundown. Only once did the men pause in their exertions, and that was to pose for a photograph made by Professor John Carbutt, the official *viewist*. At dusk the workmen retired to their crude tent camp to dine on beans and fatback while the excursionists gathered in their luxurious encampment to enjoy lamb with green peas, roasted antelope, and Chinese duck, all washed down with champagne. After dinner Colonel Seymour brought out a case of fireworks, sending up rockets, exploding stars, and pinwheels to keep boredom away until bedtime. Those track builders who were not too weary to stay awake could, of course, share in this heavenly spectacle.

On the return trip the next morning, the train halted beside the 100th meridian arch, and for an hour the dignitaries and their wives posed in various groupings for the official photographer. In one of the prints that has survived, Dr. Durant can be seen in a hunting costume, a rifle thrown nonchalantly across his shoulder as he leans against one of the arch supports. Standing slightly apart from him are five other directors of the Union Pacific in long-tailed coats and black silk hats. Behind them is the balloon-stacked Iron Horse decorated with large flags and elkhorns, its tender heaped high with lengths of cottonwood.

Late that evening they were back in Omaha, and as Colonel Seymour reported in his best booster style, "thus ended the most important and successful celebration of the kind that has ever been attempted in the world." From his viewpoint and that of the other directors of the U.P., the excursion did prove to be a profitable investment. After the return of the politicians and financiers to the East, the attention of the nation was soon fastened upon the activities of the Union Pacific, and millions of dollars in bonds were quickly sold. Many important newspapers began sending correspondents out to the Great Plains, and most of these journalists were treated like visiting royalty by the railroad's representatives. Virtually every report sent back to be published depicted the Union Pacific as a *national* endeavor, a heroic undertaking by the people of America, with the Plains Indians cast in the role of villains. No matter that the Iron Horse was invading traditional hunting grounds of a dozen native tribes, frightening away their food supply of wild game, and tracking across land held sacred for generations—if the "redskins" resisted, they were evil, because they stood in the way of the compulsive drive toward the Western Sea. In this atmosphere of noble purpose, it became a patriotic duty to invest one's money in Union Pacific stock (even though Credit Mobilier was siphoning off most of the profits) and to defend the transcontinental railroad against subversive detractors, who might have pointed out that although the people of America were paying for the railroad it did not belong to them.

Late in November, with the blizzard season imminent on the plains, the Casement brothers ordered their men into winter quarters at the confluence of the North and South Platte rivers. They named the place North Platte; it was 290 miles west of Omaha. When the construction crew of more than two thousand men erected their tent city, the only permanent structure was the railroad station. But because North Platte was the end of track, it immediately became the staging point for overland traffic to the West. Mormon emigrants bound for Utah gathered in canvas shelters awaiting the spring; soldiers, goldseekers, and settlers waited for stagecoaches; freight piled up under mounds of protective sailcloth awaiting wagon trains.

Within a few weeks a hundred buildings were erected—hotels, warehouses, saloons, and bordellos. North Platte became the first of the wild, riproaring railroad towns that would follow the tracks to the West. Gamblers, harlots, and other camp followers who had preyed upon soldiers during the Civil War at last found them again in North Platte.

"The larger part of the floating population is made up of desperadoes," reported one correspondent, "who spend their time in gambling of all kinds, from cards to keno to faro. Day and night the saloons are in full blast, and sums of money varying from five dollars to fifty and even one hundred change hands with a rapidity astonishing to one who is not accustomed to the recklessness which their wild frontier life invariably begets." A traveler passing through North Platte that winter noted laconically: "Law is unknown here." And then he added that the inhabitants "were having a good time gambling, drinking, and shooting each other."

When Henry Morton Stanley, then a reporter for the *Missouri Democrat*, stepped off the train at North Platte the following spring he found the place in a lively uproar. "Every gambler in the Union seems to have steered his course for North Platte, and every known game under the sun is played here. The days of Pike's Peak and California are revived. Every house is a saloon, and every saloon is a gambling den. Revolvers are in great requisition. Beardless youths imitate to the life the peculiar swagger of the devil-may-care bull-whacker and blackleg. . . . On account of the immense freighting done to Idaho, Montana, Utah, Dakota, and Colorado, hundreds of bull-whackers walk about, and turn the one street into a perfect Babel. Old gamblers who reveled in the glorious days of 'flush times' in the gold districts, declare that this town outstrips all yet."

Although the track layers went into winter quarters in

The Central Pacific's first timetable (New York Public Library Picture Collection)

CENTRAL PACIFIC RAILROAD.

No. 1,   TIME CARD   No. 1.

To take effect Monday June 6th, 1864, at 5 A. M.

TRAINS EASTWARD.				STATIONS.	TRAINS WESTWARD.		
Frt and Pass No 3	Frt and Pass No 2	Pass & Mail No 2			Frt and Pass No 1	Pass & Mail No 2	Frt and Pass No 3
5 PM leave	1 PM leave	8.45 A M, L		Sacramento	8.45 A M arr	12 M arr.	6.40 P M ar.
5.30 } mt frt	3.15	8.85	18	Junction	18	11.20	5.55 } mt Ft
6.09	2.38	7.03	22	Rocklin	4	7.40	11.07	3.37
6.22	2.65	7.13 mt F	23	Pino	3	7.18 mt pass	10.56	3.22
6.40	3.30 PM arr	7.30 A M arr	31	Newcastle	6	5.45 A M, L	10.30 A M, L	3 P M, L

Trains No. 2 and 3 east, and 1 and 3 west, daily, except Sunday.
Trains No. 1 east and 2 west, daily.

LELAND STANFORD, President.

November, they continued to lay rails when weather permitted, and at year's end Jack Casement reported that the track reached to Milepost 305. For the new year of 1867, the Union Pacific also acquired a new president, old John A. Dix having departed to serve as minister to France. For Dix's replacement, Durant the kingmaker chose the wealthy Massachusetts shovelmaker, Oliver Ames, brother of Congressman Oakes Ames. At the U.P. meeting that elected Oliver Ames president, Oakes Ames sponsored a new director. He was fifty-five-year-old Sidney Dillon, who had been a railroader all his working life, and who had scented the money in Durant's Credit Mobilier. Soon after he became a director in the company, Dillon and the Ames brothers began buying up as many shares of Credit Mobilier as they could find loose on the underground market. Soon they would challenge the financial dictatorship of Dr. Durant.

Meanwhile in California, without benefit of very much publicity in the East, the Central Pacific seemed to be playing the role of tortoise in the race with the suddenly harelike Union Pacific. On the day that the U.P. laid its first rail at Omaha (July 10, 1865) the C.P. was fifty miles out of Sacramento and was building an advance camp at Cisco, forty-two miles farther up the western slope of the Sierras. Sacramento lay at thirty feet above sea level, Cisco at almost six thousand, which explains the difficulties the graders, bridge builders, and tunnelers faced in bringing an Iron Horse to the seven-thousand-foot elevation of the Sierra summit before it could descend to the Nevada plateau. (The owners of the C.P. were somewhat compensated for this difficult passage by receiving $48,000 per mile from the government as compared with the $16,000 per mile the U.P. received for its track across the level plains.)

Another major problem faced by the Central Pacific was a shortage of labor. Most Californians could earn more than the two or three dollars per day that the railroad offered, and arrivals from the East tended to seek their fortunes in gold and silver mines. The C.P.'s oxlike general superintendent, Charlie Crocker, stormed about in a futile search for laborers until he finally decided to employ some Chinese out of San Francisco. He took the idea to his construction superintendent, James Harvey Strobridge, who indignantly refused. Strobridge was a professional railroad builder, a Vermont Irishman with the same compulsion to get things done as Jack and Dan Casement, and he did not hold a high regard for Crocker, the former dry-goods merchant. Strobridge had started as a track layer on the Fitchburg Railroad, which ran near Walden Pond, but by the time the whistles of the Iron Horses on that line were annoying Henry Thoreau, he was on his way to California to dig for gold. Instead of becoming a miner, he worked on short-line railways, and Crocker hired him in 1864. The two men had much in common, being bluff, direct, physically powerful, and inclined to settle arguments with their fists.

At first Strobridge scorned Crocker's proposal to hire Chinese to build a railroad. Crocker, however, pointed out that they would work for thirty-five dollars a month, much cheaper than the drifters they were using and who were always threatening to strike. But the Chinese were too frail, Strobridge protested, they ate nothing but rice; no Chinaman was strong enough to move earth and stone and dig tunnels. "Did they not build the Chinese Wall," Crocker shouted, "the biggest piece of masonry in the world?" Strobridge had to admit they had. "All right," he said, "let's hire fifty Chinese on a trial basis. If they can't cut the mustard, that's it."

After Strobridge had worked the first gang of Chinese for a long twelve-hour day, he notified Crocker to send him fifty more. Within a few weeks Crocker had agents out in all the California towns, signing up every Chinese male they could find. Strobridge, who would have readily admitted to being a slave driver, said that they were the best workers in the world. "They learn quickly, do not fight, have no strikes that amount to anything, and are very cleanly in their habits. They will gamble, and do quarrel among themselves most noisily—but harmlessly." At the end of 1865, after the Central Pacific had employed virtually every able-bodied Chinese in California, the railroad's president, Leland Stanford, was attempting to import fifteen thousand more from China.

Popular though the Chinese may have been with the owners of the C.P., they were heartily disliked by the other

Chinese camp at Brown's Station (California State Library)

Chinese laborer in typical blue-dyed cotton clothing and basket hat at Tunnel No. 8 (California State Library)

More workmen arriving from China to build the Central Pacific (New York Public Library Picture Collection)

workers, many of whom would throw down their tools and walk away at sight of the Chinese dressed in their neat blue-dyed cotton clothing and umbrella-shaped basket hats. When Samuel Bowles of the *Springfield* (Mass.) *Republican* visited the Central Pacific in the summer of 1865, he was told that of the four thousand men at work on the railroad, nine-tenths were Chinese, and that five thousand more Chinese would soon be employed.

Bowles was one of several newspapermen traveling with Schuyler Colfax, then Speaker of the House of Representatives and soon to become Vice-President under President Ulysses Grant. Like all congressmen, Colfax enjoyed traveling luxuriously at government expense, and on this particular junket he was probably making up his mind which end of the transcontinental railroad would offer the most returns for his political insight and favors. The Central Pacific had its own version of the Union Pacific's money-making Credit Mobilier; it was called the Credit and Finance Corporation, but it was even more closely held than Credit Mobilier. The Big Four—Stanford, Huntington, Crocker, and Hopkins—kept this golden goose all to themselves. They acknowledged the visit of the Speaker of the House of Representatives by giving the name Colfax to a station at the end of track, to perpetuate his memory as a friend of railroad owners. But this was not enough for the Speaker. He preferred cash above honors, and back in Washington he eagerly accepted a bundle of Credit Mobilier stock from his fellow congressman Oakes Ames, and thus became a loyal friend of the Union Pacific.

Because of distance and relative inaccessibility, the Central Pacific was unable to compete with the Union Pacific in free excursions for politicians, financiers, and newspapermen, but it did serve as a useful model to inspire Union Pacific employees to work longer and harder. After the Central Pacific won the right from Congress in 1866 to extend its tracks as far beyond the California-Nevada border as was necessary to meet the Union Pacific tracks, Crocker and Strobridge began driving their workmen as hard as the Casement brothers were driving theirs. Each mile covered by iron rails immediately turned into money and land, and the greed of each competing company was intensified by the race across the continent, thus proving that there is nothing like a sense of rivalry to make men commit reckless deeds in war and in love, in business or in engineering.

As the Chinese rolled tons of earth and stone in wheelbarrows to build embankments around the sides of mountains and chipped away at the granite rock of tunnels, the Big Four fretted over the slow pace at which track miles were being added across the Sierras. In the autumn of 1866, while the Union Pacific was leaping a mile a day across the level plains, the Central Pacific work crews climbed doggedly yard by yard toward the snow-clad summits. In November they reached Cisco, ninety-two miles from Sacramento. Determined to use the winter for tunneling, Strobridge hauled hundreds of Chinese a dozen miles up the wagon road and put them to work digging, blasting, and hauling away the rock debris at both ends of Summit Tunnel, designed to run a quarter of a mile through the stony heart of the last mountain.

To mark the new year of 1867, the *Sacramento Union* reported that the Central Pacific was in daily operation to Cisco, "5,911 feet above the level of the sea—a higher altitude than is attained by any other railroad in America. . . . Twelve tunnels, varying from 800 to 1,650 feet in length, are in process of construction along the snow belt between the summit and Truckee River, and are being worked night and day by three shifts of men, eight hours each, every twenty-four hours—employing in these tunnels an aggregate of 8,000 laborers."

In the snows of the Sierras and the blizzards of the Great Plains, the race slowed perceptibly, but the coming of spring 1867 would see its renewal, a continuation of the greatest engineering and construction effort undertaken since the arrival of the first Europeans on the American continent.

CHAPTER 5

The Era of the Cowboy Is Born

Soon after the Kansas railroad known as the U.P. Eastern Division lost the race to the 100th meridian, its directors decided to change the name to Kansas Pacific Railroad and to petition Congress for permission to alter the survey of its original route. Instead of turning northwestward into Nebraska to connect with the main line of the Union Pacific, the Kansas Pacific would continue straight west up the valley of the Smoky Hill River and then on to Denver.

By taking the Smoky Hill route, the railroad intruded upon the heartland of Indian hunting country, the food preserve of numerous tribes and subtribes of the Sioux, Cheyenne, and Arapaho. For this reason, from 1867 to 1869 Indian resistance on the Kansas plains reached a peak, and although tradition has it that workers on the Union Pacific were under constant attack from Indians, the men who bore the brunt of these skirmishes were workers on the *Eastern Division,* or the Kansas Pacific. (Not until 1880 was this railroad finally merged permanently with the Union Pacific.)

"From Leavenworth I took railway to Topeka, fifty-eight miles," wrote Albert D. Richardson in the autumn of 1866. "The road climbs ridges like saw-teeth; jolts one like corduroys, and rocks him like a rough cradle. It leads through the old Delaware reservation, not long open to settlement, but great cornfields and herds of cattle already appear. The remaining members of this and other Kansas tribes will soon be removed to the Indian Territory, or some other remote region. The whites want their lands—and have the power."

Later that year, the railroad's tracks reached Fort Riley, where Lieutenant-Colonel George Armstrong Custer had just arrived to assist in the organization of the Seventh Cavalry; the regiment's reason for being was to drive the Plains Indi-

*William J. Palmer (The State Historical
Society of Colorado Library)*

ans from the path of the railway. In that same autumn, William J. Palmer organized an excursion party to rival that of Durant and Train in Nebraska. As treasurer and director of construction of the road, Palmer became its driving force after John C. Frémont left it to sink the remainder of his fortune in the Atlantic & Pacific Railroad.

One of those many youthful brigadier generals produced by the recent Civil War, William Palmer's chief claim to fame was that he had led a Pennsylvania cavalry unit in pursuit of the fleeing President of the Confederacy, Jefferson Davis, and had assisted in his capture. Palmer was still in his twenties, dynamic, handsome, and unusually belligerent for a man of Quaker antecedents. A decade later he would be involved in the first Western railroad war, an armed conflict between the Santa Fe and the Denver & Rio Grande.

In 1866, Palmer's job was to raise money for completion of the railroad into Denver. To impress prospective financial backers and the accompanying newspaper writers, Palmer arranged for them to travel in one of George Pullman's first experimental "sleeping cars," which they boarded in Chicago. "The car cost twenty thousand dollars!" one of the passengers exclaimed, and he was even more astonished to learn that Pullman was spending thirty thousand on a more advanced model. "Every comfort which can be placed in such a vehicle is to be found within its wooden walls. The seats, the sides of the car and the ceiling are exquisitely adorned in *marquetrie* or inlaid woods, while the gilded glass frames, in *ormolu*, and the general tone of color, are truly artistic. It is heated by a separate furnace beneath, and its lounges and mirrors, with every other luxury, make it in fact a rolling palace."

For most of the journey across Kansas to Fort Riley, the party was awash in champagne, the constant popping of corks accompanied by "the merry laughter of lady voices." As there was no dining car or station restaurants west of Topeka, the train stopped occasionally for the cooks to build a fire beside the track and prepare open-air meals of buffalo steaks and other choice viands. At Fort Riley they found the end of track, but they journeyed on by stagecoach to inspect part of the fifty miles of grading that ran straight toward the Colorado line.

One of the reporters was so delighted by the energetic enterprise, and by the vitality and buoyancy of spirits that he found everywhere along the railroad, that he resolved to abandon his plans to travel in Europe and instead return later to follow the track farther westward. "The world," he said philosophically, "in each of its great stages of development has had one *grand route*, which has been the real world of man while it lasted." After listing several famed travelers' routes used in past centuries, he added: "Now we are building another road—the most wonderful of all—through regions once unknown, and men call it the Pacific Railway."

That General Palmer's excursion was helpful in raising more cash was indicated by a burst of energetic building that resumed along the line early in 1867. By March the rails were laid into Abilene, and in June they reached the north bank of Smoky Hill River, eighty-three miles west of Fort Riley. Here was another military post, Fort Ellsworth. For some reason the name was changed to Fort Harker and a land speculator divided the ground to the west into town lots and named the village Ellsworth. When Henry M. Stanley reported its birth for his St. Louis newspaper, he wrote: "The population of the town of Ellsworth is estimated at forty men, four women, eight boys and seven girls. There are also fourteen horses, and about twenty-nine and one-half dogs. . . . As Ellsworth is part and parcel of this great and progressive country, it is also progressive—for no sooner has the fifth house begun to erect its stately front above the green earth, than the population is gathered in the three saloons to gravely discuss the propriety of making the new town a city, and of electing a mayor." Neither Stanley nor anyone else could have foreseen that within six years, thousands of Longhorn cattle and hundreds of cowboys coming up the trails from Texas would change Ellsworth into a wild and woolly cow town.

"Wonderful indeed, is the rapidity with which the rolling hills are cleft, roads graded, ties laid down, and the rails secured to their places by the railroad-makers," Stanley continued. "Squads of Irishmen under energetic taskmasters, are scattered all along working with might and main as if they had an interest in the road apart from their daily bread or monthly wages. 'Excelsior' is the motto all round, and westward do empire and civilization wend their way."

The "squads of Irishmen" in the advance construction camps increased to twelve hundred men, and General Palmer ran low on bacon and beef with which to feed them. His meat contractors, Goddard Brothers of Kansas City, sent out a twenty-one-year-old marksman named William F. Cody to hunt buffalo for the workmen. For five hundred dollars a month young Cody guaranteed to supply all the buffalo meat the construction gangs could consume. One day a hunting party of Army officers from Fort Harker came upon a herd of eleven buffalo, but before they could bring their rifles into action, they saw Cody come up at a gallop and slay the entire herd with twelve shots. According to legend, the amazed officers nicknamed the Kansas Pacific's meat hunter Buffalo Bill, and so was born one of the American West's most enduring folk heroes.

Contemporary with Buffalo Bill the hunter and scout was the American cowboy. Undoubtedly the cowboy would have flourished at some time in the late nineteenth century, but the Kansas Pacific Railroad brought him upon the scene early with the establishment of cattle shipping points in towns west of the settled areas—Abilene, Ellsworth, and finally Hays City. The first of the Kansas Pacific's cattle towns was Abilene. When Joseph McCoy, an Illinois livestock trader, arrived there in the early summer of 1867 he described it as "a very small, dead place consisting of about one dozen log huts, low, small rude affairs, four-fifths of which were covered with dirt for roofing. . . . The business of the burg was conducted in two small rooms, mere log huts, and of course the inevitable saloon, also in a log hut, could be found."

McCoy's visit to Abilene had been brought about by a livestock debacle in 1866, the first year in which Texans drove large herds of Longhorn cattle north in search of markets after the Civil War. The markets were there; in fact, a shortage of beef existed in the postwar North. Transportation was the problem; there were no railroads south of Missouri and Kansas. Although the Texans overcame the difficulties of driving their cattle overland through storms and across the rivers of Indian territory, as soon as they reached the settled areas of eastern Kansas they encountered real trouble. Between them and the nearest railheads the country was being homesteaded by farmers, many of them recent battlefield enemies of the Texans. The settlers did not want their fences wrecked and their crops trampled, and they used force in stopping the Texans from driving cattle across their properties. By summer's end of 1866, hundreds of thousands of cattle were stalled between Indian territory and the nearest Missouri railhead. The grass was quickly grazed off, and herds died or were abandoned before they could be sold.

To Joseph McCoy, who was eager to buy cattle for the expanding Chicago meat-packing industry, and to the Texans who wanted to sell cattle, the westward thrust of the Kansas Pacific Railroad offered a solution to the dilemma. McCoy chose Abilene because it was beyond settled farming country, because it bordered a river full of water for thirsty cattle, and because a sweeping sea of grass for miles around could be used for holding and fattening stock at the end of overland drives. To reach Abilene, the Texas cattlemen had only to follow a trail from Red River to the Wichita trading posts on the Arkansas, a trail pioneered by a Cherokee trader named Jesse Chisholm. Chisholm's Trail it was called, and it ran north from the Chickasaw Nation across the relatively shallow Washita, Canadian, and Cimarron rivers.

From the Wichita trading posts, Abilene and the Kansas Pacific Railroad lay a hundred miles farther north across a treeless plain, and while McCoy was building a shipping yard and a three-story hotel from lumber brought all the way from Hannibal, Missouri, a surveyor was extending the Chisholm Trail. Using a compass and a flagman, the surveyor ran a straight line of heaped-up earthen mounds that the Texas trail drivers could follow from the Arkansas River to Abilene. Late in the summer the first herds came in, and on September 5 the first shipment of twenty cattle cars rumbled eastward on the railroad. Before the brief season ended, thirty-five thousand cattle were driven into Abilene. During the following winter, McCoy sent agents across Texas to distribute circulars and place advertisements in newspapers extolling the advantages of Abilene as a cattle-shipping point. The season of 1868 began early, with endless lines of Longhorns splashing across the Smoky Hill River into Abilene's loading pens. Each year the numbers doubled, the Kansas Pacific being hard-pressed to find enough cars in which to ship out the cattle.

Abilene boomed into a town of forty saloons. Legions of audacious Texans rode up the Chisholm Trail to that garish trail oasis, where they celebrated the end of their overland journeys with whiskey, dance-hall girls, and gambling. At first the riders were called "drovers" or simply "Texans" (McCoy named his hotel the Drover's Cottage) but soon they were "cowboys" and they made songs about themselves—"I'm Bound to Follow the Longhorn Cows," "The Dying Cowboy," "Get Along Little Dogies," "The Old Chisholm Trail," and of course "The Railroad Corral," in which they sang about rousting steers from the long chaparral and driving them far to the railroad corral, using the tune of "The Irish Washerwoman."

Joe McCoy was proud of what he had accomplished. To him it was a successful business venture, nothing more. He probably never realized that he and the K.P. Railroad on its way to the Western Sea had played a large part in the creation of that most romantic folk creature of the New World—the American cowboy. Without the railroad and the trail town, the image of the cowboy never would have become fully formed. He would have been only a stock handler on horseback, a man wearing a big hat, a bandanna, boots and spurs. Without the trail town he would have had no destination, no relationship with the Calico Queens and Painted Cats, the dance-hall girls of a dozen Bull's Head Taverns & Gambling Saloons, Long Branches, Alamos, and Lady Gays. He would have had no town marshals to challenge to the death in thousands of legendary walkdowns and shoot-outs on the Texas Streets that fronted the railroad tracks. He might have lived and died without ever seeing the steaming, smoking Iron Horse that hauled away the bawling Longhorns he drove up from Texas. Without the Iron Horse, the trail town, and the cowboy, a larger part of the myth of the American West would have faded into history, never to be perpetuated in multitudes of yellow-backed dime novels and millions of feet of film flicking shadows on motion-picture and television screens.

Cowboys driving longhorns into Abilene, Kansas (Author's Collection—Frank Leslie's Illustrated Newspaper 1878)

Shipping point for Texas cattle, Abilene (Missouri Historical Society, The Gardner Collection)

The American Indian was there, too, cast in the villain's role of Cowboys & Indians, the stereotyped conflict immortalized in a children's game that has become a universal symbol of good and evil. Along the Chisholm Trail and other overland routes to the railroad towns, cowboys and Indians occasionally exchanged gunfire. More often than not, the Indians wanted nothing more than a few beeves to replace the buffalo that the cattlemen had driven from their land; sometimes the tribes of Indian territory demanded a toll (ten cents per head was the going rate) for Longhorns crossing their reservations. Cowboys and Indians seldom sought out each other; the shifting overland cattle trails usually ran west of settlement but east of the Plains tribes' hunting grounds. As the tribes were pushed west, the trails moved west behind them.

A few hundred railroad workers in Kansas and Nebraska probably took more punishment from Indians than did all the thousands of cowboys from Texas to Montana. It was the Iron Horse that the warriors hated, the snorting, whistling monster that violated their natural sanctuary and drove away their wild game. As soon as iron tracks invaded the High Plains west of Salina, the Indians began to fight, challenging surveyors, graders, track layers, and even train crews. In the spring and summer of 1867, hunting parties of Cheyenne, Sioux, and Arapaho raided along the stretch of track between Ellsworth and Fort Hays. Graders at Wilson's Creek and

*Sometimes Indian war parties attempted to stop
the Iron Horse. (Culver Pictures)*

Bunker Hill took casualties in several attacks during June, and farther west at Monument Station a thousand men exchanged their shovels for rifles and refused to work until a regiment of Kansas volunteer cavalrymen arrived to shield them from angry swarms of Plains Indians. At Brookville, only sixteen miles west of Salina, a war party surrounded a temporary roundhouse containing a locomotive and train crew, and then tried to set the building afire. In an attempt to escape, the engineer got up steam and crashed his Iron Horse through the flimsy roundhouse door. The noise of splintering wood and the appearance of the hated monster with its shrilling whistle and jangling bell frightened the attackers into hasty flight.

Reacting to this determined resistance to the railroad by the Plains Indians, General William T. Sherman ordered an expedition into the area, under the direction of General Winfield Scott Hancock. Sherman, who was in command of military forces in the West, had devised a plan to drive all the

Plains Indians north of the Platte and south of the Arkansas River, leaving a broad belt between for the transcontinental railroads and ultimate settlement of the Indian lands that the roads would acquire as they laid their tracks westward. During the summer of 1867, Hancock with George Armstrong Custer of the Seventh Cavalry chased Indians across Kansas, burning tepee villages and killing indiscriminately. By autumn the Great Plains on both sides of the Kansas Pacific Railroad was in a turmoil that signaled the beginning of a long and bloody Indian war.

Although Hancock was recalled and the federal government through its Interior Department attempted to pacify the aroused tribes with treaty signings at Medicine Lodge, Kansas, and Fort Laramie, Wyoming, the more militant Indian leaders remained adamant against the railroads. Small war parties continued raiding, the most effective group consisting of about two hundred Cheyenne Dog Soldiers with a few Sioux and Arapaho allies. A visitor to the town of Sheridan at the end of track in 1868 reported that the place was in a state of siege. "Several days before, a large war party of savages had appeared upon two buttes near the town and opened fire upon the inhabitants. Everybody rushed to arms, and for the larger part of the day a spirited fusillade was kept up. The people of the place at once organized a regular corps of defenders, and detachments were on the watch day and night. On the more prominent eminences pickets were posted to signal the approach of war parties. At night the guard was doubled so as to completely encircle the town."

In a move to punish the resisting Indians, Sherman now sent the famous Civil War cavalry commander Philip Sheridan out upon the plains. Believing that the only good Indian was a dead Indian, Sheridan recruited a special company of frontier scouts at Fort Hays and ordered them to track down and kill any Indians sighted near the railroad. In September the scouts trailed a large band of Cheyenne Dog Soldiers to the Arikara fork of the Republican River. There the Indians trapped the scouts on an island and kept them surrounded for eight days until a relief column arrived. During the fighting, the famous warrior Roman Nose and Lieutenant Frederick Beecher were killed. History recorded the incident as the Battle of Beecher's Island, but the Indians called it the Fight When Roman Nose Was Killed. Continuing his war to crush Indian resistance completely, Sheridan organized a winter campaign under Lieutenant-Colonel Custer, which culminated on November 27 in the destruction of Black Kettle's peaceful Cheyenne village. Although there was practically no resistance, the Army glorified the incident by calling it the Battle of the Washita.

The ranks of the railroad defiers were growing thin now among the High Plains tribes. Through the spring of 1869, Tall Bull and his unyielding Dog Soldiers and a few small bands of Sioux and Arapaho managed to elude their pursuers. For a few weeks they fought a desperate last-ditch guerrilla war against the Iron Horse.

On May 28, about thirty Cheyennes armed with rifles and bows caught seven track repairmen west of Fossil Creek Station (now Russell, Kansas). One of the workmen, Adolph Roenigk, said the Indians came dashing out of a ravine "yelling like demons." Roenigk and his companions grabbed their rifles and ran for a handcar. "We tried to get the car under headway, but had gone only a short distance when more Indians came out of the ravine ahead of us, and the next minute we were surrounded and they were firing into us from all sides . . . I thought it impossible to reach the station alive. The Indians were pressing us hard. When their guns were empty and no time to reload, we received a shower of arrows." (Artist Jacob Gogolin later painted scenes of this incident from Roenigk's descriptions.) Before the railroad workmen were halfway to the safety of the station dugout, two of them were shot and fell from the handcar. Four of the five survivors were wounded, and only the intercession of the station agent with his Spencer carbine enabled them to reach the dugout.

Some of the Indians kept the repairmen pinned down there while others tore up a section of track by breaking off the heads of spikes and removing several rails. After darkness fell, the besieged railroad men could still hear sounds of the Indians and their ponies. Near midnight, the headlight of an approaching train appeared on the eastern horizon. To warn the engineer of the broken rails, the station agent tossed a

*Jacob Gogolin's painting of a Cheyenne attack upon track repairmen
on the Kansas Pacific (Kansas State Historical Society)*

bale of hay onto the middle of the track and set it afire. The
engineer, however, did not sight the blaze in time to avoid
overturning into a ditch. Thus did the Cheyennes hamper the
Iron Horse. But they could not destroy that hated symbol of
the white man's technology; two days later, a wrecking crew
lifted the monster back up on its repaired tracks and brought
it once again to steaming life.

A hundred miles farther west and about two weeks later,
a similar party (possibly the same warriors) ripped up the
track near Grinnell. When the locomotive of the eastbound
train was derailed, the Indians swarmed down upon the cars,
but by this time the Kansas Pacific had introduced the practice of arming its passengers. A volley of shots from the car
windows forced the attackers into a hasty retreat.

Surveyors, being the "point men" of an advancing
railroad, were viewed as hostile spies by the people whose
country they were marking off for invasion. Because of constant attacks upon them as the Kansas Pacific moved west
from Fort Wallace into Colorado, surveyors refused to go into
the field without the protection of at least a platoon of sol-

diers. And if the engineers grew careless in their work, this armed guard offered little security.

"We were running some rapid trial lines north of Sheridan, and were fifteen or twenty miles out in a rolling country," a transit man recorded in June 1869. "Our progress was as rapid almost as a man would walk at a moderate pace, and we were exceedingly vulnerable to attack, as we were all separated, strung out over a distance of a mile or more." The man in front that day was Philip Schuyler, a twenty-five-year-old engineer. He was on horseback, riding slowly to choose the best grade route, when he suddenly discovered that he was entering a V-shaped ambush with mounted Indians swarming up from left and right out of deep narrow ravines. A bullet flesh-wounded Schuyler's horse, and what followed was one of those classic chases so relished by writers of Western fiction and directors of Western cinema.

Putting spurs to his horse, Schuyler forced the animal to leap across one awesome ravine after another, but just as he thought he was escaping to level ground, another formidable array of Indians blocked his passage and he was again quickly surrounded. The circling warriors rode closer and closer, shaking their weapons and taunting the young engineer. Schuyler raised his rifle and fired at the nearest man. As the Indian fell, Schuyler spurred his horse into a sudden charge and broke through the line. In the pursuit that followed, Schuyler's bleeding horse was wounded again, his field glass was shot away, bullets struck the breech of his rifle and pierced his clothing, and the shaft of a hurled lance almost knocked him from his saddle. To add a cinematic finish to the incident, when Schuyler at last reached his fellow surveyors, he found them engaged in a fight with another war party and had to help drive away these attackers. "We were unanimous in the opinion that it was folly to continue work without a larger escort and a personal bodyguard," the transit man recorded. "Consequently it was decided to turn our faces in the direction of Sheridan, which we did, arriving there late in the afternoon, the Indians following us all the way."

During the month succeeding this incident, several cavalry columns patrolled the railroad and combed the High

Plains with orders "to treat all Indians as hostile." On July 11, 1869, eight troops of cavalry and a battalion of Pawnee mercenaries stormed Tall Bull's summer encampment at Summit Springs. They charged in a double encirclement from east and west, trapping the Cheyennes in a deadly crossfire, and when the assault ended a few minutes later, Tall Bull and most of his defiant young haters of the railroad were dead. From that day, the Iron Horse thundered freely across the High Plains of Kansas.

During the Hancock and Custer campaign along the Kansas Pacific in 1867, a number of Indian raiders shifted their operations northward to the Union Pacific in Nebraska. There they achieved only one notable success, the legendary train ambush at Plum Creek on August 6. Long afterward, a Cheyenne named Porcupine told why they wrecked the train: "The soldiers had defeated us and taken everything that we had and had made us poor. We were feeling angry and said among ourselves that we ought to do something. In these big wagons that go on this metal road, there must be things that are valuable—perhaps clothing. If we could throw these wagons off the iron they run on and break them open, we should find out what was in them and could take whatever might be useful to us."

The day after the wreck occurred, Henry M. Stanley happened to be in Omaha, and he interviewed a survivor, a fellow Briton named William Thompson, who worked for the Union Pacific as a telegraph repairman. Thompson and four other men had been sent out after nightfall on a handcar from Plum Creek to find and repair a break in the telegraph line. Unknown to them, the wire had been torn down by Porcupine and the other Cheyennes, and part of it was used to fasten a railroad tie to the track. The tie was meant to derail an Iron Horse, but instead the handcar carrying the telegraph repairmen struck it and the Indians rose up out of the high grass to surround the men.

In the pursuit that followed, four of the five repairmen were quickly killed. A Cheyenne shot Thompson in the arm, knocked him to the ground, and then scalped him. Although the pain was excruciating, Thompson pretended to be unconscious. "I can't describe it to you," he told Stanley. "It just felt as if the whole head was taken right off. The Indian then mounted and galloped away, but as he went he dropped my scalp within a few feet of me, which I managed to get and hide. The Indians were thick in the vicinity, or I might then have made my escape. While lying down I could hear the Indians moving around whispering to each other, and then shortly after placing obstructions on the track. After lying down about an hour and a half I heard the low rumbling of the train as it came tearing along, and I might have been able to flag it off had I dared."

The Iron Horse and several freight cars plunged into the ditch, killing the engineer and fireman. The conductor and three other men in the caboose escaped and ran back down the track to warn a second freight train, which was following close behind the first. William Thompson meanwhile took advantage of the Cheyennes' preoccupation with the loot that they were digging out of the wrecked freight cars. He crawled away through the grass, still clutching his scalp, and then jogged fifteen miles to Willow Island Station. After his fellow workers dressed his wounds, Thompson made his way to Omaha, carrying his scalp in a pail of water to prevent it from drying out. "The scalp," reported the observant Stanley, "was about nine inches in length and four in width, somewhat resembling a drowned rat as it floated, curled up, on the water." Thompson hoped to find a doctor who could reset it on his head, but the effort failed. He then had his scalp tanned, and after returning to England, for some reason known only to himself, he shipped it back to Omaha, where it was exhibited for years in the public library's museum.

Reprisals upon the Union Pacific such as the Cheyennes' Plum Creek ambush were abominations to General Sherman, who had come to regard the railroad as a holy endeavor that must be defended at all costs against such "a worthless set of scamps" as the Plains Indians. He ordered out more infantry units to guard the graders and track layers and more cavalrymen to patrol the completed tracks. "No interruption to work upon the line of the U.P. will be tolerated," he assured Dr. Durant. "Eastern people must not allow their sympathy with the Indians to make them forget what is due to those

William Thompson's scalp (Omaha Public Library)

who are pushing the 'frontier' further and further west. These men deserve protection and they must have it."

One of the railroad's medical officers reported from Fort Sedgwick that military protection seemed adequate but that "the Indians laugh and hoot at the infantry and boldly ride within reach of their muskets, then ducking under the bellies of their fleet ponies pat their breech clouts defiantly. They seem to exhibit more respect for the cavalry."

As an example of the railroad company's hardening attitude toward Indian resistance to invasion of their hunting areas, the scalps of Sioux and Cheyenne Indians taken by the hired Pawnee scouts were displayed freely to travelers. George Francis Train obtained a scalp that still had an ear attached, and during an 1867 springtime excursion he enjoyed startling the Easterners by exhibiting it along with the arrow that had killed its luckless owner.

The excursionists on this tour were the first to journey by rail all the way to Council Bluffs; the Chicago & Northwestern had at last brought its tracks to the Missouri River, which the travelers easily crossed by ferry to the muddy streets of

Omaha. Those who had come from New York City reached Omaha in only sixty-nine hours, a feat that the newspaper correspondents hailed as epochal. The party was invited to inspect the Union Pacific's recently completed machine shops, which extended three miles along the bank of the Missouri and contained stalls for twenty locomotives, and their car works, which turned out two flatcars and one freight car each day and was beginning construction of crude passenger cars for the use of immigrants who would soon be arriving to buy hundreds of thousands of acres of the railroad's land along the right-of-way.

Two hundred ninety miles to the west, or twelve hours by train, North Platte was sobering up from its winter of gambling, drinking, and fornicating, and was preparing to move westward. The energetic Casement brothers established a new camp near Julesburg, Colorado, and put two thousand graders to work; they hired eighteen hundred woodchoppers and haulers and sent them to the forested areas of Wyoming. By the season's end they would have 100,000 ties ready for the rails entering Wyoming. As midsummer approached, North Platte's population shrank from five thousand to three hundred. The gamblers and whores moved on to Julesburg to live off the railroad workmen.

When Henry Stanley visited "sinful Julesburg" in August 1867, he found a comfortable hotel filled with well-dressed guests. "Everybody had gold watches attached to expensive chains, and several wore patent leather boots. I vow I thought they were great capitalists, but was astonished to find they were only clerks, ticket agents, conductors, engineers. . . . I walked on till I came to a dance-house, bearing the euphonious title of 'King of the Hills,' gorgeously decorated and brilliantly lighted. . . . The ground floor was as crowded as it could well be, and all were talking loud and fast, and mostly everyone seemed bent on debauchery and dissipation. The women appeared to be the most reckless, and the men seemed nothing loth to enter a whirlpool of sin . . . . The managers of the saloons rake in greenbacks by hundreds every night; there appears to be plenty of money here, and plenty of fools to squander it . . . . These women are expensive articles, and come in for a large share of the money wasted. In broad daylight they may be seen gliding through the sandy streets in Black Crook dresses, carrying fancy derringers slung to their waists, with which tools they are dangerously expert. . . . The population of Julesburg is rapidly growing, and the town, like its predecessor of North Platte, may be epitomised as a jumble of commencements, always shifting, never ending."

Meanwhile, another 140 miles to the west, a new camp was being established on Crow Creek in Wyoming. In honor of the Indian tribe that had challenged the invasion of the Iron Horse with more fury than had any other, the surveyors named the camp Cheyenne. General Grenville Dodge predicted that rails would be laid to Cheyenne before the first snows of winter, but few of his engineers believed this to be possible.

On through the late summer and autumn, the well-organized gangs of workers pushed the rails ever westward, a mile a day, two miles a day, sometimes four miles a day. The rail terminus at Council Bluffs eliminated the slow shipments of iron and other supplies by steamboat up the Missouri. The ferry to Omaha shuttled back and forth with carloads of rails and spikes that could be loaded right onto the U.P. tracks for swift passage toward Wyoming. When Dr. Henry C. Parry passed through Cheyenne on October 7, he was astounded at the changes he found there: "When I left here last July all the land was bare, and the only habitations were tents. Cheyenne has now a population of fifteen hundred, two papers, stores, warehouses, hotels, restaurants, gambling halls, etc."

All this occurred even before the rails reached Cheyenne. Four thousand people were there a few weeks later when Jack Casement's headquarters train rolled to a stop beside the brand-new Cheyenne station. Awaiting him was a speaker's stand with brilliant banners mounted above it: OLD CASEMENT, WE WELCOME YOU. THE MAGIC CITY GREETS THE CONTINENTAL RAILWAY.

The next day, the first passenger train arrived, and from it poured a considerable portion of the gamblers and dance-hall girls of Julesburg. A few hours later, a long train of flat-cars rumbled into the station. Every car was loaded high with knocked-down buildings, storefronts, dance-hall floors, tents, wooden sidings, and entire roofs. According to legend, as a brakeman dropped down onto the station platform, he shouted to the waiting crowd: "Gentlemen, here's Julesburg!"

It was Samuel Bowles, that widely traveled publisher of the *Springfield* (Mass.) *Republican,* who first put into print the name for these movable towns: "As the Railroad marched thus rapidly across the broad Continent of plain and mountain, there was improvised a rough and temporary town at its every public stopping place . . . these settlements were of the most perishable materials,—canvas tents, plain board shanties, and turf-hovels,—pulled down and sent forward for a new career, or deserted as worthless, at every grand movement of the Railroad company. . . . Restaurant and saloon

Cheyenne, Wyoming, when it was a Hell on Wheels railroad town (Photo by A. J. Russell, The Oakland Museum)

keepers, gamblers, desperadoes of every grade, the vilest of men and women made up this 'Hell on Wheels,' as it was most aptly termed." Thus did the Hell on Wheels town enter the American language.

At the end of 1867, the Union Pacific was 540 miles from Omaha, 240 miles closer to the Western Sea than it had been in January. Almost every citizen of the nation gloried in this mighty achievement, but there were exceptions. Dr. Thomas Durant was unhappy because Oliver Ames and Sidney Dillon voted him off the board of directors of Credit Mobilier and were boldly attempting to remove him as executive vice-president and general manager of the U.P. And so began a power struggle for access to the fountains of gold flowing from the building of the "people's" transcontinental railroad.

The men most disturbed by the remarkable progress of the Union Pacific were the Big Four of the Central Pacific. In 1867, while the U.P. was laying two hundred forty miles of track, the C.P. laid only forty miles. To accomplish this, Crocker's and Strobridge's Chinese workers had to bore thousands of feet through the solid stone of the Sierras and move thousands of cubic yards of gravel in wheelbarrows, while fighting snowdrifts and dodging avalanches during several months of the year. This was substantially the same barrier that had tragically stopped the Donner party coming from the East twenty years earlier; those California-bound emigrants were reduced to cannibalism before rescuers reached them.

Learning that an engineer spying for the Union Pacific had visited the tunnel sites and reported that three years would be required to complete Summit Tunnel alone, the resourceful Strobridge ordered a shaft sunk so that his tunnelers could dig from four sides simultaneously. For several months during 1867 he kept eight thousand Chinese tunnelers working in around-the-clock shifts seven days a week. Nevertheless, there were rumors from New York that Dr. Durant was boasting that the Union Pacific would reach the California line before the Central Pacific could work its way out of the Sierras.

Reacting to this with their usual ingenuity, the Big Four decided to bypass the tunnels temporarily and push the Central Pacific tracks down the eastern slope of the Sierras and across the line into the level Nevada desert. Once there, they could sweep across the miles to Salt Lake City before the Union Pacific track layers reached Utah.

To accomplish this, Strobridge took three thousand Chinese over the summit to grade and bridge the eastern slope to the Nevada line. But the greatest feat of all was the dismantling of three locomotives and forty cars and the transportation of them over the summit on sledges. It was an accomplishment equal to Hannibal's crossing of the ice-clad Alps, with the Iron Horses sliding and foundering in the snow somewhat like Hannibal's armored elephants.

"We hauled locomotives over," general manager Crocker later recalled, "and when I say we, I mean myself. We hauled them on sleighs . . . we hauled some of them over on logs, because we could not get a sleigh big enough." After the Iron Horses and their tenders and cars were brought slipping and sliding down the slope, they had to be loaded onto wagons at Donner Lake and dragged along a rough and muddy road to Truckee. And after this was done, a cavalcade of sleds and wagons followed with tons of spikes, plows, tools, food supplies, saw mills, and iron rails—enough to lay fifty miles of track.

Adding to the hardships of a difficult year for the Central Pacific were blizzards and avalanches that dumped thirty-foot drifts on the already completed tracks. "The snow would fill up just as fast as the men could dig it out," Crocker said. To keep the road open to the summit tunnels, he employed a Scotsman, bridge-builder Arthur Brown, and ordered him to construct forty miles of snowsheds. In completing this assignment, Brown used sixty-five million feet of timber and nine hundred tons of bolts and spikes, and spent over two million dollars.

In November 1867, at the highest point of the Central Pacific, 7,017 feet above sea level, Summit Tunnel was ready for the track layers. A month later, to celebrate their triumph, the Big Four loaded ten bright yellow passenger cars at Sacramento with seven hundred Very Important People of California and hauled them up the 105-mile track to the top of the Sierras. There the excursionists engaged in a snowball fight,

*One of Arthur Brown's Sierra snowsheds on the
Central Pacific (California State Library)*

and were almost smothered by smoke when the Iron Horse
stalled in the long tunnel, but returned safely to Sacramento
to spread the news of California's marvelous railroad.

On December 13, Strobridge and his Chinese workers
on the eastern slope of the range laid the first rails across the
Nevada line. But the Central Pacific still had to lay a seven-
mile stretch of track to close in the Donner Lake area, and it
was already buried for the winter under its first snowfall. No
subsidy bonds could be collected from the government for
the miles completed beyond the gap, because according to
the law the tracks had to be *consecutive*. No doubt about it,
the Central Pacific was in a financial bind. Back to the East,
however, traveled that cold and crafty maneuverer of politicians and financiers—Collis Huntington. He stretched the
Big Four's credit to the limits, ordering railroad equipment in
such enormous quantities that at one time thirty ships loaded
with iron for the Central Pacific were circling the oceans en
route to California. Huntington knew that more than a thousand miles of empty land still lay between the ends of track of
the C.P. and the U.P., and he intended to grab for the C.P.
every mile of it that muscle and sweat could accomplish.

CHAPTER 6

The Great Race

THE GREAT RACE actually began in the spring of 1867 at North Platte, Nebraska, but it was no contest until the spring of 1868, when the Central Pacific's Chinese workers came down the eastern slope of the Sierras and began laying grades across the arid flatlands of Nevada toward the Great Basin of Utah. This green and fruitful country of the industrious Mormons was a rich prize, and the Big Four were so determined to win it that they dispatched teams of surveyors as far east as Wyoming, where they encountered the red-flag markers and theodolites of the equally eager Union Pacific surveyors.

Early in the spring of 1868, the C.P. track layers reached a newly created town named for General Jesse L. Reno of Civil War fame. Because of its strategic location adjacent to the Nevada mining country, twenty-five-foot storefront lots were soon selling for twelve hundred dollars. As soon as a station was built at end of track, construction superintendent James Strobridge shifted his crews back into the melting snows of the Sierras to complete the seven-mile gap between Reno and Sacramento. By mid-June the frozen earth and the stones were blasted and leveled, the rails were spiked down, and the gap was closed. The Big Four could now collect a fortune from the government. A newspaper reporter who was a passenger on the first train to cross the Sierras from Sacramento described the Central Pacific as "one of the most beautiful, smooth and solid roads on the continent." The Chinese laborers, he added, were "packing their traps preparatory to passing on over the summit into the great interior basin of the continent."

Not only the Chinese workers but also President Leland Stanford of the C.P. went over the mountains that summer.

Stanford's mission was to visit Salt Lake City, where he hoped to persuade Brigham Young and other Mormon leaders to build a road grade across Utah through Weber Canyon to the Wyoming line. That Young already had a $2-million contract with the rival Union Pacific to build a grade across Utah did not matter to Stanford and his Big Four partners. During the previous winter Collis Huntington had filed with the Secretary of the Interior a set of maps for a right-of-way across Nevada and Utah, labeling them as an extension of the Central Pacific line. With his usual audacity, Huntington at the same time asked the government for an advance payment of $2.4 million for construction of the line (which he never built) and he badgered officials for months until he had the bonds in hand.

Brigham Young saw no conflict in taking on two contracts, especially after Stanford guaranteed to pay the Mormons double the wages he had been giving his Chinese workers. The money of course ultimately would come from the republic's taxpayers, most of whom were unaware that during the autumn of 1868 separate crews of Mormons were hard at work hauling stone and earth to build two hundred miles of parallel road grades, one of which would never be used. The Great Race was becoming wasteful and expensive. Yet, most Americans rejoiced in the progress of what they believed to be "their" transcontinental railroad.

Strobridge and his Chinese in the meantime were driving eastward across Nevada. To avoid conflicts with Indians—such as had hampered the Union Pacific and Kansas Pacific on the Great Plains—the Central Pacific offered some of the native Americans employment and then signed a special treaty with the Paiutes and Shoshonis. "We gave the old chiefs a pass each, good on the passenger cars," Huntington said, "and we told our men to let the common Indians ride on the freight cars whenever they saw fit." Both male and female Indians worked alongside the Chinese "with nonchalance and ease," and one observer reported that the women usually outdid the men in handling crowbars and sledgehammers.

On one occasion some of the Paiutes who were working with a Chinese construction gang on the grade between Reno

Track layers on the Central Pacific moving eastward across Nevada
(Utah State Historical Society)

and Wadsworth unintentionally caused a halt in operations. Having a natural fondness for tall tales, the Indians one day told the Orientals that their Nevada desert was inhabited by snakes so large that they could swallow a man in one gulp. The result was a hasty departure that night by about five hundred Chinese, who decided to follow the railroad track back to the safety of Sacramento. An infuriated Charlie Crocker had to dispatch several men on horseback to round up the frightened Chinese and persuade them that they were the victims of Paiute humor.

On July 22, the tracks reached Wadsworth and soon afterward the first train from Sacramento rolled into the station. From there the survey line swung northeastward to work its way through the passes of the Humboldt Range. This was the desert country that overland emigrants bound for California had learned to dread. For five hundred miles it was a land of white alkali beds burned by the sun, waterless, treeless, bare of vegetation except for patches of gray sagebrush and stunted junipers. To supply timber for construction and to fuel locomotives, logs had to be hauled from the Sierra forests. Special water trains consisting of huge wooden tanks fitted upon flatcars were devised to bring that vital liquid to workmen and to fill the boilers of the advance contingent of Iron Horses.

To avoid building bridges and digging cuts—which consumed time and money—Crocker and Strobridge ran the line in snakelike curves. Each additional mile of track, after all, brought to the Big Four a profit of twice its cost to them. In a few years, millions more dollars would have to be spent to straighten those winding tracks so hastily and carelessly laid during the Great Race.

In September, after the track layers passed Mill City, a San Francisco reporter made the journey to end of track. He found that the names that the Central Pacific had bestowed upon its stations revealed the nature of the Nevada land: Desert, Hot Springs, Mirage, Granite Point. He also witnessed the lackadaisical manner in which government inspectors examined and certified the new track so that the C.P. could collect its thirty thousand dollars per mile. One inspector, said the reporter, stood on the platform of the rear car and with a small spyglass scrutinized the ties, rails, and grade as the train sped along. While he was doing this, his assistant lay down on the floor in the front of the car, shut his eyes, and composed himself to sleep. "The argument being this, that if the passengers could sleep the track must be level, easy, and all right; whereas, if too rough to sleep, something must be wrong with the work."

The C.P. was averaging a mile of new track each day now, racing frantically to beat the U.P. into Utah. Borrowing the methods of the Casement brothers of the U.P., superintendent Strobridge put together a work train of a dozen cars equipped with sleeping and dining accommodations and shops for carpenters and telegraph-line builders. The first car was Strobridge's living quarters, and his wife kept it so neat that a newspaperman dubbed her "the heroine of the Central Pacific" and declared that the domicile on wheels was equal to any home in San Francisco. A contemporary photograph shows Mrs. Strobridge standing on a porchlike platform built along the length of the car; beside her is a clothesline, hanging from which appears to be a pair of long underdrawers. A Vallejo reporter described the platform as "an awning veranda" and said that a canary bird swinging at the front door gave it a most homelike appearance. Each evening when Strobridge's work train rolled to the end of track built that day, he would have a telegraph wire run from the nearest pole into the telegraph car and would notify Sacramento of the number of miles of track laid.

No matter how hard he and Crocker drove their men, however, it became obvious as 1868 neared its end that the rival Union Pacific was going to win the Great Race into Utah and probably would have tracks laid to the key city of Ogden before the Central Pacific could push through the Promontory Range north of Great Salt Lake. Much to Brigham Young's displeasure, both railroads had abandoned plans to run their main tracks into Salt Lake City. A branch line from Ogden to Salt Lake, similar to the branch line from Cheyenne to Denver, would have to suffice. Young, however, demanded control of the spur, and he later outfitted it with rolling stock that he took from the U.P. in partial payment for the Mormons' grading contract.

At year's end the Central Pacific's tracks were approaching Carlin, Nevada, 446 miles from Sacramento; the Union Pacific's rails had been laid to Evanston, Wyoming, near the Utah border, 995 miles west of Omaha. Between these track ends were less than 400 miles, a considerable part of which had been graded in parallel lines by the rival Mormon contractors and Strobridge's Chinese workers. An air of excitement developed across America as it became apparent that the long-dreamed-of transcontinental railroad, which had been planned for completion during the nation's centennial celebration of 1876, would be joined in the new year of 1869, seven years ahead of schedule.

Although engineers for each of the rival railroads could have calculated the approximate meeting place of the track layers, their acquisitive employers insisted that the wasteful parallel grading continue across Utah. Finally, the U.P. construction men recognized the futility of continuing their grading west of Promontory toward Humboldt Wells in Nevada. After discontinuing work on this section, they brought gangs of Irish graders into Utah so that in the spring of 1869 each railroad company was grading a line between Ogden and Promontory. Grenville Dodge of the U.P. noted that considerable ill feeling developed between the Irish and the Chinese. "Our Irishmen were in the habit of firing their blasts in the cuts without giving warning to the Chinamen on the Central Pacific working right above them. From this cause several Chinamen were severely hurt. Complaint was made to me by the Central Pacific people, and I endeavored to have the contractors bring all hostilities to a close, but, for some reason or other they failed to do so. One day the Chinamen, appreciating the situation, put in what is called a 'grave' on their work, and when the Irishmen right under them were all at work let go their blast and buried several of our men. This brought about a truce at once. From that time the Irish laborers showed due respect for the Chinamen, and there was no further trouble."

The Union Pacific's race to Ogden was not won without enormous costs—in money, materials, and lives. As in war, the longer the contest continued, the more ruthless, reckless, and callous the leaders of the contending railroads became toward their common workmen. Although losses of lives by accidents were higher among the C.P.'s Chinese (between five hundred and a thousand), the U.P. undoubtedly lost the most workmen from exposure and from diseases contracted in the squalid dens of prostitution that followed the tracks westward. More U.P. workmen were murdered in the Hell on Wheels towns than were killed in accidents, a ratio of about four to one. Almost no medical facilities were provided by either railroad company. Yet, with the assistance of the national press, the railroad owners, like military commanders in wartime, kept up a drumfire of propaganda upon the populace that was designed to inspire their sweating laborers to "win" at all costs.

In the spring of 1868, the U.P. emerged from the long Wyoming winter to begin track construction west of Cheyenne. General Jack Casement's work train was lengthened to eighty cars, which now included a bakery car, a bath car, a complete feed store and saddle shop, additional kitchen, dining, and bunk cars, a combined telegraph and payroll car, and a butcher's car. The butcher's car was kept filled with fresh beef from a cattle herd that was driven each day alongside the work train as it made its way westward across Wyoming. From time to time a newspaper that followed the Hell on Wheels towns would set up shop temporarily in one of the cars, publishing whenever enough news could be collected concerning events along the way combined with occasional brief dispatches received in the telegraph car. For protection in case of Indian attacks, the Casements installed about a thousand rifles upon horizontal racks in the ceilings of the cars. Added protection was guaranteed by the railroad's good friend General Sherman, who ordered five thousand infantrymen and cavalrymen deployed at public expense from Cheyenne to the Salt Lake Valley.

During the winter of 1867–68, the Union Pacific had sent a work force of three thousand men into the Medicine Bow Range to cut ties, timbers for bridge construction, and billets to fuel Iron Horses. As the snows departed, teams of muleskinners began distributing the wood alongside the grades and survey lines. "Muleskinners," reported a contemporary observer, "yelling at reluctant animals, split the air with picturesque invective and creased tough mule hides with the business end of blacksnake whips."

At the same time, grading crews by the thousands were sent as far west as Echo Canyon in Utah. There was much boastful talk about laying track to Salt Lake before the year's end, but the realists thought the railroad would be lucky to reach the Wasatch Mountains before snow stopped construction. Edward Ordway, who was traveling across Wyoming that spring, encountered at Fort Halleck a group of brawling railroad workmen, "natives of all the civilized nations of earth," drinking up their winter's pay at the bar in the sutler's store. "Rock men, pick and shovelers, and all other necessary helpers in railroad grade making, at that time as a class were known as Navvies," he said. "All stout, healthy men, and as for their social standing or moral turpitude, all that is necessary to say is that nature had created them for a special purpose that people more delicately organized were unfit for."

During their drinking bouts, the men engaged in boxing, clog dancing, and jumping contests. They harassed stagecoach drivers, sang Irish ballads, and then to Ordway's amazement a quartet rendered "in perfect harmony Hayden's [*sic*] magnificent song 'The Heavens Are Telling.'" The men were enjoying themselves so heartily after their long winter in the timber that the gang bosses were unable to start them back to work without the assistance of a detail of cavalry from the fort, who "by a liberal use of sabers succeeded in rounding up those who were able to walk."

During April an army of graders moved out through deep patches of snow into the Wyoming Black Hills, and a thousand track layers followed. On April 16, iron rails topped Sherman Summit, 8,242 feet above sea level, a thousand feet higher than the Central Pacific's Summit Tunnel in the Sierras. Grenville Dodge had surveyed this pass to the Western Sea in 1865 and named it "in honor of General Sherman the tallest general in the service." To celebrate the crossing of what the Union Pacific boasted was the highest elevation ever reached by a railroad anywhere in the world, Dr. Durant came out from New York and personally placed the final rail. He could not resist sending a bragging telegram to President Leland Stanford of the Central Pacific, and Stanford politely replied: "We cheerfully yield you the palm of superior elevation; 7,242 feet has been quite sufficient to satisfy our highest ambition." By this time Durant was feuding bitterly with his associates Sidney Dillon and Oakes Ames, and was so furious with Grenville Dodge, because of the latter's refusal to cooperate in his devious plots to siphon funds, that Durant had determined to remove Dodge as chief engineer at the first opportunity.

While the owners celebrated at Sherman Summit, bridge builders a few miles down the western slope were nailing together a framework of timbers 650 feet long and 130 feet high across Dale Creek. It was the largest trestlework on the U.P., and when winds blew up the canyon the bridge swayed alarmingly. Government inspectors refused to approve it until they extracted a promise from Durant to lash it down with cables and replace it with an iron structure within one year. "The highest railroad bridge in the world," boasted the U.P., but to the men who first crossed it on an Iron Horse it was like spanning a structure of interlaced toothpicks.

Bypassing the incompleted bridge, Jack Casement

pushed his track layers on toward Laramie City. Silas Seymour, the dandy who was still acting as "consulting engineer," field agent, and spy for Durant, was in evidence again, accompanied occasionally by a mistress and several black servants. He and Durant were plotting something, but neither Casement nor construction superintendent Sam Reed could yet determine what was in the wind. To pick up some easy money, Durant had the townsite of Laramie surveyed into lots, and Seymour spread rumors that the division shops and roundhouse originally planned by Dodge to be located at Cheyenne would be transferred to Laramie. This of course caused a sharp increase in the demand for Laramie City lots. Within a week, four hundred lots were sold at exorbitant prices, and when the tracks came in early in May, about 8,500 of Cheyenne's 10,000 population and a large number of that town's knock-down buildings were transferred almost overnight to Laramie.

Although the rails moved swiftly on west of Laramie, the town went through a wild period, its violence intensified because of vigilante efforts to halt the general lawlessness. After the town's business leaders lynched a desperado known as "The Kid," a gun battle broke out in Belle of the West, one of the dingier dance halls. Five men were killed, fifteen wounded; the determined vigilantes captured four outlaws and hanged them from telegraph poles alongside the U.P. station. When a newspaper correspondent arrived shortly afterward to report the incident, he was told that the hanged men had broken their necks while climbing the telegraph poles. By this time, another end-of-track town, Benton, was ready for a westward shift of the Hell on Wheels, and most of the gamblers, saloonkeepers, and outlaws began leaving Laramie.

In the meantime, Durant and Seymour had aroused the anger of Casement and Reed by ordering them to make a change in Dodge's original survey. To avoid extensive grading and filling across the rough country between Laramie City and the Laramie plains, Seymour recommended a new route through the valleys of Rock Creek and Medicine Bow River. This change would add twenty miles to the railroad, but it could be speedily constructed and would

The Dale Creek bridge (Photo by A. J. Russell, The Oakland Museum)

bring almost two million easy dollars into the pockets of the railroad's builders. At this time, Dodge was in Washington serving as congressman from the Iowa district of which he claimed to be a resident. Most of his efforts were directed toward legislation favoring the Union Pacific, and he still held his title of chief engineer of the railroad. Early in May, Dodge received a telegram from Sam Reed informing him of Seymour's and Durant's interference. Dodge immediately packed his bags. He had chosen Cheyenne as a division point because that city was the most logical place for a junction with the railroad from Denver, and he was determined to block Durant's efforts to change it to Laramie. As for Seymour's new survey, Dodge viewed it as being as crooked as was its originator. Just as his predecessor, Peter Dey, had rebelled as the result of Seymour's interference in lengthening the road out of Omaha three years earlier, Dodge's professionalism could not accept the proposed change. Instead of resigning as Dey had done, however, he telegraphed President Oliver Ames of the U.P., secured his support, and then boarded a train for Wyoming, determined to have a show-down.

When Dodge arrived at Cheyenne, he learned that Durant had already ordered the repair shops moved to Laramie and that grading had begun on Seymour's winding route to the Laramie plains. Dodge countermanded Durant's order concerning the railroad shops, and then had his private car hitched to a locomotive for a fast run to Laramie. There, by chance, he met Durant walking on a street crowded with the usual gambling establishments. According to Dodge, it was not a cordial meeting. He informed Durant that he was still chief engineer of the U.P. and that he could not tolerate any interference in engineering matters. "The men working for the Union Pacific will take orders from me and not from you," Dodge quoted himself as saying. "If you interfere there will be trouble—trouble from the government, from the Army, and from the men themselves." Durant was well aware of Dodge's excellent governmental and military connections. He made no reply as Dodge turned and strode back toward the Laramie station.

Grading and filling was now too far along on Seymour's route to make a change, but as soon as the track layers reached the Laramie plains, Jack Casement set a goal of two miles a day, offering extra pay to men willing to work on moonlit nights and on Sundays. The Casements' new con-tract stipulated payment to them of eight hundred dollars per mile for less than two miles laid in a day, twelve hundred dollars a mile for over two miles a day. During that summer, the U.P. and its contractors had ten thousand men strung out across Wyoming and into northeastern Utah. After three years of trial and error, Sam Reed, the Casement brothers, and their assistants had achieved a high degree of efficiency in plan-ning and in organization. They had learned that forty carloads of supplies were required to build each mile of track, and dis-covered the importance of time-and-motion studies before that technique was given a name. Even so, the pressures upon the graders to keep ahead of the track layers resulted in what one government examiner described as "very hastily and inefficiently made up" earthen fills. After traveling over one such section, President Oliver Ames admitted that the grades and curves would have to be improved as soon as the road was completed, "though it will be a heavy additional cost."

At Mary's Creek, the U.P. had to build its first tunnel through a rugged spur of sandstone that blocked a gorge along which the tracks were to run. To avoid a delay in track construction, the resourceful Casements bypassed the spur, laying miles of rails ahead of the tunneling crew.

In the heat of July, the U.P. was platting another town, which somebody ironically decided to name for Senator Thomas Hart Benton. The late senator had spent years advocating a transcontinental railroad along the 38th parallel, and now here was his town almost astride the predestined 42d parallel. Nearby, General Sherman's Army was building Fort Fred Steele, and Dr. Durant's promoters used its presence to create an air of permanence about the city of Benton and to boost the price of lots. Although the streets were filled with burning alkali dust, and water had to be hauled three miles in wagons from the North Platte River for a dollar per barrel, the lots were eagerly and quickly bought up. Two months later, Benton was a ghost town, with nothing left there but a sidetrack for the use and convenience of the fort.

During its Hell on Wheels heyday, however, Benton had twenty-three saloons and five dance halls. Twice each day, long freight trains arrived from the East to unload tons of goods for reshipment by wagons to all points west. "For ten hours daily the streets were thronged with motley crowds of railroadmen, Mexicans and Indians, gamblers, 'cappers,' saloonkeepers, merchants, miners and mulewhackers," wrote newspaper correspondent John Hanson Beadle. "The streets were eight inches deep in white dust as I entered the city of canvas tents and polehouses; the suburbs appeared as banks of dirty white lime, and a new arrival with black clothes looked like nothing so much as a cockroach struggling through a flour barrel. . . . The great institution of Benton was the 'Big Tent.' This structure was a nice frame, a hundred feet long and forty feet wide, covered with canvas and conveniently floored for dancing, to which and gambling it was entirely devoted."

Publisher Samuel Bowles found Benton disgusting by

day, dangerous by night, "a congregation of scum and wickedness . . . almost everybody dirty, many filthy, and with the marks of lowest vice; averaging a murder a day; gambling and drinking, hurdy-gurdy dancing and the vilest of sexual commerce, the chief business and pastime of the hours,—this was Benton. Like its predecessors, it fairly festered in corruption, disorder and death, and would have rotted, even in this dry air, had it outlasted a brief sixty-day life. But in a few weeks its tents were struck, its shanties razed, and with their dwellers moved on fifty or a hundred miles farther to repeat their life for another brief day. Where these people came from originally; where they went to when the road was finished, and their occupation over, were both puzzles too intricate for me. Hell would appear to have been raked to furnish them; and to it they must have naturally returned after graduating here, fitted for its highest seats and most diabolical service."

Before Benton died, some of the tents were replaced with prefabricated buildings that had been shipped all the way from Chicago. In a dim light, a passerby would swear that they were built of brick and brownstone, but actually they were merely boards painted to simulate more-permanent materials. "The meanest place I have ever been in," was the way Jack Casement described Benton in a letter to his wife, but Casement was irritated by the August heat, which was slowing construction, and Utah was still miles and miles beyond the western horizon. Casement was also annoyed by a constant succession of excursionists brought out by Durant and Seymour to encourage sales of railroad stock. According to Casement, one excursion party contained "all the Professors of Yale College and a lot of Rail Road men with their ladies . . . a great nuisance to the work."

The most important excursion party of the summer was that of General Ulysses Grant, who as the candidate of the Republican party was campaigning for the office of President of the United States. Somewhat in the manner of modern candidates who visit foreign lands to demonstrate their breadth of vision, Grant was traveling across the West to demonstrate his interest in the transcontinental railroad and what was then called "the Indian Problem." Late in July he arrived at

Laramie City in company with a touring party of eight generals among whom were Sherman and Sheridan. By this time Durant had managed to secure from the executive committee of the Union Pacific a resolution that gave him authority to direct construction operations in the field. Armed with this weapon, Durant managed to see Grant and ask his support in removing Dodge as chief engineer. Grant refused to commit himself until he heard Dodge's side of the feud; consequently, a telegram had to be sent to Dodge, who was inspecting the Mormons' grading work in Utah, requesting his presence at Fort Sanders for a conference with Grant, Durant, Dillon, and Seymour.

Politics was a complicating intruder at this meeting. Silas Seymour's brother, Horatio Seymour, was the Democratic candidate for President, running in opposition to Grant. If Horatio Seymour should win, Durant through his connections with Silas would gain direct access to presidential powers and decisions. But only the most fanatical partisans believed that anyone could defeat Grant, the military hero of the reunited nation. And with Grant in office, his wartime comrade Dodge certainly would be the Union Pacific's man of influence with the presidency.

The confrontation occurred on July 26, 1868, in an ornately constructed log cabin used as the officers' club at Fort Sanders. Grant, Sherman, and Sheridan wore civilian clothing. Dodge, lean and sunburned, arrived wearing an engineer's cap, his boots polished to a high shine. Durant's pasty face was determined; he wore loose black summer corduroys, a gold watch chain pendant across his vest. Dillon, of Credit Mobilier, in a dark coat and gray trousers, could have been an actor cast in the role of a capitalist giant. Seymour, his hair and beard neatly trimmed as usual, kept to the background.

If we may believe Dodge's account, Grant opened the proceedings by commenting in his dry fashion upon the Army's difficulties in pacifying hostile Indians so as to keep them from attacking the railroad's graders and track layers. Having spent so much money and effort at this, he said, the government had the right to expect peaceable relations among the builders of the road.

Showdown at Fort Sanders: From left, Grenville Dodge, Sidney Dillon, and General Phil Sheridan. President Grant is standing beneath the bird cage; General Sherman is framed in the doorway. Thomas Durant, about as far away from Dodge as he can get, is leaning against the fence to the right of the top-hatted General William S. Harney.
(Photo by A. J. Russell, The Oakland Museum)

Durant plunged immediately to the attack, charging Dodge with having wasted money upon preliminary surveys, with having chosen routes too costly to construct, with ignoring the advice of his associates, and with angering the Mormons by routing the line north of Salt Lake. After Durant finished, Grant glanced at Dodge.

"If Durant, or anybody connected with the Union Pacific, or anybody connected with the government changes my lines," Dodge said calmly, "I'll quit the road."

Nobody spoke for a few moments, and then Grant broke the silence: "The government expects the railroad company to meet its obligations. And the government expects General Dodge to remain with the road as its chief engineer until it is completed."

Durant was a realist. He knew that within a few months, barring a miracle, the man who had directed those words to him would be President of the United States. Hesitating only a moment, Durant turned toward Dodge. "I withdraw my objections," he said. "We all want Dodge to stay with the road."

That of course was Dodge's story. No one else present appears to have made any record of this second showdown with Durant.

Dodge returned to Utah, and while the U.P. track layers endured the heat and desolation of Wyoming's Red Desert, he sought out his opposite number on the Central Pacific, chief engineer Samuel Montague. With his usual bluntness, Dodge told Montague that U.P. tracks would be in Ogden by the spring of 1869. To save time and money, he suggested, the two railroads should decide upon a definite meeting place somewhere west of Ogden. Montague, however, declined to name a specific place. The Great Race, with all its wastefulness, would still continue.

As the summer waned, swarms of newspapermen arrived daily from the East, dispatching bulletins "from the front" much in the manner of war correspondents. They reported each day's progress in miles and quarter miles of track laid toward the Wasatch Mountain barrier of Utah. "Sherman with his victorious legions sweeping from Atlanta to Savannah was a spectacle less glorious than this army of men marching on foot from Omaha to Sacramento, subduing unknown wildernesses, scaling unknown mountains, surmounting untried obstacles, and binding across the broad breast of America the iron emblem of modern progress and civilization."

Late in October the track layers were within a few miles of the Utah line, but each night ice rimmed the tops of the water barrels, warning that winter would come early in the mountains. In November they reached Bear River; this was the heart of the old fur-trade country of Jim Bridger and the Mountain Men. The rugged fur trappers, accustomed to the wild excitements of their annual rendezvous, would have felt right at home in Bear River City, but even they might have been astonished by the riot of November 19, when a gang of outlaws who had been driven out of town by vigilantes returned in force to burn the town's jail and sack the office of the *Frontier Index*, the peripatetic newspaper that had followed the railroad west from Fort Kearney, Nebraska.

Opinions differed as to whether the outlaws destroyed the newspaper because they believed the editor was the leader of the vigilantes or because he was a Seymour Democrat who had used his editorial columns to attack Ulysses S. Grant as a "whisky bloated, squaw ravishing, adulterous, monkey ridden, nigger worshipping mogul." At any rate, Bear River City died not long after that, and a traveler who passed through a year later said that there was nothing left to mark the place "except a few posts and old chimneys, broken bottles and shattered oyster cans."

December snows began to plague the graders and track layers after they crossed into Utah, and each day the gang foremen expected to receive orders to make winter camp. But there was to be no work stoppage in the winter of 1868–69. Alarmed by the rapid progress of the C.P. across the Nevada deserts, and greedy for the mile subsidies and land grants that might be lost to the Big Four across Utah, Durant persuaded the U.P. directors to order full speed ahead through the Wasatch Range. Now the U.P. workmen would have to endure the same hardships suffered by C.P. workmen in the

Bear River City, a short-lived Hell on Wheels town
(Photo by A. J. Russell, The Oakland Museum)

Sierras. They dragged timber out of snowbanks, moved frozen earth with picks and shovels, laid tracks on icy crusts, and learned by experience how to blast tunnels through the red sandstone of Echo and Weber canyons.

Being as eager as Durant to beat the C.P. into Ogden, Dodge did not resist Durant's orders, but he admitted that laying the track in snow and ice was done at tremendous cost, over ten million dollars he estimated. The head of the railroad's freight department complained that the track west of Bear River was "not fit to run over and we are ditching trains daily," and on one of Dodge's inspection tours he saw a train slide off a collapsing embankment and overturn. One of the few newspaper reporters hardy enough to stay in the field reported that tracks were laid on snow and ice, which then melted or evaporated, leaving ties and rails dangling in the air. Entire grades, he said, were so soft that the weight of trains would cause them to slide into rivers below. Accidents and fatalities increased rapidly, but when the men complained, their foremen used the old anti-Chinese prejudices to keep the Great Race from slowing down. Were the tarriers of the U.P. going to let the little yellow Chinamen beat them into Ogden? Never! Jack Casement found plenty of track layers willing to work after sundown by lanternlight in bitter cold.

They celebrated Christmas Day by bringing the end of track into Wahsatch, only sixty-seven miles from Ogden. Durant was there in his comfortable private car for the celebration, but snow was piled high along the tracks and correspondent John H. Beadle reported that the temperature in the dining room of the town's only hotel was five degrees below zero. "A drop of the hottest coffee spilled upon the cloth froze in a minute, while the gravy was hard on the plate, and the butter frozen in spite of the fastest eater." Twenty-eight-year-old John Beadle was a graduate of Michigan State, a Civil War veteran from Indiana, who had come to the West expecting to die from an ailment diagnosed as consumption, but he made a miraculous recovery during his zestful pursuit of news stories about the railroad for the *Cincinnati Commercial*.

When Jack Casement informed Durant that some of his

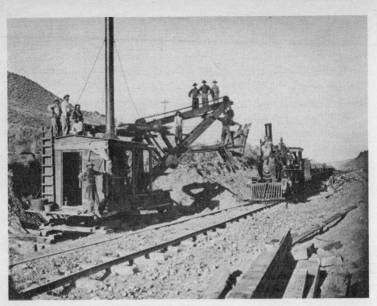

Introduced in the last weeks of construction, a steam shovel at Hanging Rock, Echo Canyon (Photo by A. J. Russell, The Oakland Museum).

Tunnel No. 3, Weber Canyon (Photo by A. J. Russell, The Oakland Museum)

men were near the breaking point, Durant told him to double the wages and keep the work going. Doubling the wages, however, meant little to the workmen, because they were already several weeks behind in receiving their pay. During Christmas week, Credit Mobilier had poured out its fifth bountiful dividend of 1868 to its tight little ring of stockholders (several of whom were congressmen), leaving the Union Pacific Railroad Company six million dollars in debt and with no funds to pay contractors and workmen. To add to the difficulties, government inspectors were refusing to certify some of the recent construction, holding up expected subsidies. In New York, Jim Fisk, a former Yankee peddler of silk goods who had become a notorious financial speculator and manipulator, was threatening an injunction suit against the railroad in a move to gain control of it. Brigham Young was pressing hard for money to pay his Mormon graders, and even the optimistic Jack Casement complained that the company owed him a hundred thousand dollars. "The banks are loaded with UPRR paper," he said, "and if The Company don't send some money here soon they will burst up the whole country."

Although Dillon of Credit Mobilier was as responsible for the railroad's poor financial condition as was Durant, the latter received much of the blame from associates who were aware of the avaricious tendencies of their vice-president and general manager. They knew that Durant and Seymour were silent partners in firms that sold supplies to the railroad at excessive prices, that Durant was receiving ten percent of many contracts and had instructed construction supervisors to report double the actual quantities of rock hauled for fills, and that Seymour was also receiving kickbacks from tie-cutting contractors and timber haulers. Herbert Hoxie, the Iowa politician who had been a beneficiary of Durant's manipulations in his 1865 contract switch to Credit Mobilier, feared that the sharp practices had gone too far and declared privately that "the entire outfit was rotten to the core."

But the U.P.'s worst blow of the winter came when the Secretary of the Interior abruptly ordered the railroad to cease construction at Echo Summit, forty miles east of Ogden. When the order reached Utah, the road already had tracks several miles west of Echo Summit and grades were approaching Ogden. The U.P.'s directors were counting on subsidies from the tracks built to Ogden, and probably beyond, to pull them out of their financial squeeze. To halt construction now might mean bankruptcy for the road. Suspecting that wily old Collis Huntington had put pressure on government officials to recognize the Central Pacific's right-of-way maps across Utah, which he had filed with the Department of the Interior, the directors of the Union Pacific decided that politics was involved in the action. They gambled on the fact that Grenville Dodge's good friend, General Grant, would be inaugurated as President within a few weeks and that a new Secretary of the Interior would be in office. And so they boldly ignored the order to stop construction, and pressed on toward Ogden. They also increased their lobbying activities among influential congressmen who were not yet receiving monetary benefits from Credit Mobilier stock.

On the morning of March 8, 1869, four days after Grant became President, Jack Casement's track gangs laid rails into Ogden, and that afternoon an Iron Horse rolled in, its whistle drowning the music of a welcoming brass band. Dodge and Reed were there to celebrate not only the railroad's capture of Ogden, but also news just received that in his first cabinet

Corinne, Utah, known briefly as "the Chicago of the Rocky

meeting President Grant had canceled the order to halt Union Pacific construction at Echo Summit.

As soon as the celebration ended, Casement had his track layers back at work, and a month later they were at Corinne. This town would be the next to the last of the tent-and-tarpaper grading camps that the arrival of rails converted to the usual roaring den of sin. A land agent for the U.P. named the town for his daughter (an act that he must have later regretted) and he promoted Corinne as Utah's future non-Mormon city, the "Chicago of the Rocky Mountains." A few weeks later when Charles Savage arrived to photograph the booming town, he said that all of Corinne was "on the wrong side of the tracks." For a time John Beadle ran a newspaper there and boasted that "the town contained eighty *nymphs du pavé,* popularly known in Mountain-English as 'soiled doves.' . . . Yet it was withal a quiet and rather orderly place. Sunday was generally observed: most of the men went hunting or fishing, and the 'girls' had a dance, or got drunk."

Only fifty miles now separated the contenders in the Great Race, and it was obvious that they must meet somewhere in the Promontory Range. Yet, no effort was being made by the leaders of either side to choose a specific meeting place. Like two weary but evenly matched armies at the end of a long war, each railroad company continued to

Mountains" (Photo by A. J. Russell, The Oakland Museum)

maneuver for advantages over the other, running their parallel grades for miles past each other, the C.P. stubbornly heading for Ogden, and the U.P. hellbent for nowhere. Notable examples of waste were the U.P.'s Big Trestle and the C.P.'s Big Fill, both of which crossed the same deep gorge within 150 feet of each other. The C.P. used 500 men and 250 teams in hauling earth during most of February and March 1869, to build the embankment across the canyon. When the U.P. reached the same point, Seymour refused to waste time on a fill and ordered Sam Reed to construct a trestle. A newspaper reporter was appalled by the flimsy structure. "The cross pieces are jointed in the most clumsy manner," he wrote. "The Central Pacific have a fine, solid embankment alongside it, which ought to be used as a track."

At last President Grant had to intercede. He summoned Grenville Dodge to Washington and asked him to arrange a meeting between representatives of both companies. If they could not decide where their tracks would join, the government would do it for them. As Huntington was in Washington, lobbying as usual, Dodge informed him of what Grant had said, and on April 8 the two men held an all-night meeting. The next morning they telegraphed officials of their respective railroads and informed them of their agreement; after receiving approval from them, they informed Congress that the Union Pacific and the Central Pacific would join their tracks at Promontory Point.

No record was kept of the Dodge-Huntington discussions, but Huntington evidently used the maps he had filed, claiming the route across Utah to Echo Summit, as a weapon to force Dodge to compromise and permit the C.P. to lease or buy the U.P. tracks from Promontory to Ogden. Thus did the C.P. gain what it had set out to achieve, a route into the Great Basin of Utah. In the end, the U.P. did not do so badly either: the company sold its tracks to the C.P. for over a million dollars and also pocketed the government subsidies for each of the fifty-three miles from Ogden to Promontory Point.

While these decisive events were occurring in Washington, the rambunctious Jim Fisk stirred up trouble in New York for the Union Pacific by filing a lawsuit on the pretext of protecting his rights as a stockholder. Fisk had smelled out the money bounty of Credit Mobilier, and charged that it was looting the Union Pacific. What Fisk wanted was to throw the railroad into bankruptcy, in the hope that he could gain control of it. He went so far as to form an alliance with the corrupt New York political boss William Marcy Tweed, and staged a raid on the Union Pacific offices to seize company records. President Oliver Ames, however, managed to transfer the books to New Jersey, out of Tweed's jurisdiction, thereby keeping the lid on Credit Mobilier's relations with the railroad—until another day. Jim Fisk had touched a sensitive nerve in the closely related financial-political establishment of America, but his reputation was so unsavory that he gained no supporters among the few honest men in Congress, who were also beginning to suspect that something was amiss in the financing of the people's railroad to the Western Sea. And so the entire affair evaporated in the atmosphere of exhilaration with which the young republic awaited the approaching day when the Great Race would end at Promontory Point.

There was one more event to be staged for the benefit of newspapermen and photographers who were gathering in that last of the railroad boom towns, Promontory City, which consisted of one long street of tents and false-fronted wooden structures set back only a few yards from the railroad track. According to rumor, Charlie Crocker had once boasted to Dr. Durant that his C.P. workmen could lay ten miles of track in a single day, whereupon Durant had bet Crocker ten thousand dollars that such a feat could never be accomplished. At any rate, as the two railroads approached each other at Promontory Point, Crocker announced that April 28 would be Ten-Mile Day.

For the railroad workmen this event was of greater importance than was the final joining of the rails, and both companies declared a holiday for all except the few hundred men engaged in the great undertaking. After distributing ties along the grade, Crocker and Strobridge planned everything like a military operation, bringing up carloads of rails, fishplates, bolts, and spikes at regular intervals, using Chinese on handcars pulled by horses to move the iron forward to the gaugers, spikers, bolters, and a picked crew of eight rail carriers. These eight iron men were of course the sporting heroes of the day, and their names—Sullivan, Dailey, Kennedy, Joyce, Shay, Eliott, Killeen, McNamara—reveal their ancestry. Every participant moved at full speed, jumping, trotting, running, dancing, pausing only occasionally to take a sip of water or tea from pails that a detachment of constantly moving Chinese carried on poles over their shoulders.

By one-thirty they had laid six miles of rails, and Crocker ordered a stop for lunch. He offered to release any track layer who had had enough. Nobody accepted the offer. An hour later they were back at work. At seven o'clock, James Strobridge signaled victory. In twelve hours, a full working day, they were fifty-six feet past the ten-mile mark. During that day, someone later calculated, the track layers had spiked 3,520 rails to 25,800 ties, and each rail handler had lifted 250,000 pounds of iron.

Although Dr. Durant was not there to witness the loss of his ten-thousand-dollar bet, Grenville Dodge was among the spectators. "I saw them lay their special ten miles on that wager," he commented, "but they were a week preparing for it, and bedded all their ties beforehand." For him it was only a stunt. The joining of the rails and the driving of the last spike would be the day of accomplishment.

Promontory Point, Promontory Summit, Promontory Station—all these names were used—lay in a waterless basin of

Ten miles of iron in a single day (Utah State Historical Society)

sagebrush, ringed on three sides by mountains. Tracks of the Central Pacific reached there on April 30, and the Californians had to wait a week before the Union Pacific track layers came into view. On May 1, hundreds of men lined up at the paymasters' cars of both railroads to receive their last wages, and thousands of others learned that they would work only one more week. "The two opposing armies," reported a newspaper correspondent, "are melting away." The Great Race was coming to an end.

Only twenty-five hundred feet of empty grading lay between the two railroads on May 7, but that afternoon, when Leland Stanford's special train arrived for the planned celebration of May 8, Jack Casement came over to inform the Central Pacific's president and several accompanying dignitaries that the joining of the rails would have to be delayed until May 10. According to Casement, heavy rains had washed out part of the U.P. tracks in Weber Canyon, and the special train carrying Durant, Dillon, and other officials could not move until repairs were completed.

But there was more to the story than that. On May 6, when the U.P. special pulled into Piedmont, Wyoming, from the East, an armed mob of several hundred railroad workmen surrounded Durant's private car, switched it onto a sidetrack, and chained the wheels to the rails. Spokesmen for the workers informed the startled Dr. Durant that he and his very important associates were prisoners until the men received their overdue wages. The amount demanded remains obscure because Union Pacific officials then and afterward maintained great secrecy about the incident, but various contemporary accounts gave estimates varying from $12,000 to $80,000 to $235,000. Some historians suspect that Mormons were leaders in this affair, as the railroad had repeatedly ignored Brigham Young's demands for payment of his grading contract. Although attempts were made to effect Durant's rescue by summoning soldiers from nearby Army posts, all telegrams to the military were intercepted, and he finally gave up and arranged for payroll funds to be telegraphed from New York headquarters.

While these events were occurring, Jack Casement felt obliged to entertain Leland Stanford and his friends from Cal-

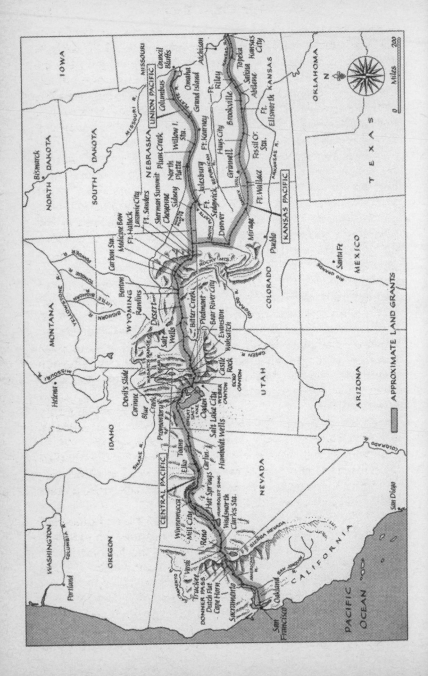

ifornia by inviting them for a sightseeing ride to Ogden on
his work train, which he had previously stocked with "a
bountiful collation and oceans of champagne." As the
weather was dismal with rain, no one objected to the delay,
and during their overnight stay in Ogden, Stanford and some
of the other orators wrote their speeches for the forthcoming
ceremonies and released them to the gathering swarm of
newspapermen.

A cold rain was still falling on Sunday, May 9, but all rails
on both approaches to Promontory, except the final connecting ones, were spiked to the ties. The next morning the
weather had cleared into an ideal day for celebration, white
clouds floating in a clean blue sky against a distant backdrop
of cedar-covered mountains, a cool breeze blowing, the temperature rising to sixty-nine degrees.

By seven o'clock the first curious spectators were assembling around the two-rail gap where a huge American flag
flapped atop an adjoining telegraph pole. Alongside the
grade, whiskey peddlers had already set up tents to sell refreshments at premium prices. At about eight o'clock a construction train arrived to unload boisterous gangs of track
layers and graders, and then backed away. Shortly after ten
o'clock, two Union Pacific trains pulled up and stopped a
short distance from the gap. The first train was Durant's delayed three-car special, and riding with him that morning
were Dillon, Dodge, Seymour, Reed, the Casement brothers,
and several other officials and guests. Aboard the second
train were four companies of the Twenty-first Infantry and its
headquarters band bound for the Presidio at San Francisco,
and also a delegation of prominent Utah citizens with a brass
band from Salt Lake City.

While these arrivals were detraining, a gang of blue-clad
Chinese workmen began leveling up the gap in the roadbed.
They laid the last ties and rails, bolted on the fishplates, and
drove all but the last few spikes. At 11:15 the Central Pacific
train puffed into view. Both Iron Horses—the C.P.'s "Jupiter" with a flared funnel stack and the U.P.'s No. 119 with
a straight cylindrical stack capped by a spark-arrester—were
now uncoupled and brought into facing positions across the
meeting place of the rails. The soldiers of the Twenty-first In-

fantry formed a double line facing the tracks and stood at parade rest.

By this time Stanford and the members of his party were shaking hands with the Union Pacific officials, and they began discussing the agenda of the ceremonies. Stanford had brought along two golden spikes, a silver spike, a combination iron, silver, and gold spike, a silver-plated sledgehammer, and a polished laurel tie, but very little planning had been done in regard to protocol. Dr. Durant, clad in a stylish black velvet jacket, and suffering from a severe headache probably brought on by excessive consumption of champagne, wished only to get done with the spike ceremony as quickly as possible, but Grenville Dodge evidently took offense at Stanford's elaborate trappings and insisted on having a simple ceremony in which *he* would drive the last spike, an iron one. Even to the very last hour, the rivalry of the Great Race would not die. It was 11:55, only five minutes before the scheduled time for beginning the ceremony, when Durant overruled Dodge and agreed to follow Stanford's program.

None of those present who recorded the events of the day agreed on the number of people gathered there. Estimates ranged from five hundred to three thousand, but judging from the photographs, the total probably was between six and seven hundred, including the understrength companies of the Twenty-first Infantry, about twenty reporters and photographers, and twenty-one women, most of whom were wives of railroad officials and Army officers. "It was not a large crowd," Sidney Dillon recalled. "In brass bands, fireworks, procession and oratory, the demonstration when ground was broken at Omaha, less than five years before, was much more imposing." But it should be remembered that in May 1869, Promontory Point was remote and difficult to reach. Virtually all of America was there in spirit that day, awaiting eagerly the telegraphic flashes that would signal the symbolic union of the continent by iron rails.

To speed this communication, a wire had been run from a telegraph pole down to a key on a small table facing the rail gap. At 12:20, telegraph operator W. N. Shilling tapped out a message to Western Union announcing that in about twenty minutes the last spike would be driven. Operators across the nation immediately began clearing their lines. While Shilling's key still chattered, James Strobridge and Sam Reed brought up the laurel tie (in which spike holes had previously been drilled) and placed it in position. The bibulous spectators pressed in so close that Jack Casement had to order them back so that photographers could set up their cameras to record the scene. "As it was," reported John Beadle, "the crowd pushed upon the workmen so closely that less than twenty persons saw the affair entirely, while none of the reporters were able to hear all that was said." Because of the boisterous jostling and shouting, only those pressed into the inner ring knew that the Reverend John Todd, who was there as a correspondent for two religious magazines, was offering a prayer. They removed their hats, while Dr. Todd's voice was drowned in the outer babble of celebrants. He kept the prayer mercifully short, and at 12:40, telegrapher Shilling tapped out: "We have got done praying. The spike is about to be presented."

Durant, his head throbbing, pushed forward to accept the two gold spikes from a representative of the Central Pacific. He kneeled and slid them into the prepared holes in the laurel tie, his eyes blinking at the inscribed silver plate: THE LAST TIE LAID ON THE COMPLETION OF THE PACIFIC RAILROAD, MAY 1869. As he arose, Stanford began speaking in the bright sunlight, his voice strong at the end: "Now, gentlemen, with your assistance we will proceed to lay the last tie, the last rail, and drive the last spike."

Grenville Dodge made the response: "Gentlemen, the great Benton proposed that someday a giant statue of Columbus be erected on the highest peak of the Rocky Mountains, pointing westward, denoting that as the great route across the continent. You have made that prophecy today a fact. This is the way to India."

While the crowd cheered and the bands played, the other spikes and the silver-headed sledgehammer were brought forward. After a telegraph wire was attached to the last spike, Stanford raised the sledge and brought it down

Moments before the last rail was laid at Promontory. Telegrapher's table

is at right center. (Photo by A. J. Russell, The Oakland Museum)

Looking eastward over the bulging stack of the Central Pacific's "Jupiter" as the rails are joined on May 10, 1869, to complete the nation's first transcontinental railroad (Photo by A. J. Russell, The Oakland Museum)

briskly, missing the spike entirely. The inebriated track layers roared with laughter. Durant put on a pair of gauntlets to protect his tender palms, lifted the sledge, and also missed. Aware that the blows of the sledgehammer had not gone out over the wire, telegrapher Shilling touched his key and tapped out: "Done." The time was 12:47, 2:47 on the Eastern seaboard. "We all yelled like to bust," was the way one of the spectators described it.

After the gold and silver spikes and the laurel tie were carefully removed, the C.P.'s "Jupiter" and the U.P.'s No. 119 eased forward until their pilots clanged together. While cheering workmen climbed up onto both Iron Horses, their engineers scrambled to the boiler fronts with bottles of champagne, to shake hands and exchange toasts. The photographers worked frantically to clear the crowd back so that the railroad's chief engineers, Grenville Dodge and Samuel

Montague, could stand before the two locomotives in another symbolic handclasp.

As soon as the wet-plate photographs were made, the "Jupiter" reversed its wheels and made room for No. 119 to cross the rail junction. Then No. 119 backed up, and the "Jupiter" with a merry whistle blast eased across to the U.P.'s tracks. The transcontinental railroad was ready for the Iron Horses to roll.

Somewhat reluctantly, the workmen who had made it all possible (most of whom were now unemployed) drifted away to the whiskey tents and dance halls of Promontory City. The well-dressed owners of the railroads gathered in Dr. Durant's private car for more champagne toasts. In all the cities of America, bells were ringing, flags were flying, whistles were blowing, cannons were firing, people were singing, and orators were declaiming: "The Anglo-Saxon and the Celt met in friendly greeting the tawny Asiatic at Promontory Point, and rejoiced together over the final consummation of the enterprise which their united labors have achieved. . . . California shook hands with New York and New England, and the mingled screams of steam whistles upon engines waked the echoes of the mountains."

In Chicago, an impromptu parade seven miles long jammed the streets of the city. In New York, a hundred guns fired salutes in City Hall Park, and Wall Street suspended business for the day. In Philadelphia, flags were hoisted everywhere and the pealing of bells on Independence Hall set off the music of church bells all across the city. In Buffalo, the populace poured into the streets to sing "The Star Spangled Banner" and fire engines assembled to blow whistles in concert. In Sacramento, thirty Iron Horses gaily bedecked and drawn up into line screeched out a concert of joy. In San Francisco, the celebration became a bedlam that lasted well into the night, and that city's leading man of letters, Bret Harte, sat down to compose a poem:

> What was it the Engines said,
> Pilots touching,—head to head
> Facing on the single track,
> Half a world behind each back?

This is what the Engines said,
Unreported and unread.

With a prefatory screech,
In a florid Western speech,
Said the Engine from the West:
"I am from Sierra's crest;
And if altitude's a test,
Why, I reckon, it's confessed
That I've done my level best."

Said the Engine from the East:
"They who work best talk the least.
S'pose you whistle down your brakes;
What you've done is no great shakes,—
Pretty fair,—but let our meeting
Be a different kind of greeting.
Let these folks with champagne stuffing,
Not their Engines, do the *puffing*.

"Listen! Where Atlantic beats
Shores of snow and summer heats;
Where the Indian autumn skies
Paint the woods with wampum dyes,—
I have chased the flying sun,
Seeing all he looked upon,
Blessing all that he has blessed,
Nursing in my iron breast
All his vivifying heat,
All his clouds about my crest;
And before my flying feet
Every shadow must retreat."

Said the Western Engine, "Phew!"
And a long, low whistle blew,
"Come, now, really that's the oddest
Talk for one so very modest.
You brag of your East! *You* do?
Why, *I* bring the East to *you*!
All the Orient, all Cathay,
Find through me the shortest way;
And the sun you follow here
Rises in my hemisphere.
Really,—if one must be rude,—
Length, my friend, ain't longitude."

Said the Union: "Don't reflect, or
I'll run over some Director."
Said the Central: "I'm Pacific;
But, when riled, I'm quite terrific.
Yet today we shall not quarrel,
Just to show these folks this moral,
How two Engines—in their vision—
Once have met without collision."

That is what the Engines said,
Unreported and unread;
Spoken slightly through the nose,
With a whistle at the close.

CHAPTER 7

First Travelers on the Transcontinental

I see over my own continent the Pacific railroad
  surmounting every barrier,
I see continual trains of cars winding along
  the Platte carrying freight and passengers,
I hear the locomotives rushing and roaring,
  and the shrill steamwhistle,
I hear the echoes reverberate through the
  grandest scenery in the world . . .

Bridging the three or four thousand miles
  of land travel,
Tying the Eastern to the Western sea . . .
                    —WHITMAN, *Passage to India*

ON MAY 15, 1869, regular train service began on America's first transcontinental railroad. Thousands of Americans who had become accustomed to train travel in the Eastern states could now journey behind an Iron Horse all the way to Walt Whitman's Western Sea. Although it was not possible—except in cases of special excursions—to board a car in an Eastern city and journey uninterrupted to California, most of these pioneer travelers seemed to look upon the necessary transfers in Chicago and Omaha, and Promontory or Ogden, as welcome breaks in an eight- to ten-day adventure.

"Every man who could command the time and money was eager to make the trip," declared that energetic traveling reporter John Beadle, "and everybody who could sling ink became correspondents." From the very beginning, many travelers did indeed seem compelled to make written records of their experiences. Their accounts were usually very sketchy until they passed Chicago or Omaha. During the first year of transcontinental service, passengers from the East arrived in Chicago on the Michigan Central Railroad, but by the mid-1870s they had their choice of connections from the Pennsylvania, Erie, or New York Central.

"Seventy-five minutes are allowed for getting from the station of arrival to the station of departure," said William F. Rae, an Englishman who made the journey late in 1869. "In my own case the times of the trains did not correspond; the one train had started an hour before the other arrived." Because he had planned to stop over briefly in Chicago, Rae was not disappointed by the enforced delay of twenty-four hours, but many of his fellow passengers were, and for another century travelers through Chicago would continue to suffer the inconvenience of changing trains and failure to make connections. During the heyday of American railroad passenger travel, one of the common sayings was that a hog could travel across country through Chicago without changing cars, but a human being could not.

To reach the Union Pacific from Chicago, travelers had their choice of two direct routes, the Rock Island or the Northwestern, and an indirect route, the Chicago, Burlington & Quincy. Knowledgeable people taking the direct routes soon learned to avoid the evening express trains, which left them stranded in Council Bluffs or Omaha for almost twenty-four hours while they awaited the departure of the U.P.'s daily train for the Pacific Coast.

Until a bridge was completed across the Missouri River in 1872, western travelers also had to endure a crossing "in a rickety old ferry boat" from Council Bluffs to Omaha. "On arriving at Council Bluffs," reported William Rae, "we found omnibuses in waiting at the station. The morning was cold and raw. But a small proportion of the passengers could get inside seats, the remainder having the option of either sitting on the roof among the luggage, or else being left behind. In itself the seat on the roof was not objectionable, provided the time occupied was brief. As nearly an hour was thus spent, the feeling of satisfaction at having got a seat at all was supplanted by a feeling of annoyance at the treatment received. Through deep ruts in the mud the omnibus was slowly drawn by four horses to the river's bank, and thence on to the deck of a flat-bottomed steamer. Seated there, a good view was had of the Missouri. It has been called mighty, which it doubtless is, considered as a stream, yet the appellation of 'Big Muddy,' which is current here, is the one which more truthfully characterises it."

And then after the bridge was built, the railroads refused to be cooperative enough to take the cars of the Eastern roads across the river to the Union Pacific station. Arriving in Council Bluffs, passengers had to remove themselves and their baggage to the cars of the Transfer Company, "whose province is to put passengers to all sorts of inconvenience and trouble in crossing over the river." John Erastus Lester of Providence, Rhode Island, who traveled West in 1872 in the hope of improving his health, said that passage by the Transfer Company "caused more hard words to be spoken than can be erased from the *big book* for many a day." He was not only disenchanted by the company's treatment of passengers but by its requirement that all freight be unloaded from Eastern cars and then repacked for shipment across the river.

Early travelers on the transcontinental railroad saw little to admire about Omaha. One found it to be "the muddiest place I ever saw," but added that "the roads are generally deep with dust." Another also described the town as being layered with mud through which "the omnibus labored slowly, the outside passengers being advised by the driver to move about from one side of the roof to another, in order to guard against upsetting the overloaded vehicle. A general feeling of relief was manifested when the station of the Union Pacific Railway was reached."

Almost all agreed that they had seldom seen such bustling confusion as that which developed at the Omaha station at the times for train departures. During the early years when the journey to the West was considered a daring enterprise, rumors were deliberately spread among the greenhorn ticket buyers of the possibility that wild Indians would attack or wreck the trains; this of course aided the Omaha railroad agents in the sale of insurance policies for the journey.

Except for a quick whistle from the engine and the conductor's cry of "All aboard!" there was no warning of the train's departure. This usually resulted in a rush of passengers who had to hop on board the moving cars. "For three or

At arrival and departure times, the Omaha station was a scene of bustling confusion. (Nebraska State Historical Society)

four miles we pass along the bluffs on which Omaha is built," John Lester recorded, "and then push out upon the open prairie, the fertile lands of Nebraska. A vast plain, dotted here and there with trees, stretches away upon every side."

In springtime, the rolling land was covered with wild flowers whose fragrance drifted into the open windows of cars moving along at twenty miles an hour; in summer, tumbleweeds by the thousands wheeled across the drying grass; and by autumn, prairie fires blazed against the horizon. "The spectacle of a prairie on fire is one of infinite grandeur," said William Rae. "For miles on every side the air is heavy with volumes of stifling smoke, and the ground reddened with hissing and rushing fire."

Travelers from abroad found the Great Plains grass shorter than they had expected, and they compared the wind-driven sweep of grayish green to ocean waves, "undulating like the Atlantic with a heavy groundswell." They also complained of their eyes wearying at the sameness of landscape, of the train seeming to be standing still in an immense void. All welcomed the first break in the monotony of the plains—the Platte River, which the railroad followed westward as had the wagon trains of earlier years.

When the transcontinental railroad opened for service, George Mortimer Pullman had been manufacturing experimental models of his sleeping cars for four years, and the Union Pacific accepted several of them in 1869. They were called Pullman Palace cars and their exteriors were painted in rich brown colors to distinguish them from the drab coaches. Everyone who could afford the additional twenty-five dollars for first-class fare and four dollars per day for a Pullman Palace car was eager to obtain a berth. First-class travelers paid one hundred dollars for the journey from Omaha to Sacramento; second-class or coach, seventy-five dollars. There was also a special rate of forty dollars for immigrants, who rode on cramped board seats. Four to five days were usually required to complete the journey by express, six to seven days by mixed train. The speed of trains varied according to the conditions of tracks and bridges, dropping to nine miles per hour over hastily built sections and increasing to thirty-five miles per hour over smoother tracks. Most travelers of the early 1870s mentioned eighteen to twenty-two miles per hour as the average. Although speeds were doubled within a decade, time-consuming stops and starts at more than two hundred stations and water tanks prevented any considerable reduction in total hours spent on the long journey.

Even in an era when the most highly skilled Americans earned less than a hundred dollars a month, demand for hundred-dollar Pullman space on the transcontinental railroad was so great that early in 1870 the Union Pacific began running three sleeping cars on some trains and still had to turn away would-be ticket buyers. Because of George Pullman's interest in the Union Pacific, he supplied that railroad with deluxe innovations long before they reached the Eastern roads. Travelers heard or read about the Palace cars and were eager to ride on them no matter what the cost. "I had a sofa to myself, with a table and a lamp," wrote one satisfied rider. "The sofas are widened and made into beds at night. My berth was three feet three inches wide, and six feet three inches long. It had two windows looking out of the train, a handsome mirror, and was well furnished with bedding and curtains."

Westbound travelers were eager to ride on Pullman Palace Cars no matter what the cost. (New York Public Library Picture Collection)

In the 1870s Pullman introduced a "hotel car" with a cooking range, but it made only one trip weekly. (New York Public Library Picture Collection)

In cold weather passengers vied for a place at the foot warmer. (Culver Pictures)

British travelers were especially impressed, and sent off earnest letters to railway directors in London, urging them "to take a leaf out of the Americans' book, and provide sleeping carriages for long night journeys." They also delighted in the freedom of movement from one car to another, although the traveler who signed himself "A London Parson" admitted that trying to dress oneself in a box two feet high was a bit inconvenient. "It was an odd experience, that going to bed of some thirty ladies, gentlemen, and children, in, practically, one room. For two nights I had a young married couple sleeping in the berth above mine. The lady turned in first, and presently her gown was hung out over the rail to which her bed curtains were fastened. But further processes of unrobing were indicated by the agitation of the drapery which concealed her nest. As the same curtain served for both berths—hers and mine—the gentleman held her portion together over my head when it was necessary for me to retire. At last all were housed, and some snores rose above the rattle of the train. I did not sleep much the first night, but looked over the moonlit prairie from my pillow."

Although Pullman introduced a "hotel car" in 1870 with a kitchen at one end from which meals were served on removable tables set between the drawing-room seats, the Union Pacific scheduled the car for only one trip each week. Until well into the 1880s the transcontinental railroad fed its passengers at dining stations along the way, allowing them thirty minutes to obtain their food and bolt it down before resuming the journey.

Judging from comments of travelers, the food varied from wretched to middling-fair. The first dining stop out of Omaha was Grand Island. "Ill cooked and poorly served," was one passenger's blunt comment. "We found the quality on the whole bad," said William Robertson of Scotland, "and all three meals, breakfast, dinner and supper, were almost identical, viz., tea, buffalo steaks, antelope chops, sweet potatoes, and boiled Indian corn, with hoe cakes and syrup *ad nauseam*." New Yorker Susan Coolidge also complained about the sameness of diet: "It was necessary to look at one's watch to tell whether it was breakfast, dinner or supper that we were eating, these meals presenting invariably the same salient features of beefsteak, fried eggs, fried potato." She was generous enough to compliment the chef at Sidney, Nebraska, for serving "cubes of fried mush which diversified a breakfast of unusual excellence." Harvey Rice of Cleveland, Ohio, described the Sidney breakfast station as a crude structure of boards and canvas. "Here the passengers were replenished with an excellent breakfast—a chicken stew, as they supposed, but which, as they were afterward informed, consisted of prairie-dogs—a new variety of chickens, without feathers. This information created an unpleasant sensation in sundry delicate stomachs."

According to William L. Humason of Hartford, Connecticut, the farther one traveled across the plains, the worse the dining stations became, "consisting of miserable shanties, with tables dirty, and waiters not only dirty, but saucy. The

This "eating house" at Wahsatch, Utah, was typical of railroad dining stops across the West. (Photo by A. J. Russell, The Oakland Museum)

Cheyenne's railroad dining room (Photo by A. J. Russell, The Oakland Museum)

tea tasted as though it were made from the leaves of the sagebrush—literally *sage tea*. The biscuit was made without soda, but with plenty of alkali, harmonizing with the great quantity of alkali dust we had already swallowed." The only dining station Humason had a good word for was at Cisco, California, where the water on the table was as clear as crystal, but he thought a dollar and a quarter was "a pretty steep price to pay for fried ham and potatoes."

At most dining stops, meal prices were one dollar, and on the California section of the Central Pacific the prices were reduced to seventy-five cents if the diner paid in silver rather than in paper money. Neither the Union Pacific nor the Central Pacific operated their eating houses, preferring to contract them to private individuals, with no required standard of service. Most of them were in rough frame buildings filled with long tables upon which large platters of food were waiting when passengers descended from the trains. Gradually the individual stations achieved reputations for certain specialties such as beefsteak at Laramie, hot biscuits at Green River, antelope at Sidney, fish at Colfax. The most frequently praised dining stop was Evanston, Wyoming, where mountain trout was the specialty. "It was kept by a colored man named Howard W. Crossley whose evident desire was to please all," wrote John Lester. He added that most "proprietors of the eating-stations ought to be promoted to higher callings; for they are evidently above running a hotel."

Because Cheyenne was listed in the guidebooks as the largest city between Omaha and Sacramento, many passengers expected superior-quality food service there. They were disappointed to find a small town of board and canvas buildings occupied by about three thousand "dangerous-looking miners in big boots, broad-brimmed hats, and revolvers." The only added feature in the dining station was a formidable row of heads of big-game animals that glared down from the walls upon the famished passengers. "The chops were generally as tough as hanks of whipcord, and the knives as blunt as bricklayers' trowels." One traveler did mention favorably the antelope steaks served in Cheyenne, but Susan Coolidge was dubious, remarking that whenever beefsteak was unusually tough, the dining stations listed it as "antelope" to give it the charm of novelty. She also noted that the rush of diners at Cheyenne was "so great that you find it impossible to catch the eye of the Chinese waiter till it is too late to make him of the slightest use." Before her journey ended she reached the conclusion that transcontinental travelers should pack lunch baskets; she recommended Albert biscuit, orange marmalade, fresh rolls, and cold roasted chicken, which could be obtained at Omaha and Ogden. Most male travelers, however, advised against lunch baskets, saying that they were always in the way and that the food was likely to spoil.

Between stops for meals, the passengers were diverted by a procession of unfamiliar wildlife along each side of the track, antelope and prairie dogs being the most commonly seen. Far more antelope than buffalo ranged along the Union Pacific tracks, and long files of these fleet-footed animals often approached very close to passing trains, "apparently racing with the cars, and always winning in the race." Although the Union Pacific frowned upon the practice, eager hunters sometimes fired upon these animals with rifles and pistols from the open windows of the cars. Few hits were recorded.

Prairie-dog villages also were close enough that passengers could observe these gregarious rodents sitting at the entrances to their burrows. "They fling themselves in the air with a gay nimbleness beautiful to see, flip a somersault, and present to the admiring gaze of the traveler two furry heels and a short furry tail as they make their exit from the stage of action."

Elk, wolves, and bears often were seen as the Iron Horse thundered across the West, and one traveler was sure that he saw a pack of wild dogs trotting along parallel to the railroad, until he learned that they were coyotes. Another unfamiliar sight were swarms of grasshoppers and crickets, which sometimes descended upon the tracks and caused the locomotive wheels to spin into a temporary stall.

Although only thinning herds of buffalo remained near the Union Pacific right-of-way after train travel began, the Iron Horses of the Kansas Pacific (less than two hundred miles to the south) occasionally were surrounded by buffalo and had to slow down or wait until the herd passed. One traveler on the Kansas Pacific told of seeing a herd that extended as far as the eye could reach. "With heads down and tails up they galloped towards the track making extraordinary exertions to get across ahead of the locomotive. In trying this strategic feat one specimen found himself forcibly lifted into the air and thrown into the ditch, where he lay upon his back, his cloven feet flourishing madly."

In its early days, before connections were scheduled with other railroads, the Kansas Pacific engineers willingly stopped trains to permit the passengers to leave the cars and shoot at passing buffalo. "Everybody runs out and commences shooting," lawyer John Putnam of Topeka wrote a friend in 1868. "We failed to bag a buffalo. I did not shoot, having ill defined ideas as to hunting rifles, which end you put the load in and which end you let it out at. . . . But I rushed out with the rest—yelled promiscuously—'Buffalo! —Stop the train'—'let me out'—'there they are!—Whoop-pey'—Give 'em thunder'—'no go'—'Come back'—'drive on' —So you see I helped a good deal."

So eager was Randolph Keim of Washington, D.C., to bag a buffalo from a train, he persuaded the engineer to let him ride up front on the Iron Horse. "Taking my rifle I posted myself on the cow-catcher, or rather buffalo-catcher of the locomotive. After proceeding about ten miles, we struck a large herd crossing the track. The locomotive pursued its course without diminution of speed. Approaching the herd rather rapidly, I did not favor the idea of receiving a buffalo in my lap, a fact growing momentarily more probable. The herd had passed. One animal lagging in the rear out of bewilderment, or reckless daring, planted himself in the middle of the track, with his head down as much as to say, 'Come on who ever you are and we'll try.' As I felt no relish to be a party to any such cranial collision, and finding no other convenient place, took a conspicuous but uncomfortable position on the steam-chest, holding on by the rail. I found the temperature as far as my feet were concerned anything but desirable, but in momentary anticipation of a rare display of buffalo meat, kept a sharp look-out for the pieces. At this moment, the whistle blew. The buffalo, startled at the shrill sound, made an effort to get out of the way. He succeeded, so far as to have his posteriors pretty well damaged, that is minus his tail, and to wind up with a series of acrobatic exercises over the embankment."

The buffalo and other animals entertained the travelers against a constantly changing background of scenery that grew more and more fascinating as they left the plains behind. The first glimpse of the snowy range of the Rocky Mountains always sent a wave of excitement through the passenger cars. "My boyish dreams were realized," one man recorded. "For hours, at the school desk, have I pondered over the map and wandered, in imagination, with Lewis and Clark, the hunters and trappers and early emigrants, away off to these Rocky Mountains, about which such a mystery seemed to hang,—dreaming, wishing and hoping against hope, that my eyes might, some day, behold their snow-crowned heights. And here lay the first great range in the pureness of white; distant, to be sure, but there it lay, enshrined in beauty."

Wyoming was filled with wonders for these journeyers from the East, but when the Iron Horse brought them through tunnels into Utah's Echo and Weber canyons, they were at a loss for superlatives to describe the towering castle-

Railroad guide books described Echo City as "not very inviting" but these tourists stopped to view the scenery. (Photo by A. J. Russell, The Oakland Museum)

like rocks. "Grand beyond description . . . castles in the air . . . fantastic shapes and profiles . . . the scene is as fearful as it is sublime." Shortly after entering the narrows of Weber Canyon, virtually everyone made note of the Thousand-Mile Tree, a single green pine in a desolation of rock and sage, marking the distance from Omaha. European travelers compared Weber Canyon to gateways to the Alps. Castle Rock, Hanging Rock, Pulpit Rock, Devil's Gate, Devil's Slide—all entered the notebooks of scribbling travelers who seemed to disagree as to whether they were creations of God or of Satan.

Along the way were occasional reminders of pioneers of a previous day—the bones of long-dead oxen and horses beside the deep-rutted trails where covered wagons had crawled, a solitary grave marker, a broken wheel, a piece of discarded furniture. "Inch by inch, the teams toiled to gain a higher foothold," said one appreciative train traveler, "inch by inch they *climbed* down the rugged passes; *now* in luxurious coaches, with horses of iron, with a skilled engineer for a driver we are carried along in comfort."

When there were no animals or scenery to entertain or awe, there was always the ever-changing weather of the West. The train on which Harvey Rice was journeying to California in 1869 ran through a typically violent Great Plains thunderstorm. "The heavens became, suddenly, as black as starless midnight. The lightning flashed in every direction, and electric balls of fire rolled over the plains. It seemed as if the artillery of heaven had made the valley a target and that we were doomed to instant destruction. But happily our fears were soon dissipated. The storm was succeeded by a brilliant rainbow."

Heavy rains were likely to flood the tracks and in the early years before roadbeds were well ballasted, the ties sank into the mud. One traveler was startled to see the car behind him churning up such a foam of mud that it resembled a boat rushing along on water. It was not unusual for hailstorms to break car windows, and tornadoes could lift a train off the track. One of the legends of the Kansas Pacific concerns a tornadic waterspout that dropped out of a massive thunderstorm, washed out six thousand feet of track, and swallowed up a freight train. "Although great efforts were made to find it," said Charles B. George, a veteran railroad man, "not a trace of it has ever been discovered."

Winter travelers could expect magnificent snowstorms or fierce blizzards that sometimes turned a journey across the continent into an ordeal. On William Rae's return trip East from California in the winter of 1870, the Iron Horse pulling his train fought a two-hour battle with a snowstorm across four miles of the Laramie plains. The delay played havoc with train schedules on the single-track Union Pacific, but Rae reported that the hot-air stove in his Pullman car kept it "as comfortable as the best-warmed room in an English house."

Rae might not have been so fortunate had he been traveling on the Kansas Pacific, which suffered as severely from blizzards as it did from thunder squalls. High winds drifted both snow and sand into cuts, leveling them across the tops, and the sturdy little wood-burning locomotives would have to back up, be uncoupled from the cars, and then run at full speed into the snowbanked cuts. This was called "bucking the snow," and usually had to be repeated several times before it was effective. Engineer Cy Warman told of bucking an eighteen-foot drift with double engines so hard that his locomotive trembled and shook as if it were about to be crushed into pieces. "Often when we came to a stop only the top of the stack of the front engine would be visible. . . . All this time the snow kept coming down, day and night, until the only signs of a railroad across the range were the tops of the telegraph poles." If the passengers were lucky, the train was backed to the nearest station, but even then conditions might be harsh. A group of snowbound train travelers who crowded into a hotel in Hays City, Kansas, spent an uncomfortably cold night and at daylight found their beds covered with snow that had drifted through cracks in walls and roof.

The universal desire of all pioneer travelers on the transcontinental was to see a "real wild Indian." Few of them did, because the true warriors of the plains hated the Iron Horse and seldom came within miles of it. After the resisting tribes finally realized they could not stop the building of the Union Pacific's iron tracks, their leaders signed treaties that removed their people from the broad swaths of land taken by the railroad. As the buffalo herds also fled far to the north and south, there was no economic reason for the horse Indians to approach the railroad. The Indians whom the travelers saw were mostly those who had been corrupted and weakened by contacts with the white man's civilization—scroungers, mercenaries, or beggars by necessity.

Except for a few acculturated representatives of Mississippi Valley tribes (who still plaited their hair but wore white man's clothing and frequented railroad stations from Chicago to Omaha), the westbound travelers' first glimpse of Plains Indians was around the Loup Fork in Nebraska, where the Pawnees lived on a reservation. Although the Pawnees had virtually abandoned their horse-buffalo culture and lived off what they could cadge from white men, the warriors still shaved their heads to a tuft, painted their faces, and wore feathers and blankets. To travelers fresh from the East, the Pawnees had a very bloodthirsty appearance, and according to the guidebooks every one of them had several scalps waving from the tops of lodgepoles.

Anywhere across western Nebraska or Wyoming, a traveler might catch a quick glimpse of a passing Sioux, Cheyenne, Arapaho, or Crow staring at the Iron Horse, but they were few and far between. Not until the train reached Nevada was there a plenitude of Shoshonis and Paiutes hanging about every station and using their treaty rights with the Central Pacific to ride the cars back and forth. Because these desert Indians were generally covered with dust and were often unbathed because there was no water readily available, the fastidious passengers found them objectionable, and the Central Pacific gradually put restrictions on their use of trains. At first they were confined to the emigrants' coaches, and then after the emigrants objected to their presence, the Indians had to ride in the baggage cars or outside on the boarding steps.

"We were regaled with the sight, for the first time, of a group of wild Indians," a traveler noted at one of the Nevada stations. "Some of the squaws were burdened with papooses strapped to their backs. They expected and received a 'shower' of donations from the passengers in the shape of 'cold victuals' and 'silver quarters.' This made them happy. Among them were some of the finest specimens of physical manhood that I ever saw." The Indian women soon discovered that the travelers on the trains were so eager to see the infants snuggled in their basket cradles that they could command from ten cents to a quarter in exchange for a look inside.

Lady Duffus Hardy was frankly more interested in the handsome males who were loading wood into the locomotive tender. "One especially attracted our attention. . . . He wore a blue blanket wrapped around him, and on his head a broad-brimmed ragged felt hat with a mass of blue feathers drooping on his shoulders. The men stood in groups, solemnly regarding us with their big black eyes, still as statues; the women squatted on the platform or peeped at us from round corners. It was not exactly pleasant, but very interesting to find ourselves amid a score or two of this savage race, the men all armed with guns and knives."

Other travelers spent a considerable amount of time worrying about what the warlike Indians might do if they put their minds to it. "It would be an easy matter," wrote an apprehensive New Englander, "for them to rush on to an unprotected portion of the road, in the night, tear up the track, withdraw until the train comes up, is thrown from the track, or brought to a standstill, then rush forward again, and tear up the track in the rear of the cars, and thus have all the passengers at their mercy." After brooding on these possibilities, he added complacently: "The poor Indian has few friends, and his days will soon be numbered."

Such perturbed passengers might better have been fretting over Anglo-Saxon train robbers, such as Jesse James, who were far more likely to wreck and rob a train in the 1870s than were the Indians. Only eighteen months after the rails were joined at Promontory, a gang of six robbers quietly boarded the eastbound Central Pacific express at Truckee, California. An hour later, at one-thirty in the morning on November 5, 1870, the train stopped at Verdi, Nevada, to take on fuel and water. Just as the engineer got his locomotive rolling again, one of the robbers dropped down from the tender into the cab, pointed a pair of pistols at the engineer and fireman, and ordered them to stop the train. At this point his five companions jumped from the first coach, uncoupled it from the express car, and a few seconds later the engine and express car with the six robbers aboard were moving rapidly away in the darkness.

With smooth efficiency the robbers broke in upon the unsuspecting express agent and took the entire Virginia City payroll—more than forty thousand dollars. After the robbers left the express car, the engineer backed his abbreviated train nine miles to Verdi, where a bewildered conductor was waiting with several cars of sleeping passengers, few of whom were aware of what had happened. This was the first robbery of a Central Pacific train, an act that was repeated only twenty-four hours later on the same train, four hundred miles farther east near Toano, Nevada. The second haul was almost as large as the first. After that, Wells Fargo Express assigned armed guards to valuable shipments; nevertheless, holdups continued for many years on the Central Pacific and its successor, the Southern Pacific.

Evidently the Union Pacific kept a tighter security on its express shipments. The first robbery on that line did not occur until August 27, 1875, near Bitter Creek, Wyoming, when two inept bandits entered a moving express car through an unbarred window. They found the express agent asleep, but instead of seizing and tying him up they tried to filch his keys from his pocket. This awoke him, of course, and in the melee that followed, several wild shots were fired, the expressman pulled the bell cord to signal the engineer to stop, and the robbers grabbed up armloads of packages and fled. They were not caught, but all they had gained for their efforts were a few articles of little value.

Three years later, Big Nose George Parrot and Dutch Charlie Burris decided to derail a Union Pacific payroll train near Rawlins, Wyoming. They loosened a rail on a curve and waited hopefully in a nearby willow thicket. As luck would have it, a railroad section boss chose that afternoon to make a walking inspection of the track. When he observed the freshly drawn spikes lying beside the loose rail, he read their meaning instantly. Suspecting that would-be train robbers were in the vicinity, he pretended not to have seen anything, until he was out of sight around the curve. Then he ran as fast as he could until he saw the train approaching and flagged it to a stop. He learned afterward that the robbers had their rifles trained on him; Big Nose George started to put a bullet in the track walker's back, but because the man did not even break his stride at the loosened rail he held his fire. A posse was soon in pursuit, but the bandits killed two of the deputies and escaped to Montana. Not until several months later were they captured, and while they were being returned to Rawlins for trial, an angry mob invaded the train on which they were riding, seized Dutch Charlie, and hanged him from a telegraph pole. The sheriff managed to get Big Nose George into a jail, but when rumors spread that the bandit had made an attempt to escape, another gang of vigilantes broke into the jail and hanged Big Nose George.

The robber whom railroad passengers most feared was Jesse James, and the very first train that Jesse robbed was carrying a load of transcontinental travelers—on the Rock Island line between Adair and Council Bluffs, Iowa, on the evening

Train robbery on the Union Pacific (Culver Pictures)

of July 21, 1873. The James boys loosened a rail, tied a rope
to it, and when the train came rumbling into view they jerked
the rail clear of the track. The locomotive plunged over on its
side, killing the engineer, and a number of passengers were
injured in the derailed cars. While some of the bandits entered the express car, others marched through the coaches,
robbing the startled travelers of their money and watches and
jewelry. They were on their horses riding hellbent for the
Missouri hills before train crew or passengers fully realized
what had happened to them.

Not all train wrecks signaled an invasion by robbers,
however, and because of the relatively slow speeds of the
early years, bruises rather than fatalities were the likely results, unless the accident occurred on a high bridge or mountain shoulder. Poor tracks and hot boxes (overheating of axle
bearings) caused many wrecks, and a surprising number of
passengers suffered injuries from falling or jumping out of

open car windows. One of the pioneer passengers of 1869 recorded how it felt to be in a train wreck in Echo Canyon: "On we bounded over the ties, the car wheels breaking many of them as though they were but pipe-stems. Every instant we expected to roll down the ravine. We ordered the ladies to cling to the sides of the seats and keep their feet clear of the floor. It seemed as if that train could never be stopped! But it was brought to a standstill upon the brink of an embankment. Had the cars gone a few rods further the reader would probably never have been troubled by these hastily written pages."

Still another westbound traveler during that first year told of being shaken out of his seat when a Central Pacific train ran into a herd of cattle between Wadsworth and Clark's Station, Nevada. The collision threw the locomotive off the track, but a telegrapher aboard climbed the nearest pole, tapped the line, and summoned a relief engine. During the eight-hour delay the hungry but resourceful passengers butchered the dead cattle, built a fire, and cooked steaks. Such encounters with cattle were among the most common causes of train wrecks in the West, and railroad men and ranchers were in constant friction for more than half a century over the rights of cattle to trespass upon railroad property.

Within a few weeks after the transcontinental railroad began operations, a flood of guidebooks for travelers appeared for sale in all the main terminals. Crofutt's, Appleton's, and Williams' were among the most popular, each publisher issuing several series. H. Wallace Atwell, who signed himself "Bill Dadd, the Scribe," led the Crofutt entries with his *Great Trans-Continental Railroad Guide*. George Crofutt claimed that he sold half a million copies of his guides during the 1870s in spite of competition from numerous imitators.

Anyone familiar with the melodramatic fiction of the nineteenth century can easily detect a similarity between the style of the dime novels, or penny dreadfuls, and that of many contemporary railroad guides. Possibly the same hack writers worked in both fields, applying the myths of the American West to that region's railroads. The guidebook writers could not resist overplaying the wickedness of Julesburg and other

Hell on Wheels towns. They lingered upon the gamblers and painted ladies, included lengthy accounts of such characters as Blacksnake Lachut, who could cut a man to pieces with his long whip, and amused himself in dance halls by flicking off the buttons that held up the straps of the dancing girls' dresses. Some guidebook writers implied that wild orgies were still constant occurrences in the former Hell on Wheels towns, although in reality little more than a water tank might remain. Even so, imaginative passengers peering from their car windows reveled in the guidebook iniquities of Julesburg, Benton, or Corinne, and scribbled in their own notebooks that "thieves, gamblers, cut-throats and prostitutes stalked brazen-faced in broad day through the streets." Walt Whitman also must have read the guidebooks, refining the dross into gold in his *Passage to India*. His account of a journey West on the Pacific railroad contains traces of guidebook phrases woven into his reverberating lines.

Thanks to energetic photographers and lecturers and the development of the magic lantern, it was possible to experience the thrills of Western railroad travel vicariously, without ever leaving one's home in Manhattan, Queens, Long Island, Connecticut, or New Jersey—these being the places where "Professor" Stephen James Sedgwick earned a handsome income during the 1870s by taking his audiences on lantern slide tours of the transcontinental railroad.

Sedgwick was a New York schoolteacher who had toyed with the magic lantern as an instructional aid, and then in the late 1860s after a gas and calcium device made it possible to project brilliant limelight pictures onto a screen for large audiences, the "Professor" abandoned his classroom and became the leading exhibitor of "lantern" shows in churches, schools, and public halls throughout the East. For almost a decade, he projected the marvelously detailed photographs of Andrew J. Russell, William Henry Jackson, Charles R. Savage, Alfred Hart, and C. E. Watkins, skillfully arranging his glass slides so that at the end of one of his lectures his audience felt as if they truly had traveled by rail to the Western Sea. These were motionless pictures, of course, but from his first slide of Russell's brilliant shot of the entrance to the Missouri River bridge, the trusses and girders of which magically drew its viewers into the infinity of the West, through hundreds of scenes of towns and bridges and mountains, alternating close-ups with long shots, Sedgwick forced a sense of movement into his imaginary journeys. Supported by the reality of the camera, Sedgwick in his lectures added to the general illusion of the American West, "the preordained home" of a people chosen by manifest destiny, hailing the builders of the railroad as noble patriots all, the Pacific being the goal of empire.

What influence Sedgwick had upon train travel to the West cannot be measured. Undoubtedly many members of his audiences were inspired to make the real journey, coming to it with a sense of prejudgment, of induced paramnesia. The scribblers among them also surely read the dime-novel guidebooks, and with a strange gullibility adopted the attitudes of the popular culture of the times, lifting entire paragraphs directly out of the cheapest paperbacks. Numerous published travel accounts of the period are permeated with guidebook legends; for example, one of the most frequently copied statements concerned the town of Wahsatch: "Out of 24 graves here, but one holds the remains of a person who died a natural death—and she was a prostitute who poisoned herself." Even that honest reporter, John Beadle, borrowed the story, increasing the number of graves to forty-three and doubling the suicides. Yet, it was not so much fictionalized "facts" that influenced readers of the guidebooks, it was the fictionalized attitudes. They swallowed the guidebooks' stories of dangers from wild Indians, lurid accounts that usually ended with a paragraph of solemn advice to buy travel insurance. This might have led cynical travelers to wonder if the publishers of guidebooks were also in the insurance business, but the reaction was more likely to be that of one reader of *Appleton's Handbook of American Travel* who asked himself: "If pleasure traveling in the United States be regarded as fraught with so much danger, is it not wiser to stay at home?"

Sophisticated travelers such as William Rae did challenge the guidebooks that assured him that at certain stops he could see Long's Peak and Pike's Peak. "It is possible that these mountain tops may have been discerned in a vision by the compilers of guidebooks," he said. "To the eye of the ordinary and unimaginative traveler they are invisible." Rae was also caustic about a guidebook's description of the Dale Creek bridge. "The grandest feature of the road," the guide-book author wrote enthusiastically, praising the bridge for its "light, airy, and graceful appearance." Rae commented that he preferred to lose a fine sight rather than risk a broken neck, and added that he did not breathe freely until the cars had passed safely over the rickety bridge.

The guides occasionally offered useful advice, especially for women who had little idea of what they would need on such a long journey. In addition to the usual baggage, it was suggested that a small valise be carried for a night-dress, clean collars and cuffs, pocket-handkerchiefs and stockings, a bottle of cologne, a vial of powdered borax to soften the West-ern water, a warm flannel sack for chilly nights, a whisk broom, a pocket pin cushion, a brandy flask, and two linen dusters. On leaving Omaha, another guide recommended, a lady should wear a light spring suit; on the second day as the train approached the Rockies, change to a winter suit was suggested. On the third day across Utah and the Nevada desert, she should don a summer suit, and then on the fourth day in the Sierras, the winter suit and "all your under-clothing" would be required. The fifth and last day of course would bring her into sunny California and the summer suit again.

Bill Dadd, the Scribe, was less considerate in his attitude toward women travelers: "It is not right or just for a *lady* to occupy one whole seat with her flounces and herself, and an-other with her satchel, parasol, big box, little box, bandbox and bundle, as we have often seen them do, while plain-dressed, hard-handed toiling men are obliged to remain standing in the crowded car. The woman who indulges in such flights of fancy as to suppose that one fare entitles her to monopolize three seats should not travel until bloomers come in fashion." Another guidebook gravely pondered the question of whether the male or female of a couple traveling together should take the window seat. In the more civilized Eastern states, proper etiquette gave the seat to the woman, but in the unrefined West where both animals and human beings performed their natural functions in the open, it was decided that the man should occupy the window seat so that if the occasion arose he could shield the view outside from his lady.

At times on the journey, said Henry Williams in *The Pacific Tourist*, one should "sit and read, play games, and indulge in social conversation and glee." By "glee" the guidebook author probably was referring to the improvised musicales and recitations that were especially popular among the Pullman passengers. In the early 1870s some Pullman cars had organs installed on them, and in the evenings amateur musicians as well as professional traveling troupes willingly gave performances. "Music sounds upon the prairie and dies away far over the plains; merry-making and jokes, conversation and reading pass the time pleasantly until ten o'clock, when we retire. . . . If people who are traveling together will only try to make those about them happy, then a good time is assured. The second night on the road we arranged a little entertainment in the car and invited the ladies and gentlemen from the other cars into our 'improvised Music Hall.' The exercises consisted principally of recitations, with the delineation of the characters of Grace Greenwood. . . . The young ladies sang for us; and we were all happy—for the time at least."

It was customary on Sundays to hold religious services in one of the cars. On a train rolling through western Wyoming in 1872, John Lester read the Episcopal service, the Reverend Mr. Murray delivered a sermon entitled "To Die Is Gain," and a choir sang "Nearer, My God, to Thee" and the American national hymn. "Here in the very midst of the Rocky Mountain wilderness," wrote Lester, "our thanksgivings were offered up; and our music floated out upon the air, and resounded through the deep caverns, and among the towering hills."

According to most travelers, the popular diversions were cards, conversations, and reading. "We had an abundant supply of books and newspapers. A boy frequently traversed the train with a good store of novels, mostly English, periodicals, etc. . . . In the evening we had our section lighted, and played a solemn game of whist, or were initiated into the mysteries of euchre, or watching the rollicking game of poker being carried on by a merry party in the opposite section."

There may have been some "rollicking" poker games on Pullman cars, but most of them were as deadly serious as the real money-making endeavors of the players in that Gilded Age of the Robber Barons. Brakeman Harry French told of witnessing such a game one evening in the course of his duties. "The car was loaded to capacity with wealthy stockmen, and I suspect, a number of fancy women. In the cramped quarters of the men's smoking room, a high-play poker game was in progress. Gold pieces and bills were the stakes, and they were very much in evidence. I was particularly interested in one of the players. Fine clothes, careful barbering, diamond-decked fingers marked him as a gambler." Poker-playing professional gamblers, fresh from the declining riverboat traffic of the Mississippi River, could indeed be found on almost any transcontinental train in the 1870s, and many a greenhorn bound West to seek his fortune lost his nest egg before reaching the end of his journey.

As in any era, travelers found plenty of entertainment in merely observing their fellow passengers. "It was curious to see a rough-booted, broad-brimmed fellow strutting up and down the train with his revolver slung behind him like a short blunt tail," said the London Parson. "But, of course, if you leave them alone they don't meddle with you. They only shoot their friends and acquaintances, as a rule." Travelers from abroad were repelled by the widespread American habit of chewing tobacco (coaches and Pullmans were furnished with an ample supply of brass cuspidors), but by the time they crossed the continent they grew accustomed to seeing fellow passengers expelling fountains of tobacco juice, and to sharing seats with burly miners who boarded the train with pockets full of tobacco plugs and whiskey bottles, which they were eager to share with their seat mates. "Smile?" a dusty-bearded Westerner might say to a well-dressed traveler, and the latter soon understood that "Smile?" was mining-country slang for "Have a drink?" The farther west the train rolled, the rougher and more unrestrained the local passengers became. "A fiercer, hirsute, and unwashed set I never saw," said one Easterner, "but for my part I found them pleasant companions, under the circumstances."

By the time the train reached Sherman Summit on the second day out of Omaha, the passengers had formed into the usual little groups and cliques, and knew one another by sight if not by name. Sherman Summit, the most elevated station on the Pacific railroad (the highest in the world, according to the guidebooks) was also the halfway point between Omaha and the Union Pacific's end of track at Ogden. If the westbound express was on schedule, the engineer would stop his panting Iron Horse longer than usual at the Sherman water tank in order to give the passengers a chance to stretch their legs, inhale the rarefied air, and enjoy the view before crossing Dale Creek bridge and plunging down the mountains into Laramie for a noon meal stop.

At Sherman, some passengers were afflicted with nose bleed from the height, or were badly chilled by the cold wind, and were glad to leave it behind. Others found it inspiring: "Never till this moment did I realize the truthfulness of Bierstadt's scenery of these hills. The dark, deep shadows, the glistening sides, and the snow-capped peaks, with their granite faces, the stunted growth of pine and cedar, all render the scene such as he has painted it." And another traveler, Dr. H. Buss, whose medical skills may have been better than his poetry, preserved the memory of his visit in verse:

> Now, Sherman on the Rocky Mountain range,
>> Eight thousand feet is raised toward the sky,
> Indian, Chinese, and many people strange,
>> Are met or passed as o'er the earth you fly.

After lunch at Laramie, where "the people around the station are more intelligent-looking than at any place since leaving Omaha," the train was soon across Medicine Bow River and into Carbon Station, where coal had been discovered and was rapidly replacing wood for fuel on the Union Pacific locomotives. Westbound travelers usually crossed Wyoming's deserts after nightfall, but even by moonlight the endless sweep of dry sagebrush and greasewood was described by various travelers as dreary, awful, lifeless. They complained of burning eyes and sore lips caused by the clouds of alkali dust swirled up into the cars, and thought Bitter Creek and Salt Wells were appropriately descriptive names for stations.

About sunrise the train arrived at Green River for a breakfast stop, and for the next hundred miles everyone looked forward to the moment of crossing into Utah Territory, the land of the Mormons and their plural wives. Wahsatch was the noon dining station, and every passenger from the East who stepped down from the train peered expectantly around for Mormons, but the What Cheer Eating House looked about the same as all the others they had seen.

A group of passengers from New England who were traveling on one of the first trains to the West in 1869 were delayed by bad tracks near Wahsatch and had to spend the night there. "What a place to stop in! No buildings—nothing but tents or shanties, and all of them 'whiskey hells' of the lowest kinds. We worked our way through the most villainous-looking crowd that man ever yet set eyes on, to an old sleeping car on a discontinued sidetrack, which proved to be densely populated with 'creeping things.'" Wahsatch was filled with several hundred discharged railroad construction workers who had just been paid off by Dr. Durant after the "capture" of his private car, and they were noisily spending their money.

"We were afraid they would attack our sleeping car and 'go through it' as the phrase is, and rob the passengers. The ladies were very much frightened; there was very little sleep in the car that night. The doors were securely locked. Some of the party had arms and stood on guard. Many times in the night some of the 'roughs' attempted to get in, and were driven away. They were apparently too drunk to form any organized plan of assault. I did not sleep, and shall long remember those sounds that made the night hideous, of howling, cursing, swearing and pistol shots. Fights occurred by the score; we could distinctly hear the blows. Knives were freely used, and the stabbing affrays were numerous. One man was shot directly under our car windows."

About fifty miles farther west, after passing through Echo and Weber canyons, was Uintah Station, a connecting point for Wells Fargo stagecoaches to Salt Lake City. As it was al-

most de rigueur for transcontinental travelers to visit the
Mormon capital, numerous passengers endured the rough
thirty-mile stage journey. The jarring and jolting was enough
"to beat a man into a jelly or to break every bone in his
body . . . I am amazed that the wheels and framework of the
coach remained unbroken and unstrained." After the rail
spur line from Ogden to Salt Lake City was completed early
in 1870, the pilgrimage to the City of the Saints was much
easier. When Lady Hardy discovered that the conductor on
her train from Ogden was a Mormon, she immediately asked
him how many wives he had. She was disillusioned by his
polite reply that he had only one. She had been under the
false impression that polygamy was imposed by the church
and that all Mormon men had several wives.

Salt Lake City was a revelation to all Easterners whose
heads had been filled with anti-Mormon propaganda. "The
city, in point of wealth and beauty, far exceeded my expectations," wrote one. "It is a perfect Eden." Another described it
as "an oasis in a desert, a blooming garden in a wilderness of
green." Almost everyone was entranced by the streams of
sparkling water that flowed along the sides of the broad

*Rail travelers from the East were surprised at the beauty of Salt Lake
City. Brigham Young's residence is on the left. (Photo by
A. J. Russell, The Oakland Museum)*

streets, melted snow brought down from the surrounding mountains to irrigate fields and gardens. Harvey Rice, who arrived there in September 1869, found ripened fruit hanging from tree limbs over the sidewalks in front of almost every cottage. The Englishman William Rae admired the extreme purity of the atmosphere, but was annoyed by the flies in the dining room of the highly touted Townsend House, which catered to these early tourists. A Finnish baroness, Alexandra Gripenberg, said the Mormons "had done a good piece of work in Utah," and admired their endurance in transforming a desert into a garden.

Few travelers, however, could resist criticizing the beliefs of Brigham Young and his followers, although those who met Young—who seemed never to refuse interviews —usually came away admiring him for his frankness and abilities. "He exhibited a degree of refinement and intelligence in his discourse which surprised me," said Harvey Rice, who decided to overlook the faults of the Mormons because they were "a quiet, orderly people." By the time the transcontinental travelers were back in Uintah or Ogden to resume their journeys to the Pacific, almost all had revised their opinions of a people who at that time were generally depicted in popular print as depraved fanatics with no redeeming qualities.

At Ogden, passengers awaiting connecting trains frequently had to spend many hours in a long narrow wooden building that had been erected between the tracks of the Union Pacific and the Central Pacific. In addition to ticket offices and a large dining room, sleeping rooms furnished only with curtains for doors were available upstairs. Lady Hardy considered her enforced stay there an adventure: "Except for the passing trains this is a most lonely, isolated spot, weird and still, lying in the heart of the mountains. In the evening a blinding snowstorm came on, and the wind, howling fearfully with a rushing mighty sound, shook the doors and rattled at the windows as though it wanted to come in and warm itself at our blazing wood fire."

Upon boarding the Central Pacific at Ogden, the first-class passengers found themselves in Silver Palace cars instead of Pullmans. Collis Huntington and his Big Four partners refused to accept George Pullman's arrangement for the use of his sleeping cars and ordered their own constructed. The Silver Palaces were attractive with their white metallic interiors, and although they were outfitted with private sitting rooms and smoking rooms, they lacked the luxurious touches that travelers from the East had grown accustomed to in their Pullmans. Passengers complained that their berths were not as roomy or as comfortable, and some said the cars were often too cold. Eventually the Central Pacific had to give up the Silver Palaces because transcontinental passengers resented having to change from their Pullmans.

The earliest experiment in running a Pullman train from coast to coast was conducted in the spring of 1870 by affluent members of the Boston Board of Trade. Participating in the event was George Pullman himself, along with 129 members of such leading families of Boston as the Rices, Peabodys, Danas, Warrens, Farwells, Houghtons, and Whitneys. The Pullman Hotel Express consisted of two sleeping cars, two hotel cars, a commissary car, dining car, smoking car, and baggage car. The smoking car was divided into four compartments, one outfitted for publication of a daily newspaper, *The Trans-Continental*, another with tables for card games, a wine room, and a barber shop. The baggage car not only carried the party's luggage and several chests of ice, it also contained a large flask of symbolic water from the Atlantic Ocean. As added complements to this prototype of luxurious trains of the future, Pullman included two libraries and two organs.

Amid a considerable amount of newspaper publicity, the Pullman Hotel Express crossed the continent in seven days (it stopped only at the larger stations and meals were served on board) and then with much ceremony the flask of Atlantic water was mingled with that of the Pacific in San Francisco Bay. After the excursion was completed, the Union Pacific scheduled the Hotel Express for a regular weekly run from Omaha to Ogden, but the general public was not yet ready to pay the added fare for such sumptuousness. Perhaps the financial depression of the period contributed to the lack of passengers. At any rate, after a few weeks the service was discontinued, to await the next decade, when elegant train travel across the West would become almost commonplace.

As they rolled westward from Ogden, travelers on the Central Pacific read in their guidebooks about the iniquities of Corinne and Promontory, but they saw little of either place because the schedule usually brought them across this part of Utah during the night. In the early months of transcontinental travel, however, when Promontory was the transfer junction between U.P. and C.P., the pioneer journeyers saw more of that historic but doomed town than they wanted. According to William Humason, who arrived there a few days after the joining of the rails, the Union Pacific conductor rudely ordered everybody out of the cars although there was no Central Pacific train waiting. "Out we were turned into the hot sun, with no shade, no hotel, no house—surrounded by no comforts but sand, alkali, and sagebrush. Many of the passengers having had no sleep the night before, looked pretty hard as they sat on their carpet-bags, nodding in the hot sun." There was a hotel in Promontory—the Pacific—but Humason and his New England companions disdained to go near that wood-and-canvas shanty. Nor did they venture into the gambling dens of that last Hell on Wheels where three-card-monte players and their "cappers" lay in wait for bored transfer passengers, and "women with few scruples to overcome and no characters to lose" welcomed gentlemen with an inclination for dalliance between trains.

The Cosmopolitan Hotel of booming Elko, Nevada, was the first dining stop west of Ogden. Alkali dust swirled in streets filled with freight wagons drawn by long mule teams hauling supplies to miners in nearby Pine Valley. Chinese workers discharged by the railroad had established a colony here and were much in evidence around the hotel. Beyond Elko was the valley of the Humboldt and then the train entered Nevada's barren deserts. In summer, passengers choked on dust if they left the windows open, or sweltered in heat if they closed them. After passing Winnemucca, the Iron Horse turned southward to the Humboldt Sink (where the river was literally swallowed up by the desert) and thereafter instead of facing the sun continued a southwesterly course to the Sierras.

By this time the passengers were beginning to show the effects of several days' travel, "a drooping, withered, squeezed-lemon appearance," as one observer put it. "There were the usual crumpled dresses, loose hanging and wayward curls, and ringlets, and *possibly* soiled hands and faces; which reduces the fair sex from that state of perfect immaculateness. . . ." Even the self-reliant Susan Coolidge admitted that after two or three days on the Pacific railroad she began to hate herself because she could not contend with the pervasive dust, which no amount of brushing or shaking could completely remove from her hair and clothing. And one of the most frequent complaints of all early travelers was the discomfort caused by "the very oppressive smoke" from the locomotives, which constantly drifted into the cars.

The bracing air of the Sierras, however, was a perfect restorative for the weary travelers. With two Iron Horses pulling the cars, the train slowly climbed the winding canyon of Truckee River, rising eighty feet to the mile. Pine and fir replaced the dreary desert sagebrush, and then came a spectacular view of Donner Lake encircled by forested mountains. The guidebooks told the travelers all about the gruesome tragedy of the Donner party during the winter of 1846–47. "After snorting and puffing, whistling and screaming, for an hour and a quarter, our pair of Iron Horses stop in the snowsheds at the station called 'Summit.' Here we have a good breakfast, well cooked and fairly served; although we could not expect waiters enough to attend in a rush such as they have when the passengers, with appetites sharpened by mountain-air and a long ride, seat themselves at table, and all with one voice cry, 'Steak! coffee! bread! trout! waiter! a napkin!'"

From the summit of the Sierras to Sacramento was 105 miles, a drop from 7,017 feet to 30 feet above sea level. According to William Humason, 50 miles of the descent was made without the aid of steam. "The conductor and brakeman ran the train with brakes on most of the way." For some travelers the ride down the western slope of the range was

terrifying, and the coasting trains made so little noise that un-
wary railroad workers, especially in the snowsheds, often
were struck and killed. "The velocity with which the train
rushed down this incline, and the suddenness with which it
wheeled around the curves," said William Rae, "produced a
sensation which cannot be reproduced in words. . . . The
axle boxes smoked with the friction and the odour of burning
wood pervaded the cars. The wheels were nearly red hot. In
the darkness of the night they resembled discs of flame."

Corresponding somewhat to the biggest drop and swing
of a modern amusement park's roller-coaster was Cape Horn,
nine miles below Dutch Flat. The guidebooks warned timid
passengers not to look down upon the awful gorge of the
American River two thousand feet below, and John Beadle
said that although Cape Horn offered the finest view in the
Sierras, the sight was not good for nervous people. "We're
nearing Cape Horn!" someone would always cry out, and the
next moment the train would careen around a sharp curve.
"We follow the track around the sides of high mountains,"
said William Humason, "looking down into a canyon of awful
depth, winding around for miles, until we almost meet the
track we have before been over—so near that one would
think we could almost throw a stone across. We have been
around the head of the canyon, and have, therefore 'doubled
Cape Horn.'"

Almost as fascinating as the scenery and the roller-
coaster ride were the Sierra snowsheds built by engineer
Arthur Brown. When passenger service began, these
sheds—built with sharp sloping roofs against the mountain-
sides so that deep snowfalls and avalanches would slide right
off them—covered forty miles of track between Truckee and
Cape Horn. After numerous passengers complained that the
walls blocked their view of magnificent mountains, the Central Pacific responded by cutting windows at the level of
those of the passenger cars. The result was a series of flick-
ering scenes somewhat like those of an early motion picture,
but even this pleasure was denied Sierra travelers during the
snowy months of winter when the openings had to be closed
again.

"A blarsted long depot—longest I ever saw," was the comment of an oft-quoted anonymous Englishman as he passed through the snowsheds, and the London Parson said he had never seen "a more convenient arrangement for a long bonfire. The chimney of every engine goes fizzing through it like a squib, and the woodwork is as dry as a bone." To prevent fires, the Central Pacific kept watchmen at regular intervals inside the sheds, with water barrels and hand pumps always ready to extinguish blazes set by sparks from locomotives. There was little they could do, however, against forest fires, which sometimes swept across sections of sheds. And sturdy though the structures were, an occasional mighty avalanche would crush one of them. The train on which Lady Hardy was traveling was delayed all night by the collapse of a shed while fifty male volunteers from among the passengers went ahead to clear the tracks.

The snowsheds not only covered the main track, they also enclosed stations, switch tracks, turntables, and houses where workmen lived with their families. Children were born in this eerie, dimly lit world where without warning a huge boulder or avalanche might crash through the roof, where trains derailed with disastrous results, and where at least on one occasion wild animals escaped from a wrecked circus train to terrify the inhabitants. As snowplows were improved, some sheds were removed, others were replaced with concrete, and the army of workmen declined to a handful of lookouts and track walkers.

Although passage through the Sierras was their introduction to California, most westbound travelers did not feel that they had truly reached that Golden Land until their Iron Horse brought them down into the blazing sunshine and balmy air of the Sacramento Valley and the flowers and orchards of the Queen City of the Plain. "We seem in a new world," said one. "The transition was sudden and the transformation magical," said another. "The sun descended in a flood of glory toward the Pacific Ocean." Sacramento was still more than a hundred miles from the Pacific Ocean, and like inspired pilgrims they determined to travel on to that legendary Western Sea. Until 1870 they transferred to the cars of the California Pacific, which took them to Vallejo, where again they had to change, this time to a steamboat running down the bay to San Francisco. After the Central Pacific completed its subsidiary Western Pacific to Oakland in 1870, the journey was easier, although they still made the final crossing by boat before reaching San Francisco and the Pacific shore. After a week of noise, dust, and locomotive smoke, the first act of those travelers who could afford it was to register at the magnificent Palace Hotel and seek out a quiet room and a warm bath.

And what were the feelings of travelers after they had completed their first journey by rail across the American continent? Those from other countries were impressed by the grandeur of the Western land, and of course they made comparisons with their own nations, sometimes favorable, sometimes unfavorable. They found travel by train across the West less tedious because they could walk about in the cars and stand on the platforms to enjoy the passing landscapes, yet at the same time they complained of the lack of privacy. They praised the comforts of the Pullman cars, but deplored the necessity for constantly changing trains; there was no such thing as a continuous Pacific railway from New York to San Francisco. They confessed that before the journey they had feared the rumored American defiance of rules and regulations and the recklessness in regard to speed, but they were pleased to find that American railway men held human life in as high regard as it was held in their native lands.

American travelers, on the other hand, were more concerned with feelings of national pride. After crossing the vastness of the American West, the endless unclaimed fertile lands, the prairies and forests, the broad rivers and towering mountains, they felt that they had seen a new map unrolled, a new empire revealed, a new civilization in the process of creation. In the first years after the Civil War, the salvation of the Union was still a glorious promise of destiny. "I felt patriotically proud," wrote one traveler to California. He saw the transcontinental railroad as a force binding the Union together "by links of iron that can never be broken." Although Americans were aware that private corporations had built this first railroad to the Pacific, they rejoiced in the belief that California was a rich prize of empire that had been won for them by those connecting links of iron. In their first flush of triumphant pride, they viewed the railroad as a coop-erative venture shared by the builders and the people. The disillusionment would come later, as would their doubts in an ever-expanding empire

For Americans and foreigners alike, there was a deep-ening sense of wonder at this final link in the encirclement of the earth by steam-power. From San Francisco they could now journey to China and Suez by steam-powered vessels, from Suez to Alexandria by rail, from Alexandria to France by water, from France to Liverpool by rail and water, from Liver-pool to New York by water, and from New York to San Fran-cisco by rail. In reaching the Western Sea, the Iron Horse had shrunk the planet.

CHAPTER 8

Railroaders West

DURING THE PIONEER DAYS of the transcontinental railroad, more than six times as many railroad men as passengers were killed or injured in accidents, and foremost among the casualties were engineers and firemen. Only men with strong nerves dared to board an Iron Horse and drive it over the poorly constructed roadbeds and flimsy bridges left after the Great Race to Promontory. Because he commanded the power of the locomotive, the engineer was the hero of the rails, a dashing and romantic figure suited to equal rank with cowboy, horse soldier, or gunfighter in the mythology of the West. By tradition the fireman was the engineer's apprentice, usually a younger man hoping to exchange his shovel handle for the throttle arm of the engine. He was responsible for keeping the brass and ironwork polished, and seeing that the Iron Horse was removed on time from its roundhouse stable, properly watered at the tank, fed on wood or coal, and harnessed to the train it was to pull across the plains and mountains.

The first locomotive engineers were the men who invented and built them, or worked as machinists in the shops, but after the growth in numbers of Iron Horses, experienced firemen were drafted as locomotive drivers or locomotive runners. Not until well along into the late nineteenth century did the "drivers" or "runners" become known again by the proud name of "engineers."

In addition to the common hazards of loose rails or washouts, engineers working the Western railroads faced such unique dangers as buffalo on the tracks and drunken cowboys in the trail towns. Trail-town saloons were built alongside the tracks, and cowboys on a night rampage could not resist firing at the lights of passing trains. Engineers soon learned to douse their headlights and lanterns, and firemen kept the firebox closed while passing through a trail town. Seasoned engineers and firemen also had to know when to "unload," or leap from their Iron Horse, when a wreck appeared inevitable. To stay aboard a moment too long usually meant the difference between life and death by collapsing wood and metal or by scalding steam from an exploded boiler.

Veteran railroad man Harry French told of how the engine crew of a Kansas cattle train escaped serious injury by unloading just before a collision in a snowstorm. "The engineer . . . hobbled up to see how much damage had been done to his beloved engine. He was a short, fat man with a protruding stomach and a thick, bush-beard that reached almost to the summit of the stomach. He had just about reached the engine when he heard the thud of hoofs behind him. Glancing over his shoulder, he beheld the glitter of long horns through the swirling snowflakes . . . he sprinted for the nearest telegraph pole with the grace and speed of a ten-second man. . . . Grasping the pole with both hands, he went up it. . . . He seemed to use that little round stomach as a sort of fulcrum for each upward heave."

To find engineers and firemen who could endure such tribulations, Western railroads recruited from the ranks of doughty frontiersmen. An example was Jim Curry, Indian fighter and survivor of the Beecher Island incident, who drove an Iron Horse for the Kansas Pacific, and before the end of his career shot and killed at least three men from the cab of his engine. Less-hardened men turned to alcohol for relief from the unbearable strain on their nerves, and pioneer engineers on the Western railroads had a reputation for heavy drinking. Whenever passengers became annoyed by a jolting train they usually blamed it on a drunken engineer, as in 1869 on the Union Pacific: "Last night our engineer was reported drunk. I cannot vouch for the correctness of the report. He certainly performed some feats not necessary for the comfort of railroad passengers, such as twitching and jerking the train suddenly forward, and stopping it suddenly—almost throwing us out of bed—sometimes scarcely moving along, then speeding up and dashing ahead as though demons

Railroad yard with crewmen assembling trains for runs to the West
(Courtesy Kenneth M. Newman, The Old Print Shop)

were in pursuit of him. Soon his boxes were on fire, and he had to make long stops to cool off. His performances were of such a nature that we were kept awake most of the night."

Nevertheless, to most travelers across the West the engineer was a heroic figure, "his hands blackened, and perhaps his face, his clothes stained with oil, his greasy cap drawn over his eyes. . . . We could not but note the engineer's bearing, as he mounted his steed. He patted the glittering brazen knobs, here and there, as a man might a favorite animal." For risking their lives each time they rode an Iron Horse to the West, engineers received sixty dollars per month, provided that during the month they drove an engine a minimum of twenty-five hundred miles. Pay was deducted proportionately for any shortage of miles, and nothing extra was given them for excess mileage. It is not surprising that engineers were the first railroad men to organize a protective association and that the first work rules of the Brotherhood of Locomotive Engineers were established on Western railroads.

Without brakemen, engineers could not move a train

across the continent, and there was always a love-hate relationship between the two, somewhat like that between sergeants and commanding officers. The brakemen resented the engineers sitting in their cabs while they had to work outside no matter what the weather, and they also envied the engineers their sixty dollars a month while they were earning only forty. Brakemen seldom became engineers, the usual route of promotion for them being yard brakeman to freight brakeman to freight conductor, or freight brakeman to passenger brakeman, and then finally passenger conductor. In the West, brakemen were sometimes called Iron Horse wranglers, a wrangler being a horse herder on a ranch; it was the Iron Horse wrangler's duty to round up and cut out the cars by coupling and uncoupling them, a difficult and dangerous task indeed until the invention of air brakes and the Janney coupler.

Before Eli Janney patented his coupler in 1873, railroad cars were fastened together by a link and pin, and a brakeman had to stand between the cars, guide the link into a socket, and then drop the pin into place. If the pin failed to drop, as it often did, the brakeman had to pound it down, and if the cars were moving in darkness and he was holding a smoky coal-oil lantern in one hand, he had to be very adroit to escape being maimed. That is why so many brakemen of the 1870s had missing fingers and hands. Dick Nelson, who worked as a freight brakeman in Wyoming, described it this way: "Judge the speed of the moving car coming toward you. Lift the link so it will enter the pocket of the draw bar. Get hands and fingers out of the way—you may need 'em some time. Damage to the equipment will result if the link goes over or under the pocket. Then you'll have to go back to the way-car [caboose], loop a bull-chain around your neck, come back, get that crippled car out of the train and onto a side track. Then get ready to catch hell from the boss because you've been so clumsy. If you'd really been clumsy and stepped under the wheels of a moving car, you'd wind up dead, or crippled for life."

Eli Janney's coupler was automatic, fitting together like the fingers of two hands, and because it operated with a lever running outside the car, brakemen no longer had to risk their

The first transcontinental trains were braked by hand, requiring brakemen to work on the tops of cars in all weather. (Culver Pictures)

Cartoonist Thomas Nast's depiction of a train butch at work
(Culver Pictures)

lives between cars when coupling or uncoupling them. It was typical of railroad management, however, that although Janney's device was available in the 1870s, the link and pin remained in use for another twenty years.

The same reluctance toward change was met by George Westinghouse while he was perfecting his air brake. Before adoption of that invention, brakemen always had to be ready to apply hand brakes. Usually two brakemen worked on each freight train. "We lived on the car tops," said Harry French. "Weather did not count." Until well into the 1880s, few freight trains were equipped with air brakes. "We had to ride out on top when the train was moving," Dick Nelson recalled. "Trainmen did the braking—not the engineers. . . . That took nerve, coordination, timing, and a perfect sense of balance, to go over the top of a freight train—winter or summer. . . . Rain, snow, sleet, ice all over the roofs and on brake wheels and handholds."

On the transcontinental railroad's sharp descents through the mountains of Wyoming, Utah, and California, brakemen had to be ready to leap from car to car, applying hand brakes. Uneven braking could cause a train to separate, an extremely dangerous situation. If brakes were set too tightly, friction so heated the wheels that they would slide along the tracks and the brakeman would have to make rapid adjustments on several cars to keep the train from gathering speed.

Westinghouse's solution to this braking problem was to place a compressed-air tank in the locomotive and run a hose from it back to the brake shoes of each car. It worked splendidly on short passenger trains, but on long freight trains the air pressure was slow in reaching the rear cars, causing them to jam into the forward cars, damaging equipment and cargo. Westinghouse solved that drawback in 1872 by installing auxiliary tanks on each car, all connected by a hose from the locomotive so that the engineer could brake his entire train simply by pulling a lever. But again, as in the case of the Janney coupler, most railroads refused to adopt Westinghouse's safety brake on freight trains for another fifteen or twenty years. Not until the late 1880s could a freight brakeman spend much of his time in a comfortable caboose. His best route of escape from the hardships and dangers was to obtain a job as brakeman on a passenger train equipped with air brakes. In that capacity he served as apprentice to the conductor, leaping off and on the train to throw switches and going through the cars to call out the stations. His alertness was now concentrated mainly on noting the exposure of a stockinged ankle when he assisted female passengers up the steps of the cars.

The railroad employee whom transcontinental travelers saw more of than any other was the train "butch," who originally was called a newsboy, train boy, or news butch, because his first function was to sell newspapers and magazines to passengers. After local peddlers, who came aboard at various stations, successfully demonstrated that fruit, lunches, handmade apparel—almost anything—could be sold on trains, the news butches added numerous items to their stock. On the Pacific railroad they sold candy, peanuts, cigars, sandwiches filled with "a piece of ham the thickness of a safety razor blade," postcards, guidebooks, jokebooks, and dime novels. Under the counter they sold sexy books such as *Fanny Hill* at any price the market would bear. A hard-working, imaginative train butch could earn as much in a week as the engineer up ahead earned in a month.

Horatio Alger, Jr., wrote dime novels about train butches, and inventor Thomas A. Edison started his working career in that occupation. Edison augmented his earnings by selling fresh bread and country butter to hungry passengers. William A. Brady, who became famous as a prizefight manager and producer of stage and motion-picture dramas, was a train butch on the Union Pacific. Brady startled his customers by shouting lines from Shakespeare's plays as he moved through the cars; he sometimes earned eighty dollars a week, or five times as much as an engineer. Ernest Haycox, writer of Western novels, learned the trick of first peddling salted peanuts and then following up with soda water, but he admitted that he was no great success as a train butch.

Not all travelers tolerated the energetic and noisy train butch. "First he offers you yesterday's newspapers," complained Major William Shepherd, a visiting Englishman. "Next time he walks through the carriage he drops two or three handbooks, guides, maps, or magazines beside each traveler; the next trip he forces the choice of apples or pears, then oranges, California grapes, dried figs, maple sugar, including an advertisement; cigars—each item nearly requires a separate trip up and down the carriage; last, he brings his basket of peanuts, and throwing two or three into everyone's lap, he has completed the round, not for the day but for the nonce; he will begin again at the beginning, for sure, after dinner. This itinerant trader certainly should be suppressed; his prices are extravagant and his office unnecessary."

Robert Louis Stevenson, too, began his transcontinental journey by heartily disliking the news butch on the Union Pacific, "a dark, bullying, contemptuous, insolent scoundrel, who treated us like dogs." On the other hand, he found the Central Pacific's train butch helpful and kind. "He told us where and when we would have our meals, and how long the train would stop; kept seats for those who were delayed, and watched that we should neither be left behind nor yet unnecessarily hurried. . . if he but knew it, he is a hero of the old Greek stamp, and while he thinks he is only earning a profit of a few cents, and that perhaps exorbitant, he is doing a man's work and bettering the world." In yet another encounter, Stevenson almost came to blows with a third train butch who kept rudely striking the author's foot as he passed in the aisle. But when Stevenson later became ill on the train, the butch made him a present of a large juicy pear. "For the rest of the journey I was petted like a sick child; he lent me newspapers, thus depriving himself of his legitimate profit on their sale, and came repeatedly to sit by me and cheer me up."

Perhaps because they were trained to be as unobtrusive as possible, Pullman porters were seldom more than mentioned by the first transcontinental passengers, and the porters themselves rarely took the trouble to record their experiences. The first Pullman porter is believed to have been a black man, probably a former slave, employed by George Pullman in 1867. For more than a century, Pullman porters were almost exclusively black, although a few Mexicans were employed as porters on Southwestern railroads and white men worked as porters on Canadian railroads. No one knows for certain why and when porters were first called "George," although it is assumed that they were given the nickname in honor of George Pullman.

Many of the first Pullman porters learned their duties on the Union Pacific, in which Pullman owned stock and for which he used to introduce many of his different models. One of the recurring problems that porters had on Western runs was persuading cowboys and miners to remove their boots before climbing into their berths. "They wanted to keep them on," one porter recalled. "They seemed afraid to take them off."

To prepare porters for their work, the Pullman Company operated a school in a sidetracked sleeping car in Chicago. After learning the art of making up and taking down beds, how to handle linen and blankets, methods of awakening passengers and storing their luggage, the beginning porters worked as apprentices on regular train runs until they were pronounced ready for a Pullman assignment at a salary of twenty dollars a month plus any tips they might receive. On the early Western runs, tips were uncertain and inadequate, barely enough to pay for uniforms and boot polish, which porters had to buy out of their own pockets.

Like the black railroad construction men who chanted the exploits of a folk hero, steel-driving John Henry, the Pullman porters told stories about Daddy Joe, who was so tall and muscular that he could make up an upper and lower berth simultaneously. Daddy Joe may have originated on the Pacific railroad when he foiled an Indian attack on a passenger train that had stopped at a water tank. According to the tale, he climbed atop his Pullman car, and in a thunderous voice addressed the Indians in their own language, after which he presented each of the surrounding warriors with a magnificent Pullman blanket while the train pulled peacefully away. But today Daddy Joe, as the Pullman car, has almost vanished in the mists of time and folklore.

Because of the likelihood of derailments, breakdowns, and other delays on the single track of the railroad to the Pacific, each train carried a telegrapher as a member of its crew. Frequently the telegrapher doubled as a baggage man, but he was always equipped with a portable instrument known as the "box relay," which could be attached to the telegraph line that ran alongside the tracks and used to send out calls for help. "It was an inviolable order that no train must leave a terminal without a telegrapher," said one veteran of Western railroading. "In some instances trains were held for hours until he could be found or became sufficiently sober for duty."

All station agents in the smaller Western towns were required to know Morse code and how to operate a telegraph. "Most of the operators in those days were boys, and right lively fellows they were," said John Cruise, who was the first telegrapher on the Kansas Pacific. "They had to send telegrams, repair breaks in the line, locate interruptions from grounding, install offices, etc. . . . When the road had been built as far west as Edwardsville a wreck occurred near the end of the line, and all hands from headquarters were ordered out. It was in the fall, and there was a drizzling rain. We built a bonfire along the side of the track. The operator shinnied up a pole and brought down a wire. Then he took a bureau from one of the wrecked cars, put an old Clark relay on the bureau, and used one post as a key by pounding it with one end of the wire. Having no umbrella, I kept my messages in one of the bureau drawers while copying them, and kept the paper covered with the cape of my military overcoat. And there we worked all day and night until the wreck was cleared up. Fancy such a telegraph office now. Oh, I tell you, we had experiences in those days!"

The goal of all ambitious railroad men was to become a conductor, "the captain of a passenger train," uniformed in a brass-buttoned blue suit and a gold-braided visored cap. A conductor on the transcontinental railroad certainly had no sinecure; not only was he responsible for the safety of his passengers and the collection of tickets and keeping of accounts, he also had to handle drunken miners and disorderly cowboys and meet complaints in a conciliatory and tactful manner. He might vary in temperament from kindly to stern and haughty, but to the passengers he represented the railroad company, and he had to maintain the air of a gentleman—diplomatic, compassionate, sometimes valiant. In the era of wood-burning locomotives, he was also expected to assist in the loading of billets so as to speed the train from one wood pile to the next.

The Union Pacific had a conductor who had lost his scalp to Indians, and another who was noted for his ability to play the organs in the Pullman Palace cars. One conductor on the Kansas Pacific never went on duty without being fully armed. "He had much experience in life on the plains," said Randolph Keim. "He always had his rifle by his side and pistols, either about his waist, or where he could conveniently put his hands upon them. He was an excellent shot, and had several bullet scars as mementoes of early conflicts."

In the West, the free-spirited local travelers refused to waste time standing in line at stations to buy their tickets; they would climb onto the train at the last minute and bargain with the conductor over ticket prices to their destinations. To handle this business, each conductor equipped himself with a small tin box of tickets, and after dark carried a lantern made with a hoop that fit over one arm, leaving his hands free and furnishing light by which to make change.

"An American conductor is a nondescript being, half clerk, half guard, with a dash of the gentleman," said Scottish tourist William Chambers. "He is generally well dressed, sometimes wears a beard, and when off-duty passes for a respectable personage at any of the hotels and may be seen lounging about in the best company with a fashionable wife. . . . One thing is remarkable about him—you do not get a sight of him till the train is in motion, and when it stops he disappears. . . . The suddenness of his appearance when the train gets underway is marvelous. Hardly have the wheels made a revolution when the door at one end of the car is opened, and the conductor, like a wandering spirit, begins his rounds. . . . All he says is 'Ticket!' and he utters the word in a dry callous tone, as if it would cost something to be cheerful."

Another British traveler, Phil Robinson, irritated by the indifference of the conductor on the Union Pacific, commented sarcastically: "What is the 'conductor'? Is he a private gentleman traveling for his pleasure, a duke in disguise, or is he a servant of the company placed on the cars to see to the comfort &c. of the company's customers? I should like to know, for sometimes I have been puzzled to find out."

Even so, most passengers respected the conductor. It was he who set the train in motion, a blue-uniformed figure of authority, standing beside the steps of his boarding car, a watch in one hand, the other raised to signal the engineer to start steam coursing through the Iron Horse. And it was that marvelous engine that veteran conductor Charles George saluted when he looked back upon his forty years of railroading in the nineteenth century: "Man's genius seems materialized in the Iron Horse, and no one can look upon a locomotive of today without having a feeling come over him that is akin to awe."

·◄❧ CHAPTER 9 ❧►·

Exit the Land Grabbers,
Enter the Stock Manipulators

THE LOVE AFFAIR of nineteenth-century Americans with their transcontinental railway lasted less than a decade—only through the passionate romance of construction and the sensual excitement of the first years of travel. Even as the scribbling journeyers to the Pacific were recording their pristine adventures, the perfidy of the promoters and their knavish allies, the politicians who dominated federal and state governments, was slowly seeping out to disillusion the American public.

During the building of the thin strip of parallel iron rails across the continent, the arrogant promoters engorged 33 million acres of the people's lands. Additional land grants to other Western railroads during that decade brought the total to 155 million acres, or more than one fourth of the Louisiana Purchase, one ninth of what was then the nation's entire land area. (Because of failure to comply with conditions of the grants, the railroads lost some of their acreage, but they still got away with about one tenth of the people's land.) This empire of landed wealth, which had been stolen from the Indian tribes, was transferred to a handful of enterprising buccaneers by members of Congress who were elected to office by the people of the nation in the innocent belief that they were choosing representatives to protect the public interest. In addition to the land, the railroad promoters received millions of dollars in subsidies and bonds, an undetermined amount of which found its way back into the pockets of the congressmen who were giving it away.

Upon completion of the first transcontinental road, a number of those who had been enriched by the people of the United States packed up their swag and departed, leaving an almost defunct railway for others to operate and for the taxpayers to pay for several times over again through subsidies, loans, bond defalcations, and high freight rates. Thomas Durant retired to the Adirondacks to live in baronial style, buying up timber and minerals, dabbling in small railroads, and then lost a good part of his fortune in the Panic of 1873, which ironically was brought on by another high-flying railroad promoter, Jay Cooke. When Durant died, twelve years later, creditors brought judgments of twenty million dollars against his estate, but his heirs managed to salvage more than a million. Oliver Ames stayed on a few years with the Union Pacific, he and Sidney Dillon becoming uneasy partners of the piratical Jay Gould. Grenville Dodge moved on to Texas for more shady transcontinental railroad dealings, Sam Reed went to Canada to engineer construction of the Canadian Pacific, and the hard-working Casement brothers continued to supervise construction gangs on the tightening network of railroads across the West.

Collis Huntington and his Big Four partners of the Central Pacific held firm and began to expand. With the fortunes they had taken from the people of the United States, they began killing off or absorbing all the rival railroads in California. Using their closely held Contract and Finance Company, they had built the Central Pacific for half what the government paid them, pocketed the remainder, and then paid themselves millions of dollars in dividends from stock that they had acquired for nothing. Eventually they ruled California, buying up politicians and judges, forcing the public to pay interest on their own bonds, selling their land back to them at exorbitant prices, taxing them through higher and higher monopolistic freight rates.

"The Pacific Railroad is already a power in the land, and is destined to be a power vastly greater than it is now," Charles Francis Adams observed during the first years of its operation. "It already numbers its retainers in both houses of Congress, and is building up great communities in the heart of the continent. It will some day be the richest and most powerful corporation in the world; it will probably also be the most corrupt." A civic leader and member of the famed New England family, Adams some fifteen years later would become president of the Union Pacific in an effort to save it from collapse after it was plundered by stock manipulators.

One of the first disillusionments of the people who had viewed the transcontinental as "their" railroad was the shocking discovery that its tracks and bridges built with their money had been so shoddily constructed that hundreds of miles would have to be bought and paid for all over again. For many miles across the level plains and deserts, ties were unballasted, the trackbed consisting only of earth thrown up by the graders' plows. Little attention had been paid to the meeting of rail joints with ties; wooden trestles and abutments lacked masonry supports; cheaply made wrought-iron fastenings soon began to work loose from the rails. Thin embankments were eroding; sharp curves needed straightening; rough grades needed smoothing.

A traveler in 1869 reported a narrow escape on the Union Pacific: "A bridge over Bitter Creek, just east of Green River, built upon abutments of soft sandstone, crumbled away under our train, precipitating the engine, tender, and express-car into the creek, and the passenger-car, in which I was, was only saved by a stringer or beam of the bridge catching into the roof and holding it suspended over the brink. One passenger was killed and several more or less injured. . . . The bridge as well as two others in the vicinity had been examined the day previous and pronounced unsafe. . . . The unanimous opinion is that it was criminal to attempt to cross. The western portion of the road is dangerous."

Isaac Morris, one of the few honest government examiners of the Pacific railroad, not only agreed that the Union Pacific's Western track was dangerous, he said that it was the worst railroad he had ever traveled over, and went on to list its deficiencies: unsafe bridges, tunnels too narrow, roadbed not properly leveled, nor were the rails aligned, roadbed not of the required uniform width of fourteen feet, cross-ties sunken in an unballasted bed. The ties, he said, were laid with great irregularity. "They appear indeed to have been pitched on, and the rails spiked to them wherever they fell. . . . No attention appears to have been paid to regularity of distance between the ties, they varying from fifteen to twenty-six inches, the distance at the ends being rarely uniform. . . . The material objection is, however, to the ties themselves. They are of soft white pine on the road I examined, as well as on the Central Pacific, the first being obtained from the neighboring mountains, the latter from the Sierra Nevada." After pointing out that government construction standards called for oak or other hardwood timber for ties, Morris accurately predicted that the white pine would quickly rot, requiring replacement of thousands of ties.

In Morris's judgment, the transcontinental railroad was only about two-thirds completed when the rails were joined at Promontory. "There is a vast difference between getting rails down so that cars can pass over them and finishing a road. . . . The right to pass over the roads, such as they are, by paying for it, is all the people will get for the enormous amount they have been compelled to contribute for their construction, and they are certainly entitled to have a 'first-class road in all respects' that they may be assured of life and limb." In summing up, Morris recommended that the government protect its interests by withholding subsidies and land grants until the road was satisfactorily completed. His report to Congress, however, like most honest reports that might interfere with the exploitation of the public, was filed away and quickly forgotten by the people's representatives in Washington.

Another disillusionment of Americans with their transcontinental railroad was its failure to accomplish the age-old dream of Western mankind to reach the legendary riches of the Indies by way of the Western Sea. Greedy old Collis Huntington was so determined to capture the teas of China and the silks and spices of India for his Big Four that he bought up a fleet of ships to bring Far Eastern goods to Oakland, where they were loaded onto "Silk & Tea Trains" for shipment across America. Although millions of pounds of tea and silk were shipped by rail to the Eastern United States during the early 1870s, the trade never developed into the lucrative enterprise that most Americans had expected. Walt Whitman hinted at the reason in his *Passage to India:*

> In the Old World the east the Suez canal,
> The New by its mighty railroad spann'd . . .

Six months after the rails were joined at Promontory, Ferdinand de Lesseps completed the Suez Canal, shortening sea lanes between the Western world and the Orient by several thousand miles. Ocean vessels could now transport at lower rates than could any railroad all the teas and silks and spices that the Western world could consume. If America's transcontinental railway was to survive, it would have to do so without the commerce of the "spicy islands off the West."

The greatest disillusionment of all, however, did not come until 1873. On September 6, 1872, the *New York Sun* published some letters that Congressman Oakes Ames allegedly had written to Henry S. McComb, one of the original trustees of the Union Pacific's Credit Mobilier. McComb had been pressuring Ames to turn over to him 343 shares of Credit Mobilier stock, which McComb claimed belonged to him, and when the congressman refused to do so, McComb released the letters to the *Sun*. It was clear from the content of the correspondence that Ames in 1868 had distributed shares of Credit Mobilier stock to a considerable number of his fellow congressmen in an effort to influence actions favorable to the Union Pacific. "I have assigned, as far as I have gone, to 4 from Mass., 1 from N.H., 1 Del., 1 Tenn., 1 Ohio, 2 Penn., 1 Ind., 1 Maine," he informed McComb in one letter. "I have 3 to place which I shall put where they will do the most good to us."

Because publication of the letters occurred amid the Grant-Greeley presidential election campaign, most Americans dismissed the implications as political mudslinging. Jim Fisk attempted to expose Credit Mobilier in 1869, but his reputation for skulduggery won him few listeners among the public. At about that same time, Charles Francis Adams tried to warn the nation in the *North American Review:* "The Credit Mobilier is understood to be building the road; but what this Credit Mobilier is seems to be shrouded in mystery as is the fate of the missing $180 million of capital stock of these roads. . . . Whoever originated this anomalous corporation, it is currently reported to be the real constructor of the Union Pacific, and now to have got into its hands all the unissued stock, the proceeds of the bonds sold, the government bonds, and the earnings of the road—in fact, all its available assets. . . . Who then constitute the Credit Mobilier? It is but another name for the Pacific Railroad ring. The members of it are in Congress; they are trustees for the bondholders, they are directors, they are stockholders, they are contractors; in Washington they vote the subsidies, in New York they receive them, upon the Plains they expend them, and in the Credit Mobilier they divide them. . . . Under one name or another a ring of some seventy persons is struck at whatever point the Union Pacific is approached. As stockholders they own the road, as mortgagees they have a lien upon it, as directors they contract for its construction, and as members of the Credit Mobilier they build it."

Adams was equally acerbic about the Central Pacific. "Managed by a small clique in California, its internal arrangements are involved in about the same obscurity as the rites of Freemasonry." At the time he published his exposures, however, Americans were still glowing with pride over completion of "their" transcontinental railroad, and considered any criticism of it unprogressive, malicious, and downright unpatriotic.

As Congress began a typically mild investigation of itself early in 1873, there appeared to be no way of concealing the fact that the Vice-President, the Vice-President-elect, chairmen of important committees in the House, a dozen Republican party leaders of both House and Senate, and the Democratic floor leader of the House had all accepted bribes in the form of Credit Mobilier stock. They included such names as Schuyler Colfax (who had been honored by having a town on the Central Pacific in California named for him), James A. Garfield of Ohio, William B. Allison of Iowa, James Brooks of New York, John Logan of Illinois, and James G. Blaine of Maine. Logan and Blaine, having gotten wind of a possible investigation, returned their stock and thus got off the hook. Under questioning, a surprising number of congressmen claimed that they could see nothing wrong in what they had done. Buying the stock was only a good investment, they said, until Ames admitted that they had not *bought* the stock; after it was given on credit to the congressmen, the directors of Credit Mobilier issued dividends more than sufficient for payment, so the stock actually cost them nothing. A headline writer of the *New York Herald* stated it succinctly:

CREDIT MOBILIER EXPOSÉ
Oakes Ames Unbosoms Himself
Shares Allotted and Dividends Paid Without Transfer
of Purchase Money

Vice-President Colfax was caught in an outright lie after inventing an elaborate story about receiving a mysterious thousand-dollar bill in an envelope. Garfield denied that he had kept the shares assigned to him, but Ames's memorandum book showed that the congressman was debited for ten shares, then was issued dividends that amounted to $329 more than the shares cost. Even then Garfield tried to wriggle out of the mire, by testifying that he had thought the $329 was a loan from Ames.

The irreverent *New York Herald* prepared obituaries and epitaphs for all those involved, printing them under suitable headlines:

CREDIT MOBILIER
Ravages of the Great Washington Plague
Terrible Mortality at the Capitol
List of the Distinguished Dead
All Stockholders of the Union Pacific Railroad
Who Received a Higher Dividend Than 750 Per Cent
Are Cordially Invited to Attend the Funeral

For the journalists of the day, Oakes Ames was now "Hoax" Ames, and Schuyler Colfax was "Smiler" Colfax because he continually smiled throughout his flimsily crafted testimony. Oakes Ames's "epitaph":

O lofty worth, whose virtues were unknown
O shining light, whose glamor was unseen,
Whose latest spasm of godlike work has shown
What men are not, but what they might have been.
Thou toldst the truth, tho' hid 'neath many cloaks
O concentrated essence of a Hoax.

Vice-President Colfax:

A beautiful smiler came in our midst
Too lively and fair to remain.
They stretched him on racks till the soul of Colfax
Flapped up into Heaven again.
May the fate of poor Schuyler warn men of a smiler,
Who dividends gets on the brain!

James A. Garfield:

Here rests his head upon its lap of earth,
A youth to fortune and misfortune known;
Mobilier frowned upon his humble berth,
And Hoax Ames henceforth marked him for his own.

As might have been expected, however, the self-investigating congressional committee produced a flood of sanctimonious oratory and then whitewashed the whole affair. After first voting to expel Ames and Brooks, the House backtracked to a resolution of censure. When Ames and Brooks died shortly afterward, their fellow congressmen eulogized them as victims of "broken hearts." Colfax did not die of a broken heart, however. His Indiana constituents passed a resolution expressing "undiminished confidence in his honor and integrity," styling him "a model statesman, temperate and faithful to principles." After leaving the vice-presidency in March, he was in such demand as a lecturer before temperance and religious groups that he traveled around the country earning more money from gullible listeners than he ever could have gained from government graft. (In addition to Credit Mobilier stock, he had taken four thousand dollars in exchange for a government contract awarded to a manufacturer of envelopes.)

James Garfield did not die of a broken heart, either. His Ohio constituents returned him to Congress three more times, and then the people of America elected him President, which might be an indication that Americans would sooner vote a rogue into its highest office than an honest man. Nor did any of the others die of broken hearts. They continued to draw dividends from their Credit Mobilier stock, enjoyed the frequent showers of money that fell upon them from other railroad stock manipulators, and gave away America. After closing the book on Credit Mobilier, they passed a law increasing congressional salaries, making it retroactive to the beginning of that session.

Realization by the public that the Union Pacific had been throughly plundered caused a sharp drop in the value of its stock. During the Credit Mobilier exposures it sank from one hundred dollars to thirty dollars a share, and after the financial panic of late 1873 it fell to fourteen dollars. This attracted the attention of one of the most power-mad Robber Barons of the Gilded Age, a man known as the Mephistopheles of Wall Street, variously described as being a double-crosser, dishonest, amoral, and rapacious. Jason Gould (he later shortened his first name to Jay) was born in that part of upstate New York around Albany that generated a large number of the exploiters of nineteenth-century America. Offspring of hard-scrabble Yankee migrants from New England, they learned early to respect the power of the dollar. Jay Gould earned his first dollar by making and selling sundials, and he probably still had it when he died forty years later. During those forty years he always found ways to use other people's money to build fortunes for himself. At the age of twenty-one, he was worth a million dollars; at thirty-six he had increased his fortune to twenty-two million; at forty-six he owned eighty million. In a time when a million was almost equal to today's billion, Jay Gould was probably the wealthiest and one of the most powerful men in the world. He left in his wake a legion of broken men who mistakenly put their trust in him—bankrupts, nerve-shaken invalids, and suicides. Along the way he also plundered dozens of railroads, leaving them so debt-ridden that some never recovered.

Gould was a mild-mannered man, frail of body, sallow-skinned, about five and a half feet tall, subject to constant chest and stomach ailments, insignificant in appearance, his voice soft and plaintive—all of which must have disarmed those who stood in his way until his sad black eyes suddenly turned searching and cold. In 1869 he joined forces with another Robber Baron who was his exact opposite physically and temperamentally, the fleshy, red-faced, womanizing Jim

Jay Gould (Culver Pictures)

Fisk. Together they seized control of the Erie Railroad, watered its stock by printing certificates on a press they kept in their basement, transferring to their personal accounts the money they received for the stock as well as most of the railroad's cash reserves. When they abandoned the railroad, it was in such poor condition and so entangled in debt that most of its stockholders died of old age without receiving a penny of dividends.

After betraying Fisk, in another financial scheme, Gould turned almost all of his efforts to Western railroads, seeing them as the keys to unlimited power and wealth. In 1873 he was quite aware of how badly the Union Pacific had been plundered by its original promoters, but being the sort of adventurer who thrives in times of financial panic by using other people's money, he decided to gain control of the Omaha-to-Ogden section of the transcontinental railroad. Later, perhaps, he would go after the Central Pacific and own all of the iron road to the Western Sea.

With less than two million of the twenty million dollars that he had at his command in 1873, Gould bought up one third of all the Union Pacific stock. The road had a large

bonded indebtedness coming due in 1874, and if the obligations were not met it would be thrown into receivership.
Gould took care of this problem by joining in a scheme with
two other large stockholders, Oliver Ames and Sidney Dillon. "I sent for them and had an interview with them," he
said afterward. "We funded the debt into bonds." The three
men put some of their own money into the bonds and increased freight rates 133%, actions that caused the stock to
begin rising on Wall Street. By buying additional blocks of
shares and declaring huge dividends—most of which were
paid to him as the largest stockholder—Gould pushed the
price steadily higher. Then he began quietly selling out at
enormous profits, totaling more than twenty million dollars
according to some estimates. Very little money went to improve the railroad's track or its equipment, and none was
used to pay the principal or interest on the debt owed to the
United States government. By 1878, Gould owned only a few
shares of Union Pacific stock, but he was not yet through with
that ravaged railroad.

His next move was to take over the Kansas Pacific, which
another group of looters had driven into bankruptcy in 1877,
and use it as a weapon against the Union Pacific in a scheme
to gain for himself still more millions. Before taking control of
the defunct Kansas Pacific, however, he encountered some
difficulties with a German-born emigrant who had changed
his name from Ferdinand Heinrich Gustav Hilgard to Henry
Villard. Villard had started his career in America by writing
for German-American newspapers. He reported the Lincoln-
Douglas debates, and accompanied Lincoln on his train ride
to Washington to be inaugurated. During the Civil War he
worked as a battlefield reporter for two New York newspapers. After the war, he sold railroad bonds in Germany, and at
the time Gould started his raid on the Kansas Pacific, Villard
represented the interests of German bondholders in that
troubled railroad and was in nominal control as receiver.

Although Gould was able to buy almost half of the
Kansas Pacific's stock for a few cents on the dollar, Villard insisted that the road was the property of its bondholders, and
refused to go along with Gould's scheme to pool all the securities and issue new stock. The struggle between these two

equally determined men continued through the late 1870s. Gould eventually decided to use flattery and cajolery, suggesting that Villard himself draw up a plan that would reorganize the finances of the Kansas Pacific and at the same time redeem the bonds at full value. Villard submitted a plan, but as usual the Mephistopheles of Wall Street outmaneuvered his opponent. Gould paid off the bondholders, but took control of the railroad away from the ambitious Villard.

Gould was now ready for a masterful financial coup. He simply informed the directors of the Union Pacific that he intended to extend the Kansas Pacific's tracks from Denver to the Pacific Coast by way of Salt Lake City, and thus destroy the transcontinental railroad's monopoly. Late in 1879, the Union Pacific directors came to Gould's house in New York to talk terms of surrender. Gould's proposal was a merger of his Kansas Pacific with the Union Pacific, for which he would receive two hundred thousand shares of Union Pacific stock. As soon as the deal was agreed upon, Gould leaked the news of the merger, and as his stock soared in value he sold it. According to Villard, Gould cleared more than ten million dollars in this manipulation before the stock crashed. Leaving the looted Union Pacific-Kansas Pacific to flounder, Gould now turned his attention to other Western railroads.

Meanwhile, one of his rivals, Thomas A. Scott of the Pennsylvania Railroad, was attempting to tie his powerful Eastern network into a route to the Pacific. For a brief time before Gould's entry upon the Western scene, Scott took over the presidency of the Union Pacific, but was unable to overcome its financial difficulties and shifted his efforts to the Texas & Pacific. This was the road, long dreamed of by Southerners, that would follow the 32d parallel from Texas to San Diego, California, with eastern connections to New Orleans and across the South to the Atlantic Coast. Seeing this system as a perfect adjunct to his Pennsylvania Railroad, Scott in 1871 acquired the charter and land grant for construction of the Texas & Pacific.

To build his road, Scott chose Grenville Dodge, who had left the Union Pacific a few months earlier. Their arrangement gave Dodge a high salary as well as an interest in the new road. The engineer responded by traveling about Texas,

Thomas A. Scott (Culver Pictures)

persuading various towns to invest their futures in railroad bonds and thus guarantee their inclusion on its westward route.

Before construction could begin, however, the Credit Mobilier scandal broke in Washington, and Dodge feared becoming involved. Acting for the Union Pacific in his last year with that railroad, he had evidently paid members of Congress about eighty thousand dollars for their cooperation in authorizing a government loan for the Omaha–Council Bluffs bridge, and he also had received Credit Mobilier stock, which was registered in his wife's name. As he feared, the investigating committee ordered him to Washington for questioning. He acknowledged the summons with an arrogant reply that he was busy at railroad building and could not come North to testify until his work was finished. Aware that years might pass before completion of the Texas & Pacific, the committee sent a sergeant-at-arms to Texas with a subpoena. When the man arrived, he was told that Dodge had already left for Washington. Instead, he had gone to St. Louis and registered in a hotel under an assumed name. When the process servers tracked him down, he slipped out, secretly boarded a train for an unknown destination in the West, and remained in hiding until the committee completed its investigations. Years afterward, when another investigating committee managed to snare him into Washington, he was scolded for his behavior in 1873. Dodge denied that he had ever left Texas. "A note to me at my office at any time would have brought me," he said with pretended astonishment. "I never knew that anybody had any difficulty in finding me." He then added with a note of offhanded pride: "I saw a statement in the papers that I had been followed 2,200 miles to get me here."

Work on the tracks of the Texas & Pacific across eastern Texas was well under way when the Panic of 1873 dried up construction funds. By using Negro prisoners rented from the state of Texas for a few cents a day, Dodge brought the rails into Dallas that year, but it was three more years before there was enough money to build to Fort Worth. In the hope of raising more funds, Tom Scott went to England and Dodge went to Washington, but neither had any luck. The Texas & Pacific was in trouble, with heavy short-term debts coming due.

Like a jackal attracted to a wounded animal, Jay Gould began circling for the kill, but found another jackal trying to move in ahead of him—Collis Huntington of the Big Four. Huntington had made up his mind to shut off any competitive threat from a transcontinental railroad across the Southwest by building it himself under the name of Southern Pacific. Huntington had already found Scott to be a formidable foe in Washington, where both men showered money on congressmen in efforts to gain access to public funds with which to build both the Texas & Pacific and the Southern Pacific. Huntington complained that Scott lobbied day and night, catching his sleep in chairs or sofas between appointments. From the sidelines, Gould watched them duel, sizing up Huntington as the more durable antagonist and wondering if he dared challenge him.

A complicating factor in these maneuvers was the Atchison, Topeka & Santa Fe, which after receiving a vast land grant across Kansas in 1863 had remained moribund until 1870. In that year, under the leadership of a Massachusetts

Yankee named Ginery Twitchell, the tracks began moving westward, reaching Newton in 1871 to take much of the Texas cattle trade away from the Kansas Pacific. The following year the railroad was extended to Dodge City, which was to become the king of the trail towns and give the Santa Fe a virtual cattle-shipping monopoly. On December 28, 1872, the railroad reached the Colorado line, its original goal, but it was obvious to the stock manipulators in the East that the Santa Fe now had transcontinental ambitions. Twitchell had raised a considerable amount of his construction funds from Boston capitalists, and one of the leading investors, Thomas Nickerson, replaced him as president in 1874. With fresh financial support, Nickerson pushed the tracks across Colorado to Pueblo in 1876, intent upon following the old Santa Fe Trail into New Mexico. Here he ran into a strong rival, none other than the fighting Quaker, William J. Palmer, who had built the Kansas Pacific to Denver in the years immediately following the Civil War.

"Young men without money can only make a fortune by connecting themselves with Capitalists," Palmer wrote in 1865. "The best place to invest capital is in the West." Establishing headquarters in Denver, Palmer connected himself with capitalists in Philadelphia, New York, and Great Britain, and organized the Denver & Rio Grande Railway, its objective being El Paso, Texas, with a possible extension into Mexico. By what route he reached Mexico was of no particular concern to Palmer. He had learned while building the Kansas Pacific that more capital could be collected from organizing land companies, laying out towns, and selling lots than from the railroad itself. That the towns might wither and die for lack of any economic base was of no concern to Palmer, either.

Sixty miles south of Denver was a pleasant little county seat called Colorado City, but before building his railroad there Palmer visited the place to buy up land. Because the land around Colorado City was too expensive for his taste, Palmer went farther out and acquired large blocks for eighty cents an acre. When Palmer built his railroad south in 1871, he bypassed Colorado City for his new town of Colorado Springs, where he made large profits by selling off lots. A few months later, Colorado City died when it lost the county seat to Palmer's Colorado Springs, because the latter was on a railroad.

The next town southward was Pueblo, and Palmer's first move was to send an agent there to warn the citizens that unless they raised $150,000 for the Denver & Rio Grande, the railroad would bypass the town. Pueblo raised the money and Palmer ran his tracks alongside the town, but he built the depot across the Arkansas River so that he could sell lots in his new town of South Pueblo.

These actions and other gouging manipulations by Palmer and his associates won the Denver & Rio Grande few friends as it continued to build southward across Colorado. Soon after the Santa Fe reached Pueblo in 1876, intense rivalry between the two railroads led to armed conflicts, with the majority of the local people siding with the Santa Fe. Both roads were determined to build south into New Mexico, but the only practical route was through the bottleneck of Raton Pass, long used by wagon trains on the Santa Fe Trail. Palmer built his Denver & Rio Grande tracks to within a few miles of the entrance, assuming that this gave him the right to use the pass.

A dozen years earlier, however, a hard-bitten old trader named Uncle Dick Wooton had secured charters from the legislatures of Colorado and New Mexico authorizing him to open a toll road through the pass. He built an inn, and lived well by collecting tolls and furnishing food and lodging to travelers. When it became obvious to Uncle Dick that a railroad was coming through his pass to put an end to his bonanza, he sided with the Santa Fe. Whether this was because he disliked the Denver & Rio Grande's high-handed methods or because the Santa Fe offered him fifty dollars a month for life is anybody's guess. At any rate, when a Santa Fe grading crew mounted on horses arrived in the pass one cold winter's night, Uncle Dick cooperated by rounding up an armed force in the area to guard the graders when they began their work by lanternlight. As Uncle Dick had expected, a thoroughly aroused band of Denver & Rio Grande engineers and roustabouts soon appeared on the scene to challenge the right of the Santa Fe to Raton Pass. They were also armed, and for a few minutes a violent clash seemed inevitable. Wooton and the Santa Fe forces held the high ground, however, and the Denver & Rio Grande outfit withdrew, losing forever the route through Raton Pass to New Mexico.

The Santa Fe now found itself engaged in a new war of nerves with the powerful Collis Huntington, who viewed the railroad's thrust into New Mexico as a flank attack upon his Southern Pacific. This was especially irritating to him because he was still engaged in a frontal war with Tom Scott's Texas & Pacific.

In the course of that struggle, Tom Scott had maneuvered himself into a strategic position in the deadlocked Hayes-Tilden presidential election of 1876. Tilden, the Democratic candidate, undoubtedly had received the most popular votes, but Hayes, the Republican candidate, claimed the most electoral votes. The disputed electoral votes were mostly in the Southern states, and the Southern Democrats were determined not to surrender them lightly to the Republicans. Because Scott had been lobbying for several years

Rivalry between the Santa Fe and the Denver & Rio Grande came close to a shooting war. (The State Historical Society of Colorado Library)

among Southern politicians, the Republicans around Hayes
sought Scott out as an ally in a political deal with the South.
Scott had won the confidence of many Southern congressmen
with assurances that if they would vote for a federal subsidy
for his Texas & Pacific he would give the South a transcontinental railroad by linking it to the Texas & Pacific. Northern
Democrats and Republicans, however, had strongly opposed
such a railroad in the recently defeated South, and it was they
who had blocked Scott's lobbying efforts.

With charges of fraud and threats of a renewal of civil war
swirling about Washington, Scott worked out a compromise
with his old enemy Huntington. Huntington agreed to withdraw opposition to Scott's Texas & Pacific, provided that the
Southern Pacific would be left in control of the California
end of that transcontinental railroad.

After this arrangement was completed, the Southern
Democrats agreed to accept Hayes as President in exchange
for an end to Reconstruction, the withdrawal of federal troops
from the South, and Tom Scott's new railway. Thus was accomplished the famed Compromise of 1877, which was in effect an alliance of Republicans, Southern Democrats, and
powerful railroad tycoons, an alliance that would control
American politics well into the twentieth century. When
Rutherford Hayes traveled to Washington for his inaugural in
March 1877, he rode in luxurious splendor aboard the private
railroad car of Tom Scott.

If Scott believed that he had won a victory over his chief
rival, however, he was soon disillusioned. Controlling the
California end of the new transcontinental railroad was not
enough for Huntington. He was determined to drive on to El
Paso and then to a seaport on the Gulf of Mexico. By the autumn of 1877, the rails of Huntington's Southern Pacific were
approaching the Colorado River; across it lay Arizona Territory. Blocking his path, however, was the Yuma Indian reservation, and he needed government authority to bridge the
river and cross Indian land. While Huntington was petitioning for a right-of-way, Scott sent a small gang of workmen
to the Yuma reservation, which was twelve hundred miles
west of his end of track in Texas, and they began grading for

the Texas & Pacific. Infuriated, Huntington rushed to Washington and demanded that the Secretary of War drive his rival off the reservation.

As soon as the government ordered the Texas & Pacific graders to suspend operations, Huntington boldly brought his own workmen in, and without permission from the government or from the Yuma Indians, he bridged the river and laid his tracks across the reservation before news of what he was doing leaked out of that remote and desolate area. "A great injustice to us," Scott complained to the War Department when he heard what Huntington had done. Huntington ignored all the charges. While the Southern Pacific's tracks continued to move across the Arizona deserts, he confidently invaded Washington.

In railroad building, a fait accompli was the same as the planting of a flag to claim territory for a king, and Huntington had no difficulty in securing an appointment with President Hayes. "He was a little cross at first, said we had defied the Government, etc.," Huntington wrote somewhat gleefully of the encounter. Huntington assured the President that he was in earnest about building the Southern Pacific to serve the people of the nation, and went on to tell Hayes how he had worked his construction gangs at night while soldiers at Fort Yuma were asleep. According to Huntington, the President laughed heartily at this clever piece of trickery.

"What do you propose to do if we let you run over the bridge?" Hayes asked.

"Push the road right on through Arizona," Huntington replied.

"Will you do that? If you will, that will suit me first rate." The President, for all his airs of Victorian respectability, talk of reform in politics, and Sunday-school platitudes, admired the Robber Barons and accepted their amorality. By endorsing Huntington's illegal entry upon Indian land for the good of the Southern Pacific, Hayes doomed the dreams of the man who had helped as much or more than had any other in the secret deal to place him in the White House. The odds against Tom Scott's Texas & Pacific ever reaching the Western Sea were now almost insurmountable.

During the summer of Hayes's first term in the White

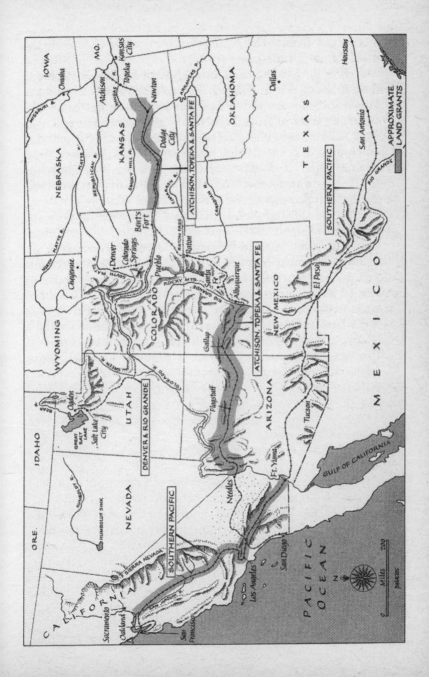

House, railroad workmen began striking in protest against wage cuts. When the railroad owners tried to break the strikes, riots spread across the country. Police and militia battled with the strikers in railroad yards, leaving many dead and wounded. On July 22, Hayes relieved soldiers on occupation duty in the South and used them to put down the strikes by force of arms. Involved in all this turmoil was Tom Scott. The riots, which had been brought on by the greed of railroad owners such as he, had cost the interlocking companies millions of dollars and left him broken in body and spirit. This was the final blow to his ambition to own a transcontinental railroad across the South and West.

Jay Gould, the jackal, now saw an opportunity for another kill, and in 1880 he took the Texas & Pacific away from Scott. For a few months he skirmished with Huntington, extending the tracks of the T. & P. toward El Paso while Huntington built eastward from El Paso. Gould knew, however, that he had met his match in Huntington. In 1881 Gould offered to abandon his plan to extend the Texas & Pacific west of El Paso if Huntington would stop his Southern Pacific at El Paso. Huntington agreed. A few months later, however, Huntington began buying up a number of small Texas railroads, tying them together until he could run his Southern Pacific trains into New Orleans, as he had planned to do all along.

By the 1880s, railroad building in America had become the national get-rich-quick game. Promoters by the score leaped into the competition, building railroads helter-skelter across the face of the land. Few of them were planned to meet any transportation needs. They were built mainly for purposes of financial exploitation, not for the people of the nation, who ultimately paid for them over and over again, through economic depressions and wars, thus perpetuating the most absurd railway system in the world.

·◄· CHAPTER 10 ·►·

Sitting Bull and the Northern Route

THROUGH THE 1860s Indian resistance to railroad construction across the buffalo ranges of the Great Plains was sporadic and largely ineffective. In Nebraska and Kansas, the Union Pacific and Kansas Pacific railroad workers skirmished with raiders from time to time, but delays in surveys and construction were of short duration. When the Northern Pacific—that long-dreamed-of route from the Great Lakes to the shores of the Pacific Northwest—finally came to life in 1870 with a flurry of track laying in both Minnesota and Washington territories, the freedom of thousands of Plains Indians who lived between these points was seriously threatened. From the 1850s to the 1870s, several preliminary surveys were made for this Northern route, but no matter which way the railroad was built, it would have to cross hundreds of miles of treaty lands and vast areas of buffalo-grazing grounds.

Both the material culture and the spiritual life of Plains Indians were based upon the buffalo. That animal, which numbered in the millions, supplied not only the basic food, shelter, and clothing needs of the tribes, it was also a folk hero and a religious symbol. Without the buffalo, the entire civilization of the Plains Indians would collapse. In the years following the Gold Rush of 1849, the tribes had seen the buffalo pushed both north and south of the white man's westward trails, and in the 1860s they had seen the railroads across the Central Plains bring devastation to once-great herds.

The free-roaming tribes had learned to hate the "bad medicine-wagon" that ran back and forth on iron tracks, frightening wild game out of the country. Some Indian leaders signed treaties and moved their people north to lands guaranteed to them in perpetuity. Other leaders such as Sit-

Sitting Bull (National Archives)

ting Bull always kept a distance from white men, signing no treaties but retreating always ahead of settlement, desiring only to be left alone.

From the time of his first knowledge of white men, Sitting Bull was continually appalled by their tendency toward violence and murder. He witnessed their cruel work in Minnesota, Dakota, and Wyoming, fighting them only when they brought their savagery to the Teton Sioux, withdrawing westward after each encounter in the hope of avoiding any further contacts with them. In the late 1860s Sitting Bull took his Hunkpapa people into the Yellowstone country west of the Black Hills where they could live in peace along the tributary Powder, Tongue, and Bighorn rivers—a land rich in buffalo and other wild game. Because of Sitting Bull's determination to remain free of reservation control and live in the traditional Indian way, large numbers of Oglala and Brulé Sioux, as well as Cheyennes and Arapaho came to join him there. They all were aware that the Yellowstone country was the last remote region in which they could truly live as Indians. White settlements and roads lay to the south, east, and west, but the land all the way north into Canada was as it had always been. They could travel back and forth to trade with Canadian half-breeds, free of any dependence upon the hated agency trading posts along the Missouri.

It was with a shock of abhorrence, therefore, that they discovered in 1871 the presence of railroad surveyors running a line through the valley of the Yellowstone. With Sitting Bull's approval, the young warriors immediately began a campaign of harassment, first letting the intruders know that they were not wanted there, and then driving them away. The reason the surveyors had come into this area was that the owners of the Northern Pacific Railroad had decided to change its route, abandoning the line through previously ceded lands and invading unceded lands without any consultation with the Indians. In 1872, the surveyors accompanied by a small military force came back to the Yellowstone country, and again Sitting Bull's followers drove them away.

This brought Sitting Bull's presence to the attention of Washington politicians and bureaucrats whose interests were close to those of the railroad's owners, and they sent out commissioners to gauge his power. None of them dared venture into his stronghold, but at the safe distance of Fort Peck they estimated that his followers consisted of seven hundred, fifteen hundred, or perhaps three thousand lodges, that he was exercising a reign of terror in the Yellowstone country, and that his warriors feared and respected him. The superintendent of Indian affairs for Montana, J. A. Viall, could not abide Indians who wanted to live as Indians, and he took the official government viewpoint that Indians off reservations were "hostile" Indians: "Should these wandering Sioux under Sitting Bull (in connection with the hostile bands of Arapahos and Cheyennes, with whom they cooperate) persist in their efforts to molest and interfere with the progress of the Northern Pacific Railroad, I sincerely trust that a sufficient military force will be sent against them to severely and sufficiently punish them, even to annihilation, should the same unfortunately be necessary. They have had fair promises, which have in every particular been carried out when any of them would accept the bounty of the Government. They know just exactly what the Department is willing to do for them; they have the evidence of three-fifths of their original numbers that the promises made are ready to be fulfilled, and a continued warfare on their part must be taken as evidence that they wish to die fighting, and are on no terms willing to live at peace with the white race. These are the only Indians in the Northwest from whom any serious trouble may be entertained, and in the event of their continuing hostile, the interests of civilization and common humanity demand that they should be made powerless."

At the request of the owners of the Northern Pacific Railroad, the War Department in the spring of 1873 ordered a powerful military force to move out of Fort Rice to serve as "protective escort" for an engineering survey party in the valley of the Yellowstone. The expedition consisted of more than 1,500 officers and men—infantry, cavalry, and artillery—353 civilian mule drivers, guides, and interpreters, 275 wagons and ambulances, and 2,300 horses and mules. It was a force capable of annihilating all Indians who might dare resist the progress of the railroad through their country.

Commanding the expedition was General David S. Stanley, and the commander of the cavalry—the Seventh Regiment—was Lieutenant-Colonel George Armstrong Custer, who three years earlier had devoted his energies to killing Southern Plains Indians who dared defy the railroads' invasion of their buffalo lands. Stanley and Custer detested each other. "He [Custer] is a cold blooded, untruthful and unprincipled man," Stanley wrote his wife one week after the expedition started. "He is universally despised by all the officers of his regiment excepting his relatives and one or two sycophants. He brought a trader in the field without permission, carries an old negro woman, and cast iron cooking stove, and delays the march often by his extensive packing up in the morning." The trader was a friend of Custer's named Balarian, who had brought along a sutler's wagon full of whiskey. The cook was Mary, a former slave who with her husband, Ham, accompanied Custer on many of his expeditions. At about the same time that Stanley was writing his opinion of Custer, the latter wrote his wife Elizabeth: "General Stanley is acting very badly, drinking . . . Major Worth found Gen'l S. dead drunk on the ground outside the camp . . . lying there in a drunken stupor."

The conflict between the two officers came to a head when Custer assumed command during one of Stanley's drinking bouts; Stanley ordered Custer court-martialed, then rescinded the order. They settled their differences by separating, Custer taking the cavalry ahead of the main column and camping each evening some distance from headquarters. In a way, Custer had the edge on Stanley because the chief engineer of the Northern Pacific, Thomas Jefferson Rosser, had been a classmate at West Point. A Texan, Rosser rose to the rank of major general in the Confederate Army, and had been an opponent of Custer in the Shenandoah Valley. After the war, Rosser took a job as ax man with one of the Northern Pacific's surveying parties, and had worked his way up to chief engineer by 1873. "We rode in our saddles 'boot to boot,'" Custer later wrote of his reunion with Rosser, "climbed together unvisited cliffs, picked our way through trackless canyons, or sat about the same camp fire." The chief engineer and the ambitious cavalry officer enjoyed themselves, reminiscing over battles in which they had fought against each other only nine years before.

It was while he and Rosser were marching ahead of the main expedition that Custer was challenged by Sitting Bull and his warriors. In retrospect, the encounters might be considered dress rehearsals for scenes from their final meeting three years later on the Little Bighorn. The principal actors were present—Sitting Bull, Crazy Horse, Gall, Black Moon, several of the Cheyenne and Arapaho war leaders. With Custer were his brother Tom, his brother-in-law James Calhoun, his favorite scouts Bloody Knife and Charley Reynolds. Custer wrote an account of the running fights along the Yellowstone for a monthly periodical, *Galaxy Magazine*, putting himself in the role of a knight battling the forces of evil. From Sitting Bull's viewpoint, Custer and his troops and Rosser and his railroad surveyors were the forces of evil.

Litton Shields, a twenty-one-year-old Irish emigrant working with the railroad surveyors, told afterward of the expedition's first meeting with Indians near the mouth of the Powder. A group of warriors called out to the soldiers from across the river, demanding a parley with their Big Chief, General Stanley. "They wanted to know what we were doing here with such a big lot of teams and wagons." When Stanley came up with an interpreter, he refused to give them any explanation for the military invasion. According to Shields, the Indians shouted back angrily that they knew "we were going to build a railroad as they had formerly lived on the Platte River and when a big train like this came through, they built a railroad and drove all the buffalo away up here, so they would have no railroads up here." Provoked by Stanley's continued evasiveness, they opened fire at him. "They got the wrong range and fired over the heads of the group, wounding a poor private, in the rear."

On August 4, probably two or three days after this meeting, Custer came close to entrapment near the confluence of the Tongue and the Yellowstone. Using decoys, a trick that had worked successfully against cavalry before (notably at Fort Phil Kearny in 1866), the Indians drew Custer out of his camp in pursuit of six darting warriors. The action was a miniature projection of what would happen at the Little Bighorn three years later. As he would do then, Custer divided his force into three groups, Captain Myles Moylan commanding the reserves, Tom Custer one troop, and General Custer himself galloping after the decoys with only Bloody Knife and one cavalryman. As Custer swept past a screen of cottonwoods along the river, three hundred warriors dashed out upon his flank. Thanks to fast horses, he was able to outrun his pursuers, pull together his scattered groups of cavalry, and drive the Indians off with the superior fire power of repeating rifles over muzzle loaders and bows and arrows. In the action, however, the regiment's veterinarian, the sutler Balarian, and a cavalryman lost their lives.

Whether Sitting Bull was in the field that day is not known, but a week later near the mouth of the Bighorn he played a large role in a daring river crossing that almost caught Custer in a fatal encirclement. According to Indians who were present and told of the fighting long afterward, Sitting Bull showed his contempt for the cavalry that day by sitting on the riverbank and calmly smoking his pipe while rifle bullets sang around him. In his official report of the action, Custer claimed that he won a victory and that Sitting Bull "for once has been taught a lesson he will not soon forget."

Jay Cooke (Culver Pictures)

The cavalry and the remainder of the military expedition departed shortly afterward, however, and Sitting Bull and his people continued to live as free Indians in the Yellowstone country. Neither the surveyors nor the military returned the next year, nor the next, but in 1876 Custer returned and it was he, and not Sitting Bull, who forgot the lesson of the 1873 fight.

If Sitting Bull believed that it was the power of his warriors that kept the Northern Pacific out of the Yellowstone country after that fierce fight in August 1873, he was mistaken. A mild-mannered, cold-blue-eyed Philadelphia banker whose name was Jay Cooke was the man whose money and power had sent the surveyors and soldiers into Sitting Bull's country, and it was the collapse of Cooke's financial power that kept them out after 1873.

On June 3 of that year, track layers brought the railroad to the Missouri River just below Fort Abraham Lincoln. Jay Cooke named the little cluster of buildings at track's end Bismarck after the German chancellor in a desperate move to attract German financing and emigration. It was a futile gesture. On September 18, while Custer was marching his cavalry to winter quarters at Fort Abraham Lincoln, the doors of Jay Cooke's banking houses in the East were closed for lack of funds, precipitating the Panic of 1873 and bringing railroad construction in the West to a sudden halt. "As soon as we got back to Bismarck," said surveyor Litton Shields, "we were all turned loose to shift for ourselves."

Jay Cooke's entry upon the transcontinental railroad scene came late. He was too busy turning over money at a fast profit to himself (three million dollars a year) as chief financier of the Union during the Civil War to share in the easy booty from early railroads. Cooke had kept an eye on the Northwest, however, and when the time came he was ready to pyramid his fortune made from the war into even greater fortunes.

As we have seen, Asa Whitney was the pioneer planner of the Northern route beginning in 1845, giving the best years of his life to it before finally abandoning the dream and becoming a dairy farmer. After Whitney there was Isaac Stevens, who led the northernmost of the Pacific railroad surveys that were authorized and financed by the federal government in the 1850s. Stevens maneuvered himself into the governorship of Washington Territory, and hungered for the road as a means to build himself an empire in the Pacific Northwest. He was killed in action during the Civil War.

Josiah Perham, a visionary from Maine, was next; he was certain that he could convince a million Americans to invest one hundred dollars each in his People's Pacific Railway, to run from Maine to Oregon. The bankers laughed at Perham, but he attracted enough supporters to persuade Congress and Abraham Lincoln to charter the Northern Pacific Railroad Company from Lake Superior to Puget Sound. The government omitted the usual subsidy for construction costs, but made up for this by giving Perham a double land grant— 12,800 acres per mile of track built across states, 25,600 acres per mile across territories. Before he could realize his dream of a people's railroad, Perham's greedy partners pushed him out of control of the company; they did not wish to share the railroad with the people. Perham died, perhaps of a broken heart, in 1868.

Jay Cooke, along with a number of other avaricious plunderers, could not resist that enormous land grant of forty-seven million acres. Cooke totted it up in his mind—a realm vast enough to swallow all the New England states and still leave room enough for Maryland!

After having secret surveys made of the route in 1869, Cooke realized for the first time the enormity of the wealth that could be obtained from sales of timber, farmland, and city lots. He also found the directors of the Northern Pacific eager to obtain his expert services as financial agent. On January 1, 1870, he signed a contract making Jay Cooke & Company sole agent for the sale of Northern Pacific first-mortgage bonds. For this he drove a sharp bargain, receiving control of three fifths of the stock, twelve-percent profit on bond sales, and one-half ownership of a land company that would sell farms and town sites along the railroad. In exchange for all this, Cooke agreed to advance half a million dollars to the company for purchase of rails, rolling stock, and other materials needed to begin immediate construction.

One significant clause that Cooke slipped into his contract required the railroad company to pay the costs of advertising and promotion. If the directors had realized how far ahead of his time Cooke was as a huckster, they probably would have red-lined that paragraph. With a cool disdain for expenses, he began issuing colorful pamphlets and broadsides appealing to investors. Employing the most-imaginative publicists that money could buy, he distributed glowing articles about the Northern Pacific to newspapers and magazines, cleverly accompanying the ballyhoo with paid advertisements. During one week he saturated the nation with blaring spreads in 1,371 newspapers, and then settled down to 140 papers a month. He favored a generous use of exclamation points in his advertising: SAFE! PROFITABLE! PERMANENT! He also sought out testimonials from important persons—heroic generals of the Civil War, statesmen, clergymen, authors—and employed prominent orators to travel around the country extolling the virtues of the Northern Pacific.

One of the phrases that Cooke made popular was "the Fertile Belt," used to describe the richness of the land through which the railroad was to run. Accompanying this publicity was a map showing the broad swath of territory that would belong to the Northern Pacific, with isothermal lines drawn to indicate that the climate was similar to that of tidewater Virginia. The exaggerated language and the banana-curved shape of the Northern Pacific's future empire brought on a considerable amount of ridicule from sophisticates who began referring to "the Fertile Belt" as "Jay Cooke's Banana Belt."

Cooke also decided to do some lobbying in Washington, hoping that he might persuade Congress to tap the Treasury for a subsidy similar to those given to other transcontinental railroads. Although he was well acquainted with the venality of Washington politicians, he knew nothing of the stratagems perfected by the veteran railroad lobbyists who preceded him, the well-entrenched marauders such as Collis Huntington, Tom Scott, and Jay Gould.

In 1870, so many schemers were trying to obtain government funds to start new railroads in the West that most congressmen's pockets were stuffed with stocks and bonds. When Cooke approached the Speaker of the House, James G. Blaine, to determine how many bonds might be required to gain that powerful politician's good will, Blaine surprised Cooke by trying to sell him a batch of worthless bonds for a projected railroad in the Southwest. Rather than buy the useless paper, Cooke "loaned" Blaine thirty-three thousand dollars, a credit that was still on the books of Jay Cooke & Company the day it was declared bankrupt.

Because of the intense competition for funds in Washington, Cooke turned his efforts toward European investors. He was rebuffed by the Rothschilds, and just as he was making plans to open branches in several European cities, the Franco-Prussian War began, bringing on a collapse of most European money markets.

Meanwhile, track laying was progressing rapidly across Minnesota. The Northern Pacific reached Brainerd before the year's end, connecting with an incompleted road to St. Paul. Cooke had already obtained an interest in a road under construction from Duluth to St. Paul, and as it was already obvious that Minneapolis-St. Paul would dominate the state of Minnesota, he also sought control of the line southward from Brainerd. The rate of expenditures was rising more rapidly than the sale of bonds.

That inveterate traveler John Beadle rode out to see Brainerd soon after service began from Duluth. He found it far superior to the raw frontier towns on the Union Pacific. "It is built of the finest lumber, and stands in a forest of slender pines. Except between the railroad track and Front Street the native pines are left standing along the roadsides—the middle of the street only being cleared—and thus the side streets look like magnificent avenues." Beadle was also impressed by the Northern Pacific's bridge across the gorge of the Mississippi west of Brainerd. "The best bridge I have seen in the West," he said.

Under the railroad's free-spending president, J. Gregory Smith, money was soon pouring out at the rate of a million dollars a month, with bond sales beginning to slacken. In the hope of increasing income, Cooke organized a land department and turned his advertising toward prospective immigrants and land buyers. He also organized a deluxe excursion to the Red River of the North, inviting the most influential newspapermen in the country to impress them with the richness of the valley's soil. As the Northern Pacific's end of track was still many miles from Red River, the excursionists had to travel by stagecoach. The weather was good, and Cooke's land agents saw that "lunch boxes were always open and liquid refreshments were always on tap." But they did not reckon on the shrewdness of journalists such as Charles Dana, Bayard Taylor, and Samuel Bowles, who instead of listening to the prepared propaganda slipped off to talk with the few settlers they found along the banks of the river.

They heard complaints about mosquitoes, lack of markets, short summers, bitter-cold winters, and over and over again anxious comments about the Indians over in Dakota and Montana. What would the Indians do when the railroad builders began pushing their tracks onto reservations and buffalo ranges that had been promised them in perpetuity? The newspapermen listened, and few of them wrote any glowing prophecies about the immediate future of the Northern Pacific.

One of Jay Cooke's fond hobbies was to entertain visiting Indians from the West in a mansion he had built in Philadelphia's Chelten Hills. He called the place "Ogontz" after a Wyandotte chief he had known during his boyhood days in Sandusky, Ohio. The Cooke family's Sandusky homeplace had been built on Wyandotte land, dispossessing Ogontz and his people, but the chief returned occasionally to visit, and the Cookes would allow him to sleep in their barn. When Jay Cooke grew rich from banking and built his fifty-room mansion with its Italian garden, for some reason he named it Ogontz. And whenever Indians of any consequence passed through Philadelphia, Cooke always invited them to Ogontz, where they must have been awed by the immensity of his drawing room, which was large enough to enclose a village of tepees.

What motivated Cooke to make these gestures is not clear. His feelings for Indians certainly were not transferable to their lands that lay in the path of the Northern Pacific Railroad. He assumed, as did everyone else engaged in the building of railroads across the West, that the Interior Department's General Land Office would extinguish any Indian claims to land along the route of the Northern Pacific, whether it be unceded hunting areas or legally created reservations. He probably was not even aware of a Supreme Court decision that declared that "whenever a tract of land has been once legally appropriated to any purpose, it becomes, from that moment, severed from the mass of public lands, and no subsequent law, proclamation, or sale, will be construed to embrace or operate upon it." (A later decision of the court in 1875 was more specific, stating that railroad land grants did not apply to those lands "which Indians, pursuant to treaty stipulations, were left free to occupy.")

The Land Office, however, was the servant of the railways. As a contemporary critic said of that bureau, instead of the Land Office managing the railroads, the railroads managed the Land Office. "The great home department of Government [Interior Department] which should be the agent and representative of the people, is rapidly becoming an appurtenance of our great railways, and a mere bureau in their service. . . . The railroad companies always have their attorneys, and of the best class. They have access to the chiefs of divisions, and their constructions of the law are generally impressed upon the minds of the clerks having the cases in charge." Western Indians knew nothing of the law, and even if they had known, they would not have been able to employ competent counsel.

In 1872 the Northern Pacific's rails reached the James River in Dakota, and track's end became Jamestown. A considerable amount of the Dakota land claimed by the railroad (25,600 acres for each mile of track) was treaty land previously assigned to the Sisseton-Wahpeton Sioux. In its usual fashion, Congress cooperated with the railroad, simply extinguishing tribal title to it, making the cession legal by agreeing to pay the Sisseton-Wahpetons ten cents per acre and then handing the land over to the Northern Pacific. A similar arrangement was made with the Crow Indians in Montana; they were forced to give up a two-hundred-mile swath through their reservation for twenty-five thousand dollars.

Immediate conversion of these thousands of acres of valuable land into cash was impossible, however, and Jay Cooke & Company was running short of funds to continue construction to the Missouri River. Bond sales almost ceased, and to keep the market from collapsing, Cooke secretly bought back ninety percent of the bonds he had sold. Discovering that the road had overdrawn almost two million dollars, much of it going to a Minnesota senator and his friends in the contracting business, Cooke arranged for the ouster of President Smith, replacing him with George Cass from the Pennsylvania Railroad. But not even the experienced Cass was able to stem the outward flow of committed funds. Money was so short in late 1872 that the workmen building the road had to be paid in scrip. By the year's end, the Northern Pacific had overdrawn five and a half million dollars from Jay Cooke & Company, money that belonged to depositors in that highly respected banking house.

To make matters worse, the Credit Mobilier scandal broke early in 1873, bringing on a public revulsion against railroads and their stocks and bonds. In April, to replace the demand deposits taken from his banks, Cooke made a desper-

ate attempt to raise money by organizing a syndicate to sell
nine million dollars in Northern Pacific bonds with a fifty-
percent stock bonus. The railroad was nearing completion of
450 miles of track to the Missouri River, Cooke pointed out in
his prospectus, and another 165 miles was built in Washington Territory. With this trackage, the road had accumulated
ten million acres, more than a fifth of its land grant. In addition, emigrants by the hundreds were arriving to buy land.
But in the spring of 1873, there were few takers for any kind
of railroad bond offer.

In June, the track layers brought the Northern Pacific's
rails to the Missouri River, to a town named for the German
chancellor, and laid down their tools. There was no more
money for wages, no more money for iron. From Philadelphia, however, Cooke boldly cabled Otto von Bismarck,
inviting him to visit the city of the future named for him at the
railroad's end of track, vainly hoping that this would inspire German investors and emigrants to favor the Northern
Pacific.

In late summer of 1873, Cooke was too busy trying to
shore up his collapsing banking empire to pay much attention to news from the West. Railroad indebtedness had now
risen close to seven million dollars, and nervous depositors
were beginning to withdraw their accounts. It no longer
seemed important that Sitting Bull's Indians in the Yellowstone country were challenging his surveyors and their military escort. Indeed, if Sitting Bull had chanced to visit Philadelphia, Cooke probably would have invited him to share
cigars in his mansion, the castle named for the Wyandotte
chief Ogontz.

Cooke did invite his friend President Ulysses Grant to
visit Ogontz in the fall. On the evening of September 17, they
dined and drank together, smoked cigars in the enormous
drawing room, and the next morning Cooke awoke to find a
batch of alarming telegrams from his New York branch
warning him that demands upon deposits exceeded holdings.
Cooke excused himself from the President and rode to his
Philadelphia bank in his carriage, still confident that he
could weather the financial storm. Within an hour, however,
another telegram arrived. His New York branch had been

Northern Pacific track layers and work train (New-York Historical Society)

forced to close. It was all over for Jay Cooke & Company. Before noon, the great banking house was declared bankrupt; before the day's end, banks and railroads and the stocks of mighty business establishments were collapsing across America. It was the most precipitant and widespread economic disaster since the birth of the republic.

For seven years the rails of the Northern Pacific's end of track at Bismarck would redden with rust. Nearby at Fort Abraham Lincoln, George Custer drilled the troops of his Seventh Cavalry, and in 1876, the year of the nation's Centennial, he led them to disaster along the Little Bighorn in Sitting Bull's Yellowstone country. Sitting Bull survived, but had to flee to exile in Canada. When he returned, the buffalo were gone from the Yellowstone, replaced by the Iron Horses of the Northern Pacific. In 1883, Sitting Bull attended the ceremonies celebrating completion of the railroad. He made a speech in the language of his people, but, as we shall see, something was lost in the translation.

CHAPTER 11

Elegance on the Western Rails

Iɴ 1876, the year of the nation's hundredth anniversary, thousands of Americans turned their backs on the depressed state of the economy and journeyed to Philadelphia to view the Centennial Exhibition. There, among all the wonders of the new industrial age, they could explore George Pullman's latest model of a hotel on wheels, the "President." This railroad car foreshadowed a new elegance in transcontinental travel that was to come during the last years of the nineteenth century.

Pullman, whose innovations were usually a full decade ahead of the men who ran the railroads, spared no expense in outfitting the "President" with exquisite appointments, elaborately filigreed woods, tastefully designed fabrics, flamboyant chandeliers, efficient washrooms, and a kitchen equipped with a mammoth roaster and broiler. While Jay Gould and his rivals manipulated railroad stocks and bonds with total disregard for the public's transportation needs, the true railroaders persisted in their efforts to improve services. Transcontinental travelers demanded speed, safety, and comfort. Impatient Americans bound westward for the Pacific Coast were unwilling to tolerate the tedious stops and transfers, the numerous delays caused by dangerous accidents, or the bodily distress that had to be endured while getting there.

During the Centennial celebrations of 1876, a pair of New York theatrical promoters, Henry C. Jarrett and Harry Palmer, decided to prove not only that the regular seven-day travel time between New York and San Francisco could be cut in half, but also that the journey could be accomplished in elegant splendor. By some miracle they persuaded five railroads to cooperate in clearing their tracks for Jarrett &

Palmer's Transcontinental Express, thus eliminating the usual four transfers. Publisher James Gordon Bennett agreed to pay half the costs in exchange for exclusive rights to news coverage in his *New York Herald,* and the promoters offered sixteen reservations for sale at five hundred dollars, which would cover the buyers' expenses en route, a week's board and lodging at San Francisco's Grand Palace Hotel, and return by ordinary train to New York. The tickets sold out immediately.

Among the passengers were three Shakespearean actors who were to present *Henry V* in a San Francisco theater the day after their expected arrival, two British Army officers, an English magazine illustrator, and correspondents for London and Paris newspapers. The train consisted of three cars—a Pullman hotel car "elegantly upholstered with hard wood elaborately carved and ornamented," a day coach, and a combination mail and baggage car painted a brilliant red and outfitted with a kitchen and ice-box.

Shortly after midnight on Thursday, June 1, bundles of that morning's edition of the *Herald* were loaded into the baggage car, and passengers began boarding to the salutes of fireworks and a brass band. The train pulled out on schedule promptly at 1:00 A.M., and twenty-one hours later rolled into Chicago's Madison Street depot. Despite a heavy rainfall, an enthusiastic crowd of railroad fans was there to greet the train with more fireworks. While fresh supplies of ice and provisions were being taken aboard, the crowd became so demonstrative that thirty policemen had difficulty maintaining order. At 10:45 the Lightning Train was moving westward out of Chicago, and all through the night across Illinois and Iowa the passengers could see bonfires burning brightly at every road crossing—signals of encouragement from admiring town and country folk.

The next morning, at Omaha, another cheering throng awaited them, but they stopped only long enough to fill water tanks. As soon as the Transcontinental Express reached the level plains, the engineer increased speed to forty-five miles per hour, then fifty, and over one long straight section hurtled his excited passengers across Nebraska at one mile per minute. Crowds waiting at ranch stops barely caught a glimpse of the train they had traveled miles to see.

At Sidney they were three hours fifty-two minutes ahead of schedule, and slowed down so that cowboys could gallop alongside, "firing a *feu de joie* from their navy revolvers." That evening at 10:40 the Lightning Train stopped in Cheyenne for five minutes while almost the entire population of the town cheered so lustily that they drowned out the crashing notes of a welcoming band.

A telegram waiting there for Henry Jarrett brought bad news. During the day a flash flood near Ogden had destroyed a section of track. Laborers were at work replacing ties and rails but there was no certainty that repairs could be completed by the time the Transcontinental Express arrived.

Throughout the following day the nation waited for news of the express. Would the washout spoil the race with time? At 8:30 P.M. on June 3, telegrams arriving in San Francisco and New York announced that the train had just passed Winnemucca, Nevada. Although it had been forced to travel slowly across the rebuilt tracks, it was still ahead of schedule.

Before leaving New York on Thursday, Jarrett had promised his passengers that they would lunch together in San Francisco on Sunday. He brought them in at 9:39 A.M., in time for a late breakfast, after a record run of eighty-three hours thirty-nine minutes. San Franciscans, eager for such rail service, turned out en masse to welcome them, as one correspondent put it, "like heroes from a battlefield."

To Jarrett and Palmer's successful combination of safety, elegance, and speed, the owners of the cooperating railroads responded with appropriate expressions of Centennial patriotism. They pondered the practicalities of regular passenger service based upon the Transcontinental Express's three-and-a-half-day schedule, but they could see no added profit in it. Not until fifty years later was such service instituted on a daily basis, about the time that commercial aviation began establishing transcontinental passenger routes. Today, in the 1970s, Amtrak offers passage from New York to San Francisco in seventy-four hours (if the trains run on time) on an obsolete system that offers neither safety nor elegance.

About a year after the running of the Transcontinental Express, that remarkable pair of nineteenth-century publishers, Frank and Miriam Leslie, undertook the most lavish of all transcontinental excursions. The Leslies were not attempting to set any speed records; the purpose of their journey was to advertise their string of weekly and monthly publications. At the same time, however, they demonstrated that railroads had made it possible to explore America's Wild West in an elegant manner, that is, if one had plenty of money.

From New York to Chicago they rode in one of Webster Wagner's Palace cars. Wagner was George Pullman's chief competitor, and was constantly involved in lawsuits brought by Pullman for infringement of patents. For years Wagner attempted to surpass his rival with arched ceilings and rococo furnishings, brocaded draperies and Oriental fabrics. He installed large divans, sofas, and mirrors in his cars. Pullman could not abide competitors, however, and finally bought out Wagner.

For their tour of the West, the Leslies took along enormous quantities of champagne, a larder of gourmet foods, and a retinue of writers, photographers, and artists to record their adventures for later publication. At Chicago, George Pullman was waiting to greet them and switch the entire expedition into the "President," the hotel on wheels that he had demonstrated at the Centennial Exhibition. "We are greeted on entering by two superb pyramids of flowers," Miriam Leslie wrote. "We are impressed with the smooth and delightful motion, and are told it is owing to a new invention, in the shape of paper wheels applied to this car." She was referring to the Allen paper wheel adopted by Pullman: a disk made of layers of paperboard glued and pressed together was fitted inside a wheel so that it bore the weight of the axle.

At Cheyenne, the Magic City of the Plains, the party stopped to explore the sights. In 1877, only nine years after four-fifths of its population rolled with its Hell on Wheels to Laramie City, the town was bustling again with what Miriam Leslie described as "wild, rough frontiersmen—miners, teamsters, drovers, Mexicans, scouts, ferocious to look upon, but lamb-like in demeanor toward quiet strangers." Cheyenne now had "a good brick hotel, five churches, a courthouse and jail, a City Hall and schoolhouse, two

theaters, and such a number of establishments openly pro-
claiming themselves concert and gambling saloons that we
ceased to count them, and prepared instead to visit them."

Visit them she did, along with Frank and their writers
and artists, and for the next several weeks the millions of
readers of Leslie's numerous periodicals were treated to a
barrage of stories and pictures of the romantic West as it
could be experienced by anyone with money enough to buy
a ticket on a railroad train, preferably with parlor-car or
sleeping-car privileges. Cowboys and Indians, the exotic
wonders of California, the wickedness of Nevada mining

*Above: Departure of the Frank Leslies on
their luxurious train tour of the West
(Culver Pictures) Left: Miriam Leslie (New
York Public Library Picture Collection)
Right: Washroom on the Leslie Excursion
Train (New York Public Library Picture
Collection)*

towns, the mysteries of Utah's Mormons, Colorado scenery—the entire panorama of the West was depicted for all the world to see from the elegant base of the Leslie Excursion Train.

In the late 1870s the public also learned of new routes through the West, and in spite of the constant siphoning of funds by greedy railroad owners, there seemed to be enough money left over to smooth some of the rough roadbeds and to add better rolling stock. Food service along the way was also improving, thanks mainly to the energies of a worthy young man named Frederick Henry Harvey, who before the end of his career was acclaimed the "Civilizer of the West."

Fred Harvey was English-born; he had arrived in the United States in 1850, at the age of fifteen, with two pounds in his pocket. He worked as a dishwasher in New York until he saved enough money to move on to New Orleans. There he learned about fine foods in famous hotel dining rooms, but soon became restless and traveled upriver to St. Louis, where he opened his own restaurant. The Civil War and a dishonest partner combined to wipe out his business, but he found employment in 1862 as a clerk on the first mail car running on the Hannibal & St. Joseph Railroad. He was in Ellsworth, Kansas, during the boom days of the cattle trade, working as a full-time railroad cattle agent and part-time hotel and ranch owner. His duties required him to travel back and forth across the West, and his epicurean tastes revolted at the food served along the way. In 1875 he opened two dining rooms at stops on the Kansas Pacific, but the next year he decided to switch to the Santa Fe. In Harvey's opinion, the men running that railroad were a dynamic group, determined to extend their tracks to the Pacific, and Harvey wanted to go with them.

One of Harvey's ideas was to convert the railroad eating stops into fine hotels with first-class dining rooms so that passengers might stop for a day or more on their journeys and see the Wild West from luxurious surroundings. He opened the first Fred Harvey House in Topeka, serving high-quality food on tables covered with snowy white linen and serviced with fine silverware. The venture was an instant success. According to one newspaper account, "traffic was blocked and it became absolutely necessary for the Santa Fe to open similar houses at other points that the West might not be settled all in one spot." The Santa Fe's management did encourage Harvey to open similar establishments, but before doing so he shrewdly insisted upon a contract. He demanded the exclusive right to manage and operate the eating houses and hotel facilities along the Santa Fe, with the profits all going to him. In addition, the railroad was to furnish fuel, ice, and water for the operation of the facilities and provide free transportation for supplies and employees of Fred Harvey.

By 1883 Harvey was operating seventeen eating stops along the Santa Fe, and their reputation for quality spread across the West. He traveled constantly up and down the line, searching out fresh butter and vegetables, tender lambs and quail, mountain trout and prairie chickens for his customers. He also made rigid inspections of the restaurants. If he found a carelessly set table he would jerk the cloth off, spilling dishes and silverware onto the floor. Then he would fire the manager. On a visit to his Raton, New Mexico, establishment, he cashiered practically the entire dining-room staff. Not being able to find enough male waiters on short notice, he employed several young women, and thus began the famed "Harvey Girls."

The handsome waitresses proved to be so popular that Harvey gradually replaced all his male waiters with females, advertising in Eastern newspapers for "young women, 18–30 years of age, of good character, attractive and intelligent." Because so many of them were immediately claimed as brides in the male-dominated West, Harvey added to their contracts a clause requiring them to forfeit half their wages if they married before the end of their first year of employment. He dressed them in black dresses with white collars and aprons, and housed them in dormitories under the care of matrons. During the last quarter of the nineteenth century, the Harvey Girls were the belles of the Southwest, and the subjects of a considerable number of legends, songs, and bad poems such as:

Harvey Houses don't you savvy; clean across the old Mohave.
On the Santa Fe they've strung 'em like a string of Indian beads.
We all couldn't eat without 'em but the slickest things about 'em
Is the Harvey skirts that hustle up the feeds.

Harvey Girls in front of a Santa Fe Harvey House (The Fred Harvey Company)
Inset: Fred Harvey (The Fred Harvey Company)

> I have viewed the noblest shrines in Italy
> And gazed upon the richest mosques in Turkey—
> But the fairest of all sights, it seems to me,
> Was the Harvey girl I saw in Albuquerque.

No matter how good service was in his dining rooms, Fred Harvey was always seeking ways to improve it. He convinced the Santa Fe's managers that passenger-train schedules must allow thirty minutes for dining stops, the time never to be shortened to adjust schedule delays. To ensure that all the travelers enjoyed their thirty minutes, he arranged for conductors to pass through approaching trains long before they reached a Harvey House, taking down each passenger's menu selection. The orders were then totaled and passed forward to the engineer, who used whistle signals to inform the Harvey House manager ahead what meals to have ready. In this way, as soon as the passengers entered the dining room, Harvey Girls would be ready with the first courses. "Meals by Fred Harvey" soon made the Santa Fe a popular route for

travelers across the West, forcing the other transcontinental
railroads to upgrade their dining services.

About a dozen years after the Eastern newspaper
reporter Charles Leland predicted in 1866 that the Pacific
railroad would become the *grand route* for the world, travelers from everywhere were crisscrossing the West. Conductors could pick up bits of extra money by furnishing lists
of their famous passengers to representatives of the Associated Press at certain stations along their routes, and the
names would be telegraphed ahead to California newspapers. Among the passengers' names that made news in the
1870s and 1880s were Oscar Wilde, Rudyard Kipling, Henry
Ward Beecher, John C. Frémont, Tom Thumb, Bret Harte,
an assortment of U.S. Presidents, distinguished military officers, various members of the British Parliament, and travel
writers Helen Hunt Jackson, Emily Faithfull, and Richard
Harding Davis.

Oscar Wilde's railroad tour of the West in 1882 aroused
the curiosity of virtually all the inhabitants of every town and
city that he visited. He was then only twenty-seven, the
emissary of a new cult that he called aestheticism. Wearing
his hair to his shoulders, he dressed in black velvet knee
breeches, black silk stockings, silver-buckled shoes, and
white lace cravat—a costume that was strange indeed on
trains crossings the rugged West. To top all this off, Wilde
often wore a sunflower in his lapel and carried a symbolic
lily.

At Corinne, Utah, one of the last of the Hell on Wheels
towns, a crowd of practical jokers, dressed in costumes
roughly approximating Wilde's, tried to board his car, but
were repelled by alert trainmen. At Denver, Colorado, however, the fun-loving editor of the *Tribune*, Eugene Field, was
more successful with his prank. As soon as Field learned
what train Wilde was arriving on, he dressed himself like the
visiting lecturer, using a wig of curly auburn hair, a brilliant
cravat, a rose-colored handkerchief in the outer pocket of his
coat, a fur-collared overcoat, and a broad-brimmed felt hat.
Then he drove to a station outside Denver and boarded a
train running just ahead of Wilde's. As Field had hoped, a reception committee was waiting at the Denver station, and

when he stepped off the train he was hailed with a cheer, to which he responded with a grave bow. He was conducted to a carriage, and as it drove through the streets of Denver he lounged in the seat in a studied imitation of Wilde's manner, waving languidly to the cheering crowds along the sidewalks. When the carriage stopped in front of the *Tribune* office for a scheduled interview, Field was recognized by one of his own reporters, and the hoax ended, to the delight of the editor and the mortification of the Wilde reception committee, which had to hasten back to the station to meet the real Oscar Wilde.

Wilde's main complaint about train travel in the West was the constant bustle and confusion at stations. "Everybody seems in a hurry to catch a train," he said. "This is a state of things which is not favorable to poetry or romance. Had Romeo or Juliet been in a constant state of anxiety about trains, or had their minds agitated by the question of return tickets, Shakespeare could not have given us those lovely balcony scenes which are so full of poetry and pathos."

When he was asked if he found any beauty in America, he replied that there was beauty in America only where Americans had not attempted to create it. "Perhaps the most beautiful part of America is the West," he said, "to reach which, however, involves a journey by rail of six days, racing along tied to an ugly tin-kettle of a steam engine. I found but poor consolation for this journey in the fact that the boys who infest the cars and sell everything that one can eat—or should not eat—were selling editions of my poems vilely printed on a kind of gray blotting paper, for the low price of ten cents."

Rudyard Kipling, who traveled the *grand route* across the West a few years after Wilde, was appalled by the open tracks at railroad stations and the carelessness with which Americans crossed them in front of approaching trains. "Long use has made the nation familiar and even contemptuous towards trains to an extent which God never intended. Women who in England would gather up their skirts and scud timorously over a level crossing in the country, here talk dress and babies under the very nose of cow-catchers, and little children dally with the moving car in a manner horrible to behold."

Like all Pullman passengers, Kipling found it somewhat difficult to undress lying down, and commented that it was "easier to get out of a full theatre than to leave a Pullman in haste." He was impressed by the profusion of nickel plating, plush, and damask, but did not think they compensated for the overheating and lack of ventilation that prevailed on most of the cars in which he traveled. He also worried about the skills of the trainmen, the condition of the brakes, and especially the tunnels, which reminded him of mine shafts shored up with match sticks. He was unnerved when he heard water and bits of stone falling from tunnel ceilings onto the roof of his car. The scenery along the Western railways he found sublime, but he said that the real wonderland was inside the trains. "We were a merry crew. One gentleman announced his intention of paying no fare and grappled the conductor, who neatly cross-buttocked him through a double plate-glass window. His head was cut open in four or five places. A doctor on the train hastily stitched up the biggest gash, and he was dropped at a wayside station, spurting blood at every hair—a scarlet-headed and ghastly sight. The conductor guessed that he would die and volunteered the information that there was no profit in monkeying with the North Pacific Railway."

Typical of American writers who explored the West by train was Richard Harding Davis. "An Eastern man is apt to cross the continent for the first time with mixed sensations of pride at the size of his country," he said, "and shame at his ignorance concerning it." Davis not only rode Pullmans on the transcontinental railroads, he also ventured onto out-of-the-way roads to experience mixed freight-and-passenger trains that "rolled off across the prairie, rocking from side to side like a line of canal-boats in a rough sea."

He regretted missing the excitement of earlier railroad travel when he might have seen gunfighters or train robbers. "I met the men who lynched them or who remembered them, but not the men themselves." Although there was no more shooting at buffalo from train windows in the 1880s, Davis witnessed a substitute for that sport on a Texas train: "The young man with the broad shoulders and sun-browned face and wide sombrero in the seat in front raises the car window, and begins to shoot splinters out of the passing telegraph poles with the melancholy and listless air of one who is performing a casual divertisement."

One of the most observant of foreign travelers in the 1880s was Baroness Alexandra Gripenberg of Finland, who came to America to attend an international women's congress and to study the suffrage movement. In Chicago she joined a group of schoolteachers bound for California aboard a Pullman car. "The women immediately took off their best hats and dresses, and the men put off their frock coats and derbies, and everyone put on a dustproof suit made of light cloth, and caps. We did not have to be afraid of buffaloes, grizzly bears, and Indians, that we knew—no, heat and dust would be our worst enemies on the western prairies, 'the plains' as they are called."

From her car window she was spellbound by the sights, sounds, and odors of the West. "A peculiar, sharp smell of hay, dust, and cattle strikes one. Some pleasant smells are interfused with it, too, just like the fragrance of dried spices. The whole endless sea of grass with its gentle, wave-like contours has a monotonous, grayish gleam of color; gray buffalo grass sways there and also whitish-yellow prairie grass; white and mottled cattle stand motionless in the heat; here and there the light felt hats worn low over the head by bold-eyed cowboys on horseback flash by. . . . All noises seem to bound back from that silent, soft sea of grass over which rests an unexplainable, passive sadness. . . ."

Alexandra Gripenberg was delighted with the comfort of the Pullman "with its two sofas which could be changed into beds," the large container that was continually filled with ice water, and the general cleanliness and order. Her only complaint was "the lack of a door or curtain in front of the washroom, and generally there was a row of seventeen people in front of it with their hand towels, waiting their turn, watching how their neighbor washed his ears."

The Pullman washroom was a grievance to many other travelers, such as Helen Hunt Jackson, who disliked having to stand in line in dishabille. "The only drawbacks we found to be the scramble in the morning for the washing apparatus," commented a touring Englishman, "and there seemed to be some difficulty about the ladies' hair-drying which was sometimes performed rather too publicly." And according to George Sala, still another problem confronted travelers crossing the West during winter: "Frequently during our journey the water in the toilet rooms on board the car was frozen, and washing was an impossibility."

On the whole, however, passengers both foreign and domestic admired the elegance and comfort of the improved Pullman cars. Henry Hussey Vivian, member of Parliament, compared the car he traveled in to a yacht and declared that the beds were as good as any he had ever slept in. He was especially pleased by the "saloon or observatory, with a sofa and arm chairs, plate-glass windows the full size of the sides and ends, and a door opening on to the outside platform, capable of holding four chairs, and enclosed by an iron railing. . . . we sit on the platform for hours in this fine climate and have an unbroken view of the scenery."

Several travelers who found the luxurious Pullmans comfortable for sleeping grumbled about the discomfort of the seats after the beds were folded away. "The attempts of passengers to rest their heads by curling themselves up on the seats or lying crosswise," said Phil Robinson, "are as pathetic as they are often absurd, and give a Palace car the appearance on a hot afternoon, of the ward in some Hospital for Spinal Complaints."

"It would be simply impossible," said another British tourist, "for human nature to travel such immense distances, without the comforts and conveniences which the Pullman cars supply." As for privacy-loving Helen Hunt Jackson, she found the Pullman drawing-room cars helpful in relieving the wear and tear of railroad travel caused by too much contact with people. "Be as silent, as unsocial, as surly as you please, you cannot avoid being more or less impressed by the magnetism of every human being in the car. Their faces attract or repel; you like, you dislike, you wonder, you pity, you resent, you loathe. In the course of twenty-four hours you have expended a great amount of nerve force, to no purpose."

Travel writer Emily Faithfull also favored drawing-room cars "in which for a few extra dollars, you enjoy plenty of space and better air, magnificent upholstery, dressing-rooms, iced water, grand mirrors, etc." On her first journey across the West she fretted over the lack of privacy after the sleeping-car beds were made up, and resented "being packed up for the night in this promiscuous fashion." Eventually, however, she became reconciled to sleeping cars. "The long journeys across the Plains," she said, "would be impossible without the rest it affords, and at last I learned to slumber as peacefully in a Pullman sleeper as in an ordinary bed, and almost to prefer night to day journeys."

Helen Hunt Jackson, however, did not agree with her English counterpart. "I dislike the sleeping-car section more than I ever have disliked, ever shall dislike, or ever can dislike any thing in the world," she said, and went on to describe the torments of trying to dress while sitting cross-legged, of spilling toiletries on her clothing, of losing a shoe, and then, when the car gave a sudden lurch, of falling head first through the bed curtains upon an outraged English gentleman who happened to be passing in the aisle.

In 1886 George Pullman introduced a "vestibuled" train, enclosing the ends of his cars with elastic diaphragms on steel frames. When the cars were connected, the diaphragms pressed firmly against each other. The resulting vestibule eliminated dust, cinders, and blasts of hot or cold air, made it possible for passengers to move easily from car to car, prevented swaying, and reduced the danger of cars telescoping in the event of a collision.

A French traveler in 1888 described the vestibule as "a concertina-pleated arrangement . . . You pass from one carriage to the other without having to expose yourself to cold or rain; children may play about and run from carriage to carriage with perfect safety. Everything has been thought out, everything has been carried out that could conduce to the comfort of travelers, and unless the Americans invent a style of dwelling that can be moved from one place to another (and they will come to this, no doubt, in time), I do not see that one could desire, or even imagine, more agreeable, more elegant, or safer railway carriages."

Many visitors from abroad, in recording their experiences while crossing America, made interesting comparisons with the railways of their own countries. Most were awed by the long distances covered by rails across the West, but generally agreed that the tracks had been built too rapidly. To these seasoned travelers, the roadbeds appeared crudely constructed, accounting for bumpier rides than those they had experienced in Britain or on the European continent.

One Briton commented on the unannounced departure of trains from stations along the transcontinental railroads. "This silent, casual departure of trains is a perpetually recurring surprise to me. Would it be contrary to republican principles to ring a bell for the warning of passengers? One result, however, of this surreptitious method of making off, is that no one is ever left behind. . . . In England people are being perpetually 'left behind' because they think such a catastrophe to be impossible. In America they are never left behind, because they are always certain they will be."

American trainmen also were said to be ruder than those abroad. "When a railway servant has succeeded in insulting you, he is quite proud, and plumes himself on his smartness," said the Frenchman Paul Blouët. "He looks at his mates and seems to say: 'Did you hear how I spoke up to him?' He would be afraid of lowering himself by being polite. In his eyes politeness is a form of servility, and he imagines that by being rude to well-bred people, he puts himself on a footing with them, and carries out the greatest principle of democracy, equality."

The remarkable efficiency with which train luggage could be checked from city to city for thousands of miles across America brought high praise from Walter Marshall, a much-traveled Englishman. "The baggage-man," he said, "will take the boxes you wish to transport and fasten to each a leather strap, to each of which is affixed a small brass plate, which is numbered, and has 'Boston' and 'San Francisco' plainly stamped on to it; at the same time he will hand over to you two duplicate brass plates, having numbers corresponding with those of the checks which have been attached to your boxes." Marshall was irritated, however, by Westerners who gathered around him to stare whenever he chose to step off the train in his knickerbockers, which "disclosed a fine view of my calves." Nor did he care for the American Iron Horse. "Massive and clumsy-looking, it has a monster black funnel resembling a wine-strainer, very wide at the top and tapering toward the bottom. It is called a 'smoke-stack,' not a funnel. In like manner, you seldom hear a engine called an 'engine' but a 'locomotive.'"

And some foreigners liked nothing about train travel across the American continent. After a trip from New Orleans to California on the Southern Pacific, William Saunders wrote: "I am bound to say that I greatly prefer the English carriages. . . I would rather spend seven days and nights in a European first-class carriage than in a Pullman car." He went on to accuse American railroads of introducing the Pullman car system for the purpose of enabling them to charge high rates. "No distinction of class is recognized in American railway legislation, but by providing special carriages at a separate cost the railway companies get over the limits of the maximum charge."

One student of railway statistics of the period, a tourist who traveled extensively both in the United States and in Europe, declared that, in proportion to the number of passengers carried, railroads in the United States killed sixteen times more passengers than did those in the United Kingdom. He also found that American trains ran at much faster speeds, but that European trains were more punctual, and in general American railroads charged higher fares than did those abroad.

Until well into the 1880s the transcontinental railroads continued the practice of supplying food service at scheduled eating stops. Except for the Santa Fe's Harvey Houses ("we were served a fine dinner made up of French foods," said Alexandra Gripenberg) the quality varied from stop to stop. Excellent food was prepared on special excursion trains such as the Leslies': "We sip our oyster soup, discuss turkey and antelope steak and quail, and trifle with ice cream and *cafe noir*." And during the 1880s the more elaborate drawing-room cars introduced a buffet at one end, where, according to Emily Faithfull, "good bread and butter, cold meats, tea and coffee can be obtained whenever passengers require."

Traveling Britons missed their tea, and most refused to drink it cold. Such tea might be all right for sportsmen out hunting buffalo, said George Sala, but on board a transcontinental railway car it was "simply a mockery, a delusion, and a snare." Phil Robinson was not only unhappy about a lack of tea, he felt that scheduled stops at eating houses were unsuitable for travelers who usually had irregular appetites. "Some people *can* not eat when they have the opportunity, and when they *could* eat, do not get it. Some day, no doubt, a horrible cannibalic outrage on the cars will awaken the directors to the peril of carrying starving passengers, and the luxury of the hotel-car will be instituted."

With more and more prosperous travelers visiting the West, it was inevitable that tourist traps should begin to flourish at every railroad stop. From moss-agates in Cheyenne to Indian jewelry, fabrics, and pottery in the Southwest, the sightseers were assailed with a multitude of gimcracks and relics, most of them worthless, the peddlers persistent and annoying. And along with these wares came the unrestrained advertisers, splashing painted signs on walls, posts, trees, and rocks, precursors of the forthcoming despoilment of the Garden of the West brought on by the proliferation of railroads.

As early as 1880, traveler George Sala was protesting against "the coarseness and indecency of the quack-salvers' announcements. . . which alarm and disgust the eye at every turn. . . the loveliest spots in the scenery of this vast continent are blighted with these loathsome stigmata—the portents of shameless imposture and rapacious greed for gold. . . . From New York to San Francisco you are pursued by the quack and his revolting lotions, pills and plasters." The age of elegance on the transcontinental railroads ended almost before it began, and by the time most Americans now living were born, it existed only in the memories of the very old and in the hyperbole of travel brochures distributed halfheartedly by the dying railroads.

CHAPTER 12

The Immigrant

"**E**VERY FOREIGN labourer landing on our shores is economically valued at 1,500 dollars," a government report estimated in the 1870s. "He rarely comes empty-handed. The Superintendent of the Castle Garden Emigration Depot has stated that a careful inquiry gave an average of 100 dollars, almost entirely in coin, as the money property of each man, woman, and child landed in New York." The bureaucrat was arguing in favor of more government land grants and construction funding for more railroads across the West, and went on to calculate that in less than ten years the railroads would attract enough immigrants to add $4.8 billion to the wealth of the nation.

Immigrants were needed by the millions in the 1870s to keep the Western railroads financially afloat, and during the last quarter of the nineteenth century a veritable dragnet was cast across Europe in search of people who were sturdy, hardy, and industrious enough to bear the drudgery of an agrarian frontier existence and yet had enough money in their pockets to buy railroad acreage. "It is difficult to make progress anywhere without capital," the Chicago, Burlington & Quincy Railroad's land department bluntly advised prospective immigrants, "and nowhere is the need of money more keenly felt than in a new settlement . . . a few hundred dollars to start with—sufficient to meet the expense of putting up at first a low-cost house, to purchase a pair of horses, a wagon, cow, pigs, tools, etc., and such outfit as is needful for a beginner and his family." (The Chicago, Burlington & Quincy was a combination of several smaller railroads owning extensive land grants throughout the Plains states from Iowa to Colorado and Montana. Its land department was one of the most aggressive in the West.)

Almost every handbook prepared by the Western railroads for prospective buyers of their land warned foreigners not to come unless they were willing to work, possessed a pair of stout arms, and knew how to make a living at agriculture or some mechanical trade. "Persons accustomed to living by their wits alone are not wanted. . . . Every one of the so-called learned professions is overstocked. There are more doctors, apothecaries, lawyers, literary men, architects, teachers, clergymen, and other men of liberal education in the United States than can make a decent living . . . even in the Western States, where their services are less required, the supply, though not of a high order, exceeds the demand. . . . Clerks ought not to think of coming unless they have thoroughly made up their minds to lay down the pen and to take to the spade or the plough."

And of course they stressed the advantages of the Western over the Eastern states, which were depicted as being deficient of all opportunities. Go West, the guidebooks told the immigrants, where a working man not only can earn more but will spend less for the necessaries of life. There was no truth in this, but the railroad land agents learned the art of false advertising early in the game. They also touted the low-cost fares on immigrant trains, but for an immigrant crossing the continent with a large family, the $26.80 fare from New York to Omaha and then perhaps more than that to the final destination could wipe out a lifetime's savings. It was no bargain, either, considering the nature of immigrant trains, with bodies packed ninety to a car on hard board seats, the trains constantly shunted onto sidetracks to make way for expresses and freights, so immigrant passage usually required ten days from Omaha to San Francisco. And once they reached their western destination, they found that there were no low-cost fares back to the East. If they did not like the West, they had to pay full rates or stay where they were.

The immigrants caught only fleeting glimpses of the elegance of drawing-room and parlor cars; indeed, the railroads, which boasted that there were no separate classes of passenger service in democratic America, seemed to conspire to keep immigrants and Pullman passengers out of each other's view as much as possible. They did not entirely succeed in

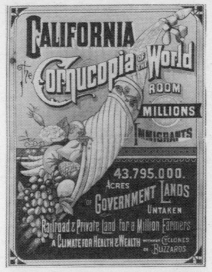

California put in its bid early for immigrants
(*The New-York Historical Society*)

this, especially at the larger railroad stations, and the general public was so appalled at what they saw that in 1873 a bill was introduced in Congress to forbid the railroads to transport human beings as if they were livestock. Nothing was done, however. Too many members of Congress were either lackeys of the railroad owners or feared their power.

In 1879, a twenty-nine-year-old Scottish writer named Robert Louis Stevenson journeyed on immigrant cars from New York to California. Stevenson had met Fanny Vandegrift Osbourne in France, fell in love with her, and decided to follow her to the Pacific Coast. At that time he had achieved little fame and lacked sufficient funds to travel by Pullman. He described himself as an "amateur emigrant," viewing his fellow travelers sympathetically yet realistically. "They were mostly lumpish fellows, silent and noisy, a common combination; somewhat sad I should say, with an extraordinary poor taste in humour, and little interest in their fellow creatures beyond that of a cheap and merely external curiosity." Among the foreigners in his car was a German family and "a knot of Cornish miners who kept grimly by themselves, one

reading the New Testament all day long through steel spec-
tacles, the rest discussing privately the secrets of their old-
world, mysterious race."

In the car ahead of Stevenson were about fifty Chinese,
also bound for California, and he reflected upon the irony of
immigrants from hungry Europe and hungry China meeting
face to face in the American West. "As we continued to steam
westward toward the land of gold, we were continually passing other emigrant trains upon the journey east; and these
were as crowded as our own . . . whenever we met them,
the passengers ran on the platform and cried to us through
the windows, in a kind of wailing chorus to 'come back.' On
the plains of Nebraska, in the mountains of Wyoming, it was
still the same cry, and dismal to my heart, 'Come back!' That
was what we heard by the way about the good country we
were going to."

One of Stevenson's compatriots, Lady Hardy, recorded at
about this same time her sudden meeting with a trainload of
immigrants as she stepped off her Pullman car at the Omaha
station. "The platform overflows with them, they are everywhere, all with a more or less travel-stained look. Having
been penned up so long in such close quarters they are glad
to get out and stretch their legs and rinse the dust from their
grimy faces. Swarthy men with bare arms are splashing
about in buckets; some are performing their ablutions under
the pump, or in anything that comes handy. . . . The women
as a rule look faded, wan, and anxious; the men energetic and
strong, confident and assured, with a bright, never-say-die
look upon their faces. . . . It is a strange gathering, that flock
of varying nationalities, all bound on one adventurous er-
rand—a wave of the Old World breaking on the shores of the
New."

Miriam Leslie, on her luxurious tour in 1877, also found
the Omaha platform crowded with immigrants, one of the
strangest and most motley groups she had ever encountered.
"Men in alligator boots, and loose overcoats made of blankets
and wagon rugs, with wild, unkempt hair and beards, and
bright resolute eyes, almost all well-looking, but wild and
strange as denizens of another world." When she observed

the women, Mrs. Leslie had the same reaction as Lady Hardy: "The women looked tired and sad, almost all of them, and were queerly dressed in gowns that must have been old on their grandmothers, and with handkerchiefs tied over their heads in place of hats; the children were bundled up anyhow, in garments of nondescript purpose and size, but were generally chubby, neat and gay, as they frolicked in and out among the boxes, baskets, bundles, bedding, babies'-chairs, etc., piled waist high on various parts of the platform."

Being a true journalist, Mrs. Leslie mingled with the immigrants, talked with them, visited the lodging house and outfitting shop that the Union Pacific had built for them, and dined in their segregated eating room, pronouncing the meal to be good, substantial, and neatly served at twenty-five cents a plate.

A year later, Helen Hunt Jackson was describing the same scene—big bundles of feather beds tied up in blue check, red chests corded with rope, flurried immigrants shouting in German, Gaelic, French, and Spanish. "Inside the wall was a pathetic sight—a poor German woman on her knees before a chest, which had burst open on the journey. It seemed as if its whole contents could not be worth five dollars—so old, so faded, so coarse were the clothes and so battered were the utensils. But it was evidently all she owned; it was the home she had brought with her from the Fatherland, and would be the home she would set up on the prairie. The railroad-men were good to her, and were helping her with ropes and nails. This comforted me somewhat; but it seemed almost a sin to be journeying luxuriously on the same day and train with that poor soul."

At one stage of his journey "from sea to sea," Rudyard Kipling was unable to obtain a Pullman berth and was forced to travel across part of Montana in an immigrant car. "It was a nightmare," he said. "There was a row in our car toward morning, a man having managed to get querulously drunk in the night. Up rose a Cornishman with a red head full of strategy, and strapped the obstreperous one, smiling largely as he did so, and a delicate little woman in a far bunk watched the fray and called the drunken man a 'damned hog,' which he

Newly arrived immigrants registering at Castle Garden
(The New-York Historical Society)

certainly was, though she needn't have put it quite so coarsely.
Emigrant cars are clean, but the accommodation is as hard
as a plank bed."

Another British traveler was surprised to meet at the
Ogden station in Utah a ten-year-old girl who had traveled
alone by immigrant train from St. Louis and miraculously survived. She was an orphan bound for Salt Lake City to join her
relatives, and was carrying an extraordinary assortment of
"bags and bundles and baskets, an old tin kettle, a three-
legged stool, and a very shabby looking-glass, with half the
quicksilver rubbed off its back." She explained that the
reason she was wrapped in an old mangy buffalo robe was
that while the immigrant train was crossing the Rockies a
gang of "road agents" had boarded the cars and plundered
the passengers. They had taken her blankets, and but for the
kindness of the conductor who gave her the buffalo robe, she
feared she might have frozen to death.

As the railroad land companies became skilled at
matching immigrants with acreage, they found it more efficient to transport entire colonies of Scandinavians, Germans,
Britons, and Russians. A single family set down upon the
bleak plains tended to become bewildered and defeated, but

a group of families speaking the same language and following the same customs could sustain one another in their adversities. By the early 1880s, the Northern Pacific, Santa Fe, and other transcontinental railroads possessing enormous tracts of land that they wished to convert into cash were running trains with as many as fifty cars filled with immigrants and their baggage, all from the same locality and all traveling to the same destination.

Most westbound immigrants from abroad first set foot on American soil in the port of New York, after being hustled off their ship and into an enclosed bedlam that bore the romantic name Castle Garden. According to a handbook given to many of them aboard ship, there was a smooth-running bureaucracy at Castle Garden consisting of a boarding department, which welcomed immigrants to America before they left their ship, and also a landing department, which examined their physical condition, weeded out lunatics, and then directed them into a vast rotunda where they were sorted into separate compartments according to languages and nationalities. There, the registry department recorded their names, origins, and intended destinations, forwarding them on to the information department or a registered agent of one of the transcontinental railroad companies. After obtaining tickets and checking baggage, the immigrants were transferred to a railroad station where they boarded a train for the West—all accomplished very smoothly thanks to the efficiency of Castle Garden and its friendly officials. At least, that was the way the handbook described the operation.

Robert Louis Stevenson did not find it that way at all. Instead, Castle Garden was overrun by a swarm of confused, frightened human beings, loaded with bundles, jostling one another frantically as they were herded like animals into lines that moved very slowly past callous functionaries. "A bearded, mildewed little man, whom I take to have been an emigrant agent, was all over the place, his mouth full of brimstone, blustering and interfering. It was plain that the whole system, if system there was, had utterly broken down. . . . I followed the porters into a long shed. . . . It was dark, the wind blew clean through it from end to end, and here I found a great block of passengers and baggage, hundreds of one and tons of the other. . . . I may say that we stood like sheep, and that the porters charged among us like so many maddened sheep dogs; and I believe these men were no longer answerable for their acts."

After he finally reached his designated railway station, in a driving rainstorm, Stevenson found himself in another crowd of immigrants who seemed to be approaching panic madness. "There was no waiting room, no refreshment room; the cars were locked; and for at least another hour, or so it seemed, we had to camp upon the draughty, gaslit platform. I sat on my valise, too crushed to observe my neighbors; but as they were all cold, and wet, and weary, and driven stupidly crazy by the mismanagement to which we had been subjected, I believe they can have been no happier than myself . . . at last we were admitted into the cars, utterly dejected, and far from dry."

The immigrant cars that Stevenson and his companions boarded were very old coaches—springless, poorly ventilated, and filled with rattles. Most had been converted from obsolete day-coaches, a few from more elaborate cars such as the famous Lincoln car that Thomas Durant exchanged for a deluxe special during his years with the Union Pacific. The Lincoln car with its rebuilt wooden seats was still carrying immigrants across the West well into the late 1870s.

Immigrant cars varied from railroad to railroad, some containing double rows of narrow backless benches placed close together so as to squeeze in as many passengers as possible. Usually a coal-burning stove stood at one end of the car, a dangerous fire threat even in a minor accident. Passengers traveling in these cars had to sleep on the floor beneath the benches or in the aisles.

The transcontinental railroads introduced immigrant "sleeping cars" consisting simply of two tiers of boxlike wooden cubicles built along each side of the car and in which passengers could lie or sit as they chose, but they had to furnish their own bedding. For some reason, in the West they were called Zulu cars. In the 1880s a few minor improvements were made. Cooking stoves were placed in the Zulu cars so that the immigrants could prepare their own food during the long journey; wooden straight-backed seats were

A Zulu car bound west across the Great Plains
(The New-York Historical Society)

installed in pairs facing each other so that boards could be
placed across them to form beds, and above these double
seats were slatted berths supported either by heavy posts or
by chains. Upholstery was seldom used in Zulu cars.

Although passengers on immigrant cars were handled
as if they were freight rather than human beings, it was the
custom to separate the sexes by cars. Exceptions were sometimes made when large families were journeying together.
The train on which Stevenson traveled was segregated also
by race, the Chinese being confined to one car. William
Spalding, a young drop-out from the University of Michigan
(who later became a famous California newspaperman), traveled West as an emigrant in 1873 and was pleased to be in an
all-male car because he "escaped that most intolerable nuisance of miscellaneous traveling, crying babies." There were
no sleeping accommodations on his car, but the seats were
more comfortable than usual, being made of woven rattan.
Spalding found that he could stretch out nearly full length in
his seat by flexing his knees, and with his overcoat for a
pillow and a blanket for covering he somehow survived ten
nights of travel.

G. F. Byron, an English immigrant who traveled West from New Orleans on the Southern Pacific, found that the seats on his Zulu car were rough slats with no upholstery, hard but clean. The car also contained wooden cubicles along each side, into which the travelers could climb and stretch out for the night. For $1.25 Byron purchased a mattress from a railroad agent who assured him that he could sell it for at least the same price when he reached San Francisco. "The mattress was of curious build, a flattened square bag of straw, stiff, unwieldy, and lumpy, but somehow I managed to force mine into some sort of position, and I certainly found it soothing to sit on." Robert Louis Stevenson's Zulu car was one in which boards had to be placed across the backs of the seats, and for this crude bed he paid $2.50 for a board and three straw cushions. Sleep was almost an impossibility, with his fellow travelers sprawled on boards, seats, and flooring, all being continually shaken by the rough motion of the train, groaning and muttering in their half slumber.

At journey's end, those immigrants who had been solicited by a railroad land agent usually found temporary shelter in an emigrant reception house owned by the railroad and built like a station alongside the tracks. These lodging houses were located near unsold land grants, and newly arrived immigrants could leave family members there while they searched for a place to build a home.

A great deal of rivalry developed among the transcontinental railroads in their constant quest for immigrants to fill up the empty plains and generate cash for the money-grubbing owners. They vied with one another in spreading flamboyant advertisements across the Eastern states and Europe; they bought up newspapers or founded new ones to broadcast their messages of "flowery meadows of great fertility clothed in nutritious grasses and watered by numerous streams" or "the Cornucopia of the world—2,000,000 acres of farming land." They dispatched agents all over Europe, armed with posters, circulars, and lantern slides.

They overlooked no possible outlet, placing their propaganda in schools, railroad stations, consular offices, and on steamships. They were constantly stretching the truth, if not overlooking it entirely. One agent recalled that he always emphasized *"free* homes for the millions" because of the inherent desire in human nature to get something for nothing. "That was my slogan, or rallying phrase. It headed every circular, folder, and poster which I issued, and I issued them by the million. I spread them everywhere, and in every possible publication and newspaper, printed in black, blue, and red ink, in the English and German languages."

During the 1870s, the Union Pacific advertised land sales in more than two thousand newspapers and magazines. At the height of the Northern Pacific's campaign for land buyers, it was advertising regularly in two hundred English-language newspapers, sixty-eight German, and thirty-two Scandinavian. The N.P. distributed hundreds of thousands of maps, circulars, and a company magazine translated into several languages. The railroad also established newspapers in Germany, Switzerland, and England, and dispatched agents with stereopticons to travel about Europe giving free lectures with photographs of its marvelous low-cost lands in the American West. The Burlington Railroad outdid its rivals by commissioning an artist to paint eighty-five views much more resplendent than black-and-white photographs, each covering 250 square feet of gaudy canvas. They were exhibited to audiences abroad by a traveling lecturer who billed his show as the "Sylphorama of America by Sea, River, and Railroad."

Armies of agents swarmed over Europe, showering leaflets of their respective land companies upon the populace. A representative of the Burlington who established an office in Liverpool compiled a list of his regular activities. He boarded every transatlantic steamship before it left port, furnishing the passengers with a liberal supply of pamphlets describing the superiority of Burlington lands and climate. He visited every hotel and boarding house in the city, dispensing information to prospective emigrants. He posted on the walls of every public building maps of the Burlington route and its available lands. He canvassed the cooperative societies, obtaining names and addresses of persons interested in emigrating. He arranged for publication of articles in newspapers read by the "emigrating class," and delivered lectures to interested groups. And from time to time he visited large

manufacturing towns and agricultural districts in other parts
of England and Scotland, distributing his propaganda wherever he went.

In the early 1880s the Northern Pacific had 831 agents
in Great Britain and 124 scattered across Norway, Sweden,
Denmark, Holland, Germany, and Switzerland. They divided the countries into districts to avoid crossing one another's paths. So much proselyting was going on among the
competing land departments that one agent, in order to protect his prospects from "runners and touts," established an
emigrant home in Liverpool, where they could stay until a
ship was ready to sail. Another successful agent, an authentic
pied piper, claimed that by assembling large groups at a time
he single-handedly brought sixty thousand emigrants to
Kansas during the years he worked for the Santa Fe. The Burlington's agents used a similar colonization approach at Rochdale and Manchester, as one of their posters indicates:

To the West, To the West, to the Land of the Free
EMIGRANTS
to
Iowa and Nebraska, U.S.
The Next Colony Will Leave Rochdale for
Lincoln, Nebraska
on Wednesday June 28th, 1871

As the competition grew keener, the agents resorted to
various stunts to attract land buyers to their particular region.
One man organized an excursion of sixty Englishmen for a
buffalo hunt on the plains, with Buffalo Bill Cody as their
guide. They were expected to become missionaries on their
return to England, and perhaps emigrate later themselves.
Other agents invited selected groups of journalists to travel
along the railroads, plying them with fine foods, bourbon,
champagne, and Havana cigars to put them in the proper
mood to fill their newspapers with beneficial propaganda.
Free seed for a stated number of years was another lure, but
this stunt often backfired, the emigrants complaining that
there was more quackgrass and cockle than wheat and corn in
the free seed they planted. Ready-made houses waiting for
new arrivals more often than not also proved to be a sort of

confidence game, for the emigrants found that they were sad-
dled with excessive short-term interest rates.

Through experience, the agents found that their best
targets in Europe were racial or religious groups who were
under pressure for various reasons. Ministers of church congregations in economically depressed areas proved receptive
to emigration offers, and their followers tended to believe in
their advice. After a Swedish minister brought his entire
community to Minnesota in 1872, the Northern Pacific employed him on a commission basis to return to Sweden and
persuade other ministers to bring their congregations. The
Burlington also employed religious leaders as agents, and
that railroad's alert land office was the first to rush into
Alsace-Lorraine at the close of the Franco-Prussian War in
1871, urging farmers there to escape the "crushing heel of
militarism" by emigrating to Burlington lands in the American West.

One of the most massive transfers of emigrants was that
accomplished by the Santa Fe Railroad's Carl B. Schmidt, a
German who had come to Lawrence, Kansas, in 1864 to found
a farm-implement business. The Santa Fe employed Schmidt
in 1873, and while this resourceful agent was prowling about
Europe seeking emigrants to buy some of the three million
acres owned by the railroad, he learned of the plight of several thousand German Mennonites who were living in
Russia.

At the invitation of Catherine the Great, the Mennonites
had fled there during the eighteenth century to avoid perse-
cution. She promised them that they would be exempt from
military service, which was against their religious principles,
and also agreed that they could follow their own customs, including the use of the German language. In 1870, however,
the Russian czar annulled the Mennonites' special privileges
and notified them that they must conform to Russian
laws—"One Czar, one religion, one language."

Certain that he would find willing emigrants among the
Mennonites, Schmidt entered Russia posing as a farm-
machinery salesman and visited more than thirty villages.
As he spoke the Mennonites' language, he had no trouble

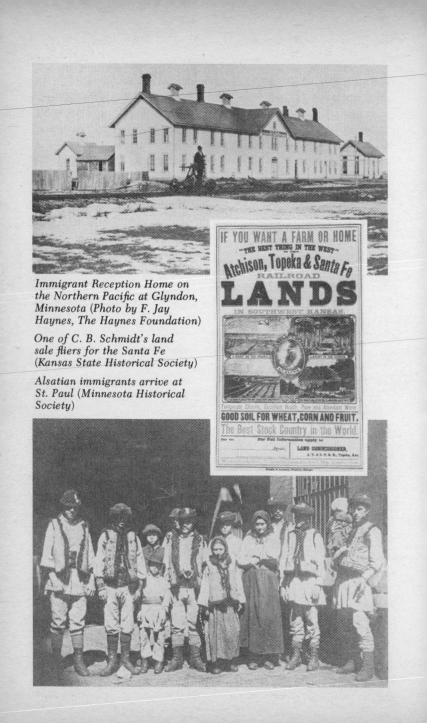

Immigrant Reception Home on the Northern Pacific at Glyndon, Minnesota (Photo by F. Jay Haynes, The Haynes Foundation)

One of C. B. Schmidt's land sale fliers for the Santa Fe (Kansas State Historical Society)

Alsatian immigrants arrive at St. Paul (Minnesota Historical Society)

IF YOU WANT A FARM OR HOME
"THE BEST THING IN THE WEST"

Atchison, Topeka & Santa Fe
RAILROAD
LANDS
IN SOUTHWEST KANSAS.

GOOD SOIL FOR WHEAT, CORN AND FRUIT.
The Best Stock Country in the World.

For Full Information apply to
LAND COMMISSIONER,
A. T. & S. F. R. R., Topeka, Kas.

convincing them that the Kansas plains were as good or better wheat lands than the Russian steppes. He allayed their fears of wild Indians, told them nothing of the periodic droughts and grasshopper invasions on the Great Plains, and returned to Kansas to await results.

On August 16, 1874, thirty-four families of Mennonites from the Russian Crimea arrived in Kansas. Before leaving Russia they had quietly converted their possessions into gold, which they managed to bring out with them and now used to buy eight thousand acres of Santa Fe land. On a level plain they graded a mile-long street, and then along it constructed a row of A-frame houses set about 150 yards apart, one for each family. They called the place Gnadenau, or Meadow of Grace.

Shortly afterward, six hundred more Mennonites arrived, and then on September 23, eleven hundred suddenly appeared in Topeka, looking for Carl Schmidt, who was now being called "the Moses of the Mennonites." The Mennonite males were generally tall and bearded, clad in Russian blouses and billowing trousers; the women wore black bonnets and long dark dresses. At first the startled Kansans ridiculed the Santa Fe for bringing human scarecrows into their state, but after word spread that these German-speaking Russians possessed two million dollars in gold, the governor of Kansas decided to hold a reception for them before the Santa Fe relieved them of their wealth in exchange for land.

Eventually fifteen thousand Mennonites came to Kansas, and their knowledge of dryland farming, which they had acquired on the arid Russian steppes, enabled them to survive the droughts of 1879 and 1880, which drove hundreds of other recent land buyers to abandon their farms. Wherever they went, these industrious emigrés from Russia planted not only wheat but orchards, shade trees, and hedges. They also planted groves of mulberry trees, imported silkworms, and attempted to established a silk culture. But it was their wheat-growing that started the conversion of the dry grasslands of Kansas into a granary. Almost every emigrating family had brought along a sealed earthen jar filled with "Turkey Red" wheat seed, and when they sowed the seed in the Kansas soil the plants not only thrived in dry weather but proved to be impervious to rust and other diseases that were destroying the crops of their less fortunate neighbors. (It should be noted as an ironic footnote that the Mennonites who remained in Russia were persecuted for years by the czars and then by their Soviet successors, who shipped large numbers of them to Siberia, where they could grow no wheat. The descendants of those who came from Russia to the Great Plains in the 1870s were growing wheat in the 1970s for export to Russia, shipping millions of bushels to ports on the railroads that had brought them to America.)

The Mennonites were considered such desirable emigrants, in fact, that other railroad land agents tried to kidnap whole parties of them while they were en route to Kansas. Years afterward, the head of the Burlington's land department, Carl Ernst, told how he met a trainload of Mennonites at Atchison, Kansas. The Santa Fe had a special train waiting for them, but Ernst directed them to a Burlington train instead. "I stole the whole bunch," he said, "except less than a dozen unmarried young men, and carried them all by special train, free, to Lincoln, Nebraska."

At almost every important railroad transfer point, agents used all sorts of ploys to divert emigrants from one land company to another. One method was to arrange for baggage to be mislaid, and then during the enforced delay, parties of emigrants would be invited on free tours during which they were told that if they purchased land along that particular railroad, free windmills would be built for them, water wells dug for them, free feed supplied to their livestock for a year, and plank roads built to their houses. If the emigrants succumbed to these promotion schemes, they usually discovered afterward that nothing had been put in writing and none of the promises was ever forthcoming.

Omaha, one of the main gateways to the West, was filled with land agents constantly besieging emigrants with claims and counterclaims. Union Pacific agents tried to frighten emigrants who were going North by relating lurid tales of blizzards and frozen earth in which crops would not grow, and those going South with stories of burning heat and deserts. To counter this propaganda, the other railroads had to install their own imaginative hucksters at Omaha. After spending a few hours there, the emigrants must have felt themselves surrounded by confidence men.

One of the more elaborate schemes to proselyte emigrants occurred during 1873 in western Minnesota. The Northern Pacific had recruited a large religious and temperance group from England and Scotland known as the Yeovil Colony and the members were being settled around the town of Hawley. Somewhere en route to Hawley, each of these emigrants was handed a pamphlet titled *Advice from an Old Yeovilian,* which warned that land located along the Northern Pacific was unfit for human habitation, that the winters were unbearably cold, the soil worthless, the growing season too short for crops, and recommended that all Yeovilians immediately turn southward to one of the other railroads. Although the pamphlet frightened away a number of colonists before the Northern Pacific agents could take steps to discredit it, most of the members had no funds with which to travel farther, and those who remained there because they could do nothing else soon discovered that the Red River country was excellent wheat land.

Bribery was another method used by land agents to assure the routing of emigrants to their respective railroads. They began with steamship agents abroad, paying them a certain amount per head for emigrants they converted from one railroad land company to another, and ended with officials at Castle Garden, who were in advantageous positions to route emigrants to the railroad that paid them the highest commissions. "We cannot compete with the other land-grant companies in our efforts to secure foreign immigrants through Castle Garden," a Northern Pacific agent reported in 1882, "unless we are willing to pay as large commissions as they do. All the officers connected with Castle Garden are in the pay of some road or other and the Company that bids highest will get the most immigrants."

In some parts of Europe by the early 1880s, the land agents were meeting strong resistance to their wholesale recruiting efforts. Russia took steps to block the exodus of its wheat-growing Mennonites, first forbidding them to take any possessions or gold out of the country, and then sending Cossacks to frighten them. On one of Carl Schmidt's last trips to Russia, secret agents of the czar followed him from village to village, but he escaped without being arrested.

In Scandinavia, where recent introduction of machinery had produced a surplus of workers, the establishment class also began to resent the wholesale depopulation of communities. Newspapers became increasingly hostile to railroad land agents from America, and a Burlington representative complained that they not only regarded him as "a robber and scoundrel of the deepest dye," but were reciting "in the most horrid manner the murders and all law breakings from America they can get hold of, but say never a word of the good things there."

Germany also tried to slow the departure to America of its poorer classes, but a land agent stationed there expressed the opinion that Chancellor Bismarck would not dare stop emigration, for fear that it might bring on a revolution. At least one group of prospective German emigrants, however, decided not to accept a Santa Fe offer after they learned about a law passed by the Kansas legislature in 1880 prohibiting the manufacture and sale of intoxicating liquors. "None of my friends can fancy themselves living under such stringent laws," said one of the reluctant recruits, "and think it can not be good where such laws are considered necessary, which are only in order for drunkards and not for sober, industrious farmers, who require a drop of liquor occasionally with their hard work."

Such disillusionment usually did not occur until after the emigrants reached their land holdings and tried to survive. Those who moved into a sod house, dugout, or cottonwood log cabin usually fared better than those who were trying to meet fifteen-percent mortgage payments on a frame house built by a railroad land company. Interest rates on the land also were excessive, and the "short credit" system used by some railroads was the downfall of many emigrants. This was a three-year plan of payment, one third down and one third due in each of the two successive years, at ten-percent interest. An emigrant whose head was filled with the rosy promises of land agents, who assured him that he could easily earn enough from his labors to pay off his debt, often found himself without a penny at the end of the first year. Santa Fe agents, for example, offered statistics to prove that a livestock raiser could earn thirty-seven percent a year on his original investment, but few beginners earned anything at all the first year, and the "land of promise" described in the flashy circulars quickly turned sour.

Almost all the railroads painted too bright a picture of the future, with overblown descriptions of abundance, crop bonanzas, and delightful climates. To counter widespread rumors of the "Great American Desert," land agents published false rainfall records, or emphasized the rainfall averages in eastern areas of the Plains states, which were twice as high as in areas west of the 100th meridian. Santa Fe agents, who evidently liked to assemble statistics, published data to prove that Kansas could support thirty-three million people in prosperity, and several companies issued pseudo-scientific reports to show that the presence of railroads in arid regions increased rainfall. One reason given was that the concussion of air caused by the rapid movement of trains affected electrical conditions of the atmosphere and brought down showers. "Rain follows the plow," was another popular slogan, its supporters claiming that the plowing of soil over vast new farming areas released moisture into the air, which was returned in the form of rain.

Efforts of trained scientists such as John Wesley Powell and Frederick H. Newell went unheeded when they tried to warn emigrants that the far western plains were subject to periodic droughts and could not be farmed without irrigation. Except for the dry periods of 1873–74 and 1879–80, the railroad lands were settled during a wet cycle, and when the great droughts came in the late nineteenth century, the settlers were unprepared for the severe privation caused by loss of crops and livestock. They were also unprepared for the fierce blizzards, or the grasshopper plagues of the 1870s, which devastated entire farms from Oregon to the Dakotas and south to Texas. To keep newly arrived emigrants from starving, the federal government had to issue a "grasshopper

appropriation" for the purchase of food and clothing to be
"divided among the naked."

No matter how difficult conditions became on the frontier, most emigrants had to stay where they were because
they had pledged everything they owned to the railroads for
their land or their town lots. Emigrants who made the mis-
take of arriving in the winter sometimes departed almost
immediately, overwhelmed by the snow, the lack of trees for
firewood, and the dreary landscape.

Sometimes entire groups of colonists who had settled on
poor land or in the middle of a drought period would try to
move to greener areas. A letter from a Nebraska colony to an
Oregon land company in May 1880, pleading for free railroad
passes, reveals the hardships experienced: "The wheat crop
has failed here for three years past and the indications are
strong for another drought as we have had no rain since last
September and the cattle here are in bad way for want of
grass, which is very scarce; and the people here are all
leaving. We live on the open prairies and the heavy winds
that prevail here are unendurable. Our houses consist of
'Dug Outs' and 'Sod houses.' Our people are all discouraged
and homesick, but too far to go back to Russia."

Immigrants who had come from Europe and the Eastern
states were often overwhelmed by the sheer vastness of the
American West, the emptiness of the land, the awesome, sur-
real world of earth and sky. "These unbounded prairies have
such an air of desolation," wrote one immigrant's wife, "and
the stillness is very oppressive." An oft-repeated remark of
plains dwellers was: "A man can look farther and see less."

For town dwellers along the Western railroads there was
also a deadly monotony in their daily vistas. The railroad land
companies, which profited from the sale of town lots, displayed no imagination in laying them out; in fact they often
used the same plans, so there was a drab uniformity noticed
by train travelers as they crossed the West—a boxlike station
painted a somber color, a water tank, a grain elevator, and a
bleak main street totally without beauty.

In addition to the austerity of their lives, they had to endure the attitudes of the railroad tycoons who regarded their
immigrant-settlers as feudal subjects who owed fealty and

their very existence to them and were expected to pay homage to the suzerains in various ways—such as high freight rates for shipments of farm produce and goods. Through the years, resentment began to build up against the railroads whose land agents had implanted dreams of great expectations among hundreds of thousands of hard-working immigrants. The image of the Iron Horse, which had brought them to settle the sweep of earth that lay between the Mississippi River and the Western Sea, would change from beneficent friend to detested foe. A whirlwind of unrest, a political revolution, would soon rage across the West, exposing the corruption and the intrinsic vulnerability of a railroad system built by buccaneers.

CHAPTER 13

Trampling the Frontier

At GOLD CREEK, Montana, on September 8, 1883, the last spike was driven to connect the rails of the Northern Pacific in its long-delayed construction from Lake Superior to the Western Sea—the fulfillment of the old failed dreams of Asa Whitney, Isaac Stevens, and Jay Cooke. The ceremonies to mark the completion of the nation's second transcontinental railroad were as elaborately staged as a theatrical extravaganza. Impresario of this carnival of the rails was the German-born financial wizard Henry Villard. Only four years earlier, Villard had lost the Kansas Pacific to Jay Gould, but in doing so he had forced Gould to pay off that defunct railroad's bondholders—an action that won for Villard the confidence of the world of big money.

Villard's carefully staged "driving of the last spike" began at St. Paul on September 3 with President Chester A. Arthur reviewing a parade of 725 wagons and thousands of marchers all carrying American flags. When the procession ended, Villard's 350 guests boarded four luxurious Northern Pacific Pullman trains draped in patriotic bunting. Among the notables were former President Ulysses Grant, Phil Sheridan and several other aging generals, Carl Schurz, who as Secretary of the Interior had assisted in extinguishing Indian claims to much of the land the railroad crossed, James Bryce, the British statesman and scholar, distinguished officials and financiers from Germany, and an assortment of bankers and congressmen. Dispersed among these special guests were numerous newspapermen, an official photographer, and a shorthand reporter. Along the way to the Far West and the last spike, "the choicest of foods, cigars, vintage wines and champagnes, were as free as the air and as plentiful as water."

Crow Indians at Last Spike ceremonies of the Northern Pacific
(Photo by F. Jay Haynes, The Haynes Foundation)

Henry Villard mounts one of his Iron Horses for the photographer
(Photo by F. Jay Haynes, The Haynes Foundation)

At Bismarck, another gala celebration awaited the excursionists. Here the leading orator was the defeated Sitting Bull, who delivered his speech in Lakota—a bitter denunciation of land thieves and liars, which was translated by an Army officer into English metaphors of benevolent hospitality. The affluent listeners, in their expensive suits, top hats, derbies, boiled shirts, and gold watch chains, gave Sitting Bull a standing ovation, and then boarded their palaces on wheels to resume the journey West.

From time to time across Dakota and into Montana they passed sheaves of grain and vegetables that Villard had arranged to have placed alongside the tracks to demonstrate the productivity of Northern Pacific land. At Billings they stopped for more speeches and entertainment, and then continued up the valley of the Yellowstone to Grey Cliff, where fifteen hundred members of the Crow tribe joined them in a mammoth barbecue. The Indians, who had lost to the railroad a considerable number of acres of their treaty land, were forced to pay for their share of Villard's broiled beef by performing a mock scalp dance, which they probably would have liked to execute in earnest.

At last the Iron Horse brought the excursionists to Gold Creek, where they detrained upon a huge wooden platform built especially for the occasion, and entered a roofed seating area decorated with mountain greenery. The Fifth Infantry band, attired in resplendent uniforms and plumed helmets, played stirring music. Beneath a sign that read LAKE SUPERIOR 1,198 MILES—PUGET SOUND 847 MILES, a group of Indian chiefs held council to cede the last of their hunting grounds to the Northern Pacific.

Instead of using a gold spike for the grand ceremony, Villard had brought a rusty spike from the first section of track built in Minnesota. He and Ulysses Grant made speeches, and everybody posed for the official photographer. Villard mounted one of the flag-draped locomotives and stood, hat in hand, staring into the camera lens—a worried-looking potentate with a flowing mustache and close-cropped hair. "The Northern Pacific," wrote one newspaperman, "fastens its magic girdle about a smiling continent, and the struggle of years is ended and the guerdon won."

In the ten years that had passed since Jay Cooke abandoned the rusting rails of the Northern Pacific on the banks of the Missouri River at Bismarck, an army of hide hunters had invaded the West to slay five million buffalo, almost bringing that native animal to extinction. During that same decade, regiments of blue-coated cavalrymen had rounded up thousands of native Americans who were left helpless because of the slaughter of their basic source of food, shelter, and clothing. Driven into reservations across Dakota, Montana, and Washington, many of them had scarcely settled into their lodges before surveyors came to take more of their land for tracks for the Iron Horse.

Whenever the Northern Pacific's westward point came to Indian land, a signal went back to Washington, and there the bureaucrats would set a paperwork ritual into motion. Acting in silent collusion, the Office of Indian Affairs, the Secretary of the Interior, the Congress, and the President of the United States arranged for a hasty extinguishment of tribal titles to the land. To keep matters legal, the government agreed to pay the Indians four or five dollars per acre for the land, but instead of paying money to the tribe, credit was assigned to them in the Treasury, a paper transaction only, "to be expended for the benefit of said Indians in such manner as the Secretary of the Interior may direct."

The final step in the ritual was for the bureaucrats to bill the railroad for the amount assigned the Indians, but after this money reached the Treasury, the Indians still had no way of obtaining it or of determining how it would be spent. Only the Secretary of the Interior could decide when or how it would be used, and few holders of that office were ever generous in dispensing funds to reservation Indians, even though the money was theirs. Nine years after the Northern Pacific was completed, members of the Yakima tribe were petitioning Congress for money due for land taken from them by the railroad. According to one official report, the right-of-way had cut a swath through farms and ranches of several Yakimas and had been appraised "without the Indians interested being allowed any voice in the selection of the appraisers. It also appears that the appraisers have estimated for the value of the land taken and the value of the improvements thereon, but nothing for the damage done to the balance of the tract or farm through which the right-of-way runs. We submit that it is often the case that the damage to the balance of the farm not taken through which a railroad runs is often much greater than the estimated value of the right-of-way through the farm. It usually involves the necessity of a large additional amount of fencing, and often many other inconveniences which are perpetual, which shows very plainly to have been the case in most, if not each one, of the tracts of land through which the railroad runs."

None of these matters concerned the champagne-drinking excursionists of September 1883, except possibly one member of the party—James Bryce, who was in a position to view events more objectively than were his companions. In that very year, Bryce began writing his classic work, *The American Commonwealth*. "The treatment of the Indians," he commented, "reflects little credit on the Western settlers who have come in contact with them, and almost as little on the Federal Government, whose efforts to protect them have often been foiled by the faults of its own agents, or by its own want of promptitude and foresight."

Bryce also must have had his host Villard in mind when he wrote: "These railway kings are among the greatest men, perhaps I may say are the greatest men, in America. They

Invader of the Indian lands (The De Grolyer Collection)

have wealth, else they could not hold the position. They have fame, for every one has heard of their achievements; every newspaper chronicles their movements. They have power, more power—that is, more opportunity of making their personal will prevail—than perhaps any one in political life, except the President and the Speaker, who after all hold theirs only for four years and two years, while the railroad monarch may keep his for life. When the master of one of the greatest Western lines travels toward the Pacific on his palace car, his journey is like a royal progress. Governors of States and Territories bow before him; legislatures receive him in solemn session; cities and towns seek to propitiate him, for has he not the means of making or marring a city's fortunes?"

On that late-summer excursion to the Western Sea, however, all was not well with the fortunes of Henry Villard. In rushing the Northern Pacific to completion so as to secure its enormous land grant before expiration date, he had spent millions of dollars of other people's money and burdened the railroad with an extraordinarily heavy debt. The purpose of the deluxe journey on rails—the parades and barbecues and the driving of the last spike—was to attract millions more dollars of other people's money to keep Villard's empire flourishing. From their Pullman windows—kept scrupulously clean by daily polishing—the financiers of the world looked out upon a thousand miles of uninhabited sagebrush and rocky mountains. "They could see nothing in the 'God-forsaken wilderness' through which they traveled to support a railroad," said one contemporary observer. "Most of them abandoned Villard's special at Portland, Oregon, and immediately telegraphed their brokers to sell their stocks and bonds without delay, and so brought on the panic that ruined 'Old Henry' Villard."

Villard's rapid rise to control of the Northern Pacific began after his deal with Jay Gould to recover Kansas Pacific Railroad investments for a group of German investors. Acting as agent for a similar group, he went to Oregon to investigate the Oregon & California Railroad, which had defaulted on its bonds. Villard immediately recognized the fortune that ultimately awaited anyone who controlled transportation in the rich Willamette and Columbia river valleys, which were rapidly filling with settlers. After a struggle with Ben Holladay, who tried to hold on to the railroad, Villard outmaneuvered the old Stagecoach King and seized control in 1879. Immediately thereafter, he reorganized his paper holdings into the Oregon Railway & Navigation Company and issued several million dollars in stocks and bonds. Because of his reputation as a financial wizard, Villard sold all his bonds before he could even draft a mortgage. He noted in astonishment on December 14, 1880: "Not a person has asked a question regarding the mortgage, form of the bond or anything."

With a plentiful supply of other people's money, Villard now began extending his railroads in Washington and Oregon, at the same time laying plans for a transcontinental line across the Northern states. The main obstacle was the Northern Pacific, which owned the land grants.

In 1875 Frederick Billings had reorganized that dormant railroad, issued new stock for old stock, and with a bit of financial legerdemain finally obtained enough credit to resume track laying. In 1880, he persuaded President Rutherford Hayes to sign a document, on July 13, removing thirty thousand square miles of land from the Arikaris, Gros Ventres, and Blackfoot tribes, so that the railroad could acquire title as rapidly as tracks could be laid across it.

Villard's first move against Billings was to obtain prior rights to strategic mountain passes and valleys that would have to be used by railroads entering Oregon and Washington. He then tried to gain control of the Northern Pacific by buying large blocks of its stock on margin, but he soon ran out of funds. To obtain more money he organized a "blind pool" in February 1881, sending out letters to about fifty wealthy speculators (including George Pullman), inviting them to subscribe to a syndicate of eight million dollars, the purpose of which he would not disclose for about ninety days. The mystery of the affair was so intriguing that the moneyed men rushed to subscribe, and within twenty-four hours the amount was oversubscribed. Villard tried to apportion the shares evenly, but the subscribers protested. All wanted more, and when news of the syndicate leaked out, avid investors stormed Villard's office, demanding shares in the secret venture, and offering the original holders fifty percent more than

Northern Pacific work crew building grade and laying track in western North Dakota (Photo by F. Jay Haynes, The Haynes Foundation)

they had paid for them. "I was almost drawn to pieces by unsuccessful applicants," Villard said on February 17. "This is the greatest feat of strategy I ever performed." To satisfy the demand, Villard agreed to accept twelve million dollars more of other people's money. He put this fortune that he had acquired with such ease into a holding company called the Transcontinental and with it he swallowed up the struggling Northern Pacific, removed Frederick Billings, and had himself named president.

To make his investors happy, Villard soon issued a huge dividend, and then began pouring out their money to complete the remaining nine hundred miles of Northern Pacific track. Villard knew very little about construction contracts and nothing about the operation of the already finished sections of the railroad. He left these matters to others and went off to Europe to sell more securities to eager investors. Crews of Chinese workers began laying tracks eastward from Washington, and gangs of Swedes and Irish moved westward across Montana. By June 1883, the westbound tracks reached Helena, but construction of tunnels and bridges through the high Rockies consumed Villard's cash faster than he could replace it. By the time set for the spike-driving ceremonies in September, the Northern Pacific was in serious financial trouble.

Between January and September 1883 the stock dropped from 83 to 52, which explains why Villard tried to make such a grand show of the spike-driving excursion. The extravaganza failed to work, however. Instead of buying, the investors sold, and a few weeks later Northern Pacific stock was down to 34. Trying desperately to stave off disaster, Villard borrowed some more of other people's money to push up the stock's price, but by December, only three months after his lavish excursion, the Northern Pacific was bankrupt and Henry Villard was forced to resign.

Like most contemporary railroad monarchs caught in such debacles, Villard claimed that his own personal fortunes had vanished along with those of his investors. If this was true, he seemed to thrive on poverty. Three years later he was dealing in millions with the Deutsche Bank and J. P. Morgan, and in September 1887 he was back on the board of the Northern Pacific. Less than two years after that, he somehow cornered a majority of the railroad's stock and was in full control again.

With the same recklessness that he had exhibited before, Villard began a rapid expansion, starting new branches and buying up uncompleted lines of potential rivals. To cover expenses, he issued third-mortgage bonds and even tried to market a fourth-mortgage. To reassure investors, he issued a dividend in 1890, but financial observers recalling his reversals of 1883 were skeptical: "Villard seems to have no faculty but that of borrowing," the *New York Times* commented, "and in that he has such genius he could borrow the United States Treasury in six months and bankrupt it in six more."

In 1893, for the second time within a decade, the Northern Pacific collapsed beneath a huge floating debt. Villard departed, grumbling and protesting about the "exhausting work, wearing anxiety and heavy pecuniary loss" he had endured while trying to save the railroad from disaster. He claimed to be the "greatest sufferer as a stock and bond holder," but the record shows that three years earlier he had used either his own or other people's money to buy the Edison Lamp Company and Edison Machine Works, and in the same year that he left the bankrupt Northern Pacific he reorganized them into the mighty General Electric Company.

In those latter years of the nineteenth century when the Iron Horse trampled the Western frontier into extinction, it seemed that whenever one buccaneer of the rails left the scene another was always ready to take his place. In 1873, after Jay Cooke crashed with the Northern Pacific, the St. Paul & Pacific also fell into bankruptcy. In addition to a section running north from St. Paul to a connection with the Northern Pacific at Brainerd, the St. Paul & Pacific also had a line running west and then north up the rich Red River Valley. Its bondholders were mainly Dutch financiers, who had little knowledge of the railroad's potential value, but its appointed receiver, Jesse P. Farley, and a close friend of his named James J. Hill knew that the road's land grant alone represented a vast fortune for whoever could gain control of it. Hill made a careful estimate and found that the St. Paul & Pacific was worth about eighteen million dollars.

When the Dutch investors sent over a representative in 1876 to see if the defunct railroad could be salvaged, Hill met him and painted a very dark picture of its prospects. Millions of dollars, he said, would be required to put the road into profitable operation, and even then, because of its location, the St. Paul & Pacific might fail again. For a year or so, Hill continued negotiating with the bondholders, and although the St. Paul & Pacific (operating under receivership) began to show a profit, Hill arranged for the records to be juggled to conceal the earnings. After he had convinced the Dutch investors that their property was almost worthless, Hill and a group of Canadian adventurers offered the bondholders a promissory note for a million dollars as a pledge of good faith against a total price of five million to take the failed railroad off their hands. Thus, without spending a penny, Hill and his associates came into complete control of a railroad with 3,848,000 acres of land and 565 miles of track.

To obtain the $5 million to pay off the unsuspecting Hollanders, the promoters simply reorganized, changed the railroad's name to St. Paul, Minneapolis & Manitoba, made Hill president, issued $8 million in new bonds to exchange for the old bonds, sold off the land grant for $13 million, and distributed $15 million in stock among themselves. Within a short time they were paying themselves seven-percent divi-

Great Northern track layers on the empty plains
(Minnesota Historical Society)

dends on stock worth $140 a share, none of which had cost them anything. Jim Hill, who had conceived this extraordinary venture, wound up with about $5 million profit before he even got started on his transcontinental railroad.

James Jerome Hill, born near Guelph, Ontario, in 1838, was roaming the United States at the age of eighteen in search of his fortune. In July 1856 he arrived at St. Paul, too late to join a brigade of westward-bound fur trappers. Hill took a job as a clerk for a steamboat company, and St. Paul became his home for the next sixty years. He grew up on the Mississippi River front, a shaggy, muscular, brawling, two-fisted fighter. He was tight with his money, and had a habit of going aboard one of the moored boats at mealtimes to cadge a free breakfast or dinner. Jim Hill was a loner, plain-spoken, a shrewd bargainer. He read everything that came into his hands, preferring biographies of men like Napoleon, Genghis Khan, or Alexander the Great, who dreamed of conquering the earth. In his photographs he seems always to be leaning forward, eager to grasp whatever was in reach, his one good eye (the other was blinded in a childhood accident) gleaming fiercely at the world.

As soon as he gained control of the St. Paul & Pacific, Hill extended it north to the Manitoba border to pick up land grants, and then began planning his railroad to the Western Sea. The Northern Pacific, swollen with land grants, was already where he wanted to be. After Hill pushed tracks west of the Minnesota boundary there would be no more land grants accruing for him. These obstacles did not seem to bother Jim Hill. He knew there was plenty of homestead land across northern Dakota and Montana, and he figured that if he could only get his tracks to a Pacific port he might put the Northern Pacific in a bind by cutting freight rates. When insiders of the railroad world heard of this scheme to build a superfluous track across the North without a land-grant subsidy, they called it "Hill's Folly."

Using comfortable three-decker bunkhouse cars for his track layers, Hill built his road (later to be called the Great Northern) slowly and as economically as possible. By occasionally joining his workmen with a spade or a sledgehammer, he won their loyalty and kept their pay low. In 1883 he and the Northern Pacific made an agreement to keep out of each other's territory, but after Villard departed, Hill ran a branch line down to Great Falls and Butte, in the heart of Northern Pacific country. Along the way he spun off other branches to pick up freight—coal, copper, timber—hauling at much lower rates than his overcapitalized rival could meet. Impartial observers saw this as wasteful competition, but by the late 1880s Hill had made up his mind to use whatever means were necessary to add the Northern Pacific to his growing empire. As he drove toward his goal, his ruthlessness matched that of his heroes Napoleon and Genghis Khan. When his tracks reached land in northern Minnesota that had been settled by homesteaders, he claimed it as part of his land grant, won a court action, and began evicting the settlers. He refused to back down until the government gave him equivalent acreage in prime timberland in the Far West.

He told friends that God favored him, but to his employees he was an irascible old lion, ruling by fear, with a temper so violent that when crossed he was known to toss equipment, furniture, and men out of windows. Yet he helped some of his few friends become millionaires like himself, an example being Frederick Weyerhauser, a German immigrant who operated a sawmill in St. Paul. Hill established Weyerhauser on one of his timber grants in Washington, and before the latter died, he converted the forests (which Congress had given away) into $300 million.

One of Hill's greatest offenses against the frontier environment resulted from his intensive campaign to fill the Montana plains with immigrants, settling them on 160-acre farms where the soil was thin and the rainfall scanty. Shack towns proliferated along his railroad tracks, but after the settlers plowed the grasslands where immense herds of buffalo once had thrived, winds began to blow away soil that was never meant for plowing. The first drought turned Jim Hill's colonies into dust bowls, and sixty thousand penniless immigrants fled the desolation and the ghost towns, cursing "that old one-eyed sonofabitch" who had brought them there. In 1890 when Hill saw an economic storm approaching, he squeezed an estimated $50 million out of his railroad holdings to keep in a safe place. He built himself a castle in St. Paul and filled it with rare books and expensive paintings.

When in 1893 Henry Villard rode the Northern Pacific to bankruptcy for the second time, Hill seized that troubled railroad, and then went after the Burlington, which would give him control of twenty-five thousand miles of track and make him emperor of one third of all the Western railroads. Eighteen ninety-three was also the year that he finished building the Great Northern to Puget Sound on the Western Sea. It was the year that the Santa Fe and the Union Pacific, methodically looted by greedy operators, fell into receivership to await another rescue by the gullible taxpaying public, for which the owners had only contempt. And it was the year that historian Frederick Jackson Turner presented his controversial thesis that the Western frontier, which had created a unique American civilization, no longer existed. Accelerated by a frenzy of railroad building in the 1880s, the settlement of land areas was so widespread that there was no longer a frontier line.

The American West now had five transcontinental railroads—the Union Pacific-Central Pacific, the Northern Pacific, Southern Pacific, Santa Fe, and Great Northern. And across Canada ran a sixth—the Canadian Pacific. In 1883, the Southern Pacific, using a patchwork of lines from El Paso

Jim Hill drives spike on his Great Northern
(The De Grolyer Collection)

across Texas, reached New Orleans for a connection to the Eastern seaboard. On February 9, 1880, the first Iron Horse came puffing into the historic town of Santa Fe, and the overland trail that bore its name was forever closed. By securing the franchise of the old 35th parallel route of the defunct Atlantic & Pacific Railroad, the Santa Fe pushed on to the Colorado River near Needles, California, in 1883. For two years, Collis Huntington blocked the Santa Fe's passage to the Pacific shore but at last agreed to a deal. In exchange for its lines in Mexico, Huntington gave the Santa Fe a route to San Diego, that long-forgotten goal during the 1850s of Jefferson Davis, William H. Emory, and the Army Corps of Engineers.

During these same years that the Robber Barons were exploiting the great transcontinental systems, hundreds of lesser promoters were looting the West with railroad schemes designed not to provide transportation but to fill their pockets with easy money from the hapless citizens of what had become a new frontier of small towns and farming

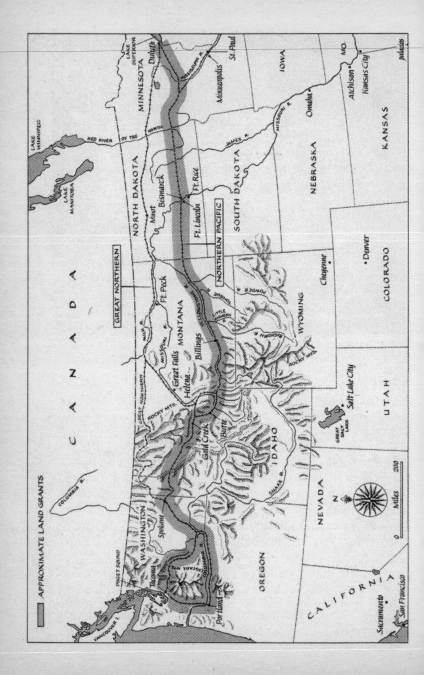

communities. Wherever on a map two towns could be found with no railroad running between them, some clever sharper would appear to organize a railroad company, convincing leading citizens of the towns and farmers of the countryside that they must have a railroad. It did not matter whether the towns had anything to ship to each other. Railroads represented progress, and the towns and townships and counties pledged their futures for a generation with bonds that enriched the promoters. Railroad construction became a mania in the 1880s with feeder lines, branch lines, and short lines running in all directions. Many were never completed, and when they were, the grading was shoddily done, the ties and rails left unballasted, so travelers who dared to board the rickety passenger cars learned to expect to be thrown from their seats several times before reaching their destination, if they ever did.

So much of the public's money was poured into unplanned and often unneeded railroads in the West that the inhabitants of the region were burdened with sharply rising taxes extending far into the future. For shouldering this debt they received poor service and high freight rates, which were another form of taxation. Westerners slowly began to perceive that the real purpose of the railroad builders was not to provide transportation for passengers and freight but to issue and manipulate railroad stocks and bonds. After the promoters had wrung as much as possible out of a road, they departed with the booty and left it in bankruptcy. The observant James Bryce was amazed at the power that American railroads had over local governments and state legislatures, which kept furnishing them with the people's money. "War is the natural state of an American railway towards all other authorities and its own fellows," he said, "just as war was the natural state of cities towards one another in the ancient world."

Had there been another frontier beyond the Western horizon, millions of settlers would have packed up and emigrated again, but there was no longer any frontier. The Iron Horse had driven it into the Western Sea, and if they wished to survive, the former frontiersmen would have to go to war with their railroads.

CHAPTER 14

The Iron Horse Assumes a Devil Image

"**WE ARE SO** used to the California of the stagecoach, widely separated from the rest of the world, that we can hardly realize what the California of the railroad will be—the California netted with iron tracks." This comment was made in 1868 by a twenty-nine-year-old San Francisco newspaperman, Henry George, who was later to become famous as a land reformer and advocate of the single-tax theory of economics. George was wondering what effect the approaching army of Iron Horses would have upon the West. He predicted that they would bring more people, more houses, more farms and mines and factories. Perhaps they would also bring more luxury, refinement, culture, and wealth—but he was doubtful if these things would be evenly distributed among the people of the West. He could understand the clamor of Westerners for immigration, for population, but if these things were so beneficial, he asked, why was it that the most populous countries in the world were the most miserable, most corrupt, most stagnant and hopeless? "The locomotive is a great centralizer," he concluded. "It kills little towns and builds up great cities, and in the same way kills little businesses and builds up great ones."

Henry George's prescient observations began to prove true within a decade after the continent was spanned with iron. Thousands and thousands of settlers who had regarded the Iron Horse with awe and gratitude for bringing them to their new homes in the West soon realized that they were now totally dependent upon a railroad for their existence. They no longer controlled their own fortunes; they were helpless before the power of a corrupt monopoly capable of using bribery, force, any means to maintain its dominion.

The merchant and professional classes in the Western

towns felt the effects of the railroads' arrogance, but farmers were the principal victims. Everything they produced had to be shipped to Eastern markets over railroads whose rates often approached extortion.

The cost of shipping grain from the Dakotas to Chicago, for instance, was greater than the cost of shipping the same grain from Chicago to Liverpool. It was also evident that the railroad titans were in league with the grain dealers. The robbery began alongside the tracks at the elevators, most of which were owned directly or indirectly by the railroads. Grain was loaded upon freight cars through the elevators, and the operators, who were in the employ of the railroads, arbitrarily assigned a grade number that determined the price to be paid by the dealers. If the elevator operator chose to assign a low grade to high-grade grain, the farmer had to accept it or his grain would not be shipped. It was common practice for the operators to assign low grades, then ship the grain to market as high-grade grain, the railroad pocketing the difference in the sale price or sharing it with the grain dealers.

As early as 1871, a Nebraska newspaper editor recognized his community's growing distrust of railroads. "People may grumble at the railroad companies, but they are a necessity of the age. What should be done is, not to attempt to destroy them nor to create a prejudice against them, but to control them by law and to appreciate their worth."

His readers, however, must have been puzzled as to how they might go about controlling the railroads by law when it was apparent that the railroads controlled the men who made the laws. An example of this was the high-handed manner in which railroads evicted settlers from homesteads by extending branch lines and claiming the homesteads as part of a land grant. In California, the Southern Pacific claimed thousands of acres of land that homesteaders had fenced, irrigated, or otherwise improved, demanding that they either pay high prices to keep the land or prepare to be evicted. When the settlers took their grievances to government land offices, the claims of the railroads were always regarded as paramount, while the rights of the individuals were viewed as of little importance.

Added to these gross impositions were the colossal debts

owed to the railroads by numerous communities that had
bonded themselves well into the twentieth century. Many of
the settlers who were paying off these debts with high taxes
and their mortgages with high interest rates also had bought
railroad stock to ensure the building of lines through their
areas. As one railroad after another was plundered of its liquid assets by unscrupulous management and then thrown
into bankruptcy, the settlers found themselves holding
worthless paper in corporations protected by the political
machinery of the states and the nation.

The railroads gained their political power through bribery, either by direct transfer of stocks or bonds or by ascer-
taining the weaknesses and wants of politicians and playing
upon them. To those in financial straits they gave "loans."
Collis Huntington, for example, made no effort to conceal his
beneficent attitude toward California legislators who had
families to support and bills to meet; he presented them with
"pleasant social gifts." Lawyers in need of cases were offered
"corporate business." Shippers of commodities were offered
secret low freight rates. Politicians in need of favorable publicity to help win elections found themselves being praised
in newspapers and magazines controlled by the railroads.

Railroad corporations subsidized hundreds of newspapers, sometimes buying them outright, and if they did not
own an influential newspaper they offered subtle bribes to its
editors, reporters, and correspondents. Retainers from railroads became so common that journalists expected to receive
them, and if they did not they used the power of the press
to ensure that rewards were forthcoming.

From the lowliest local elections to the national campaign for the presidency, the railroads were always involved,
using their power to defeat any candidate suspected of being
hostile to them. In recalling his youth during the 1880s, William Allen White, the famous Kansas newspaper editor, told
of rounding up voters for the Santa Fe Railroad. "Santa Fe
money had provided a tub of iced and bottled beer, as a rallying point, and cigars were so lavishly plentiful that men
grabbed in a box and took two and three and four."

As for national elections during this period, the railroad
titans boasted that they elected James A. Garfield in 1880;

Garfield had been involved in the Credit Mobilier scandal ten years earlier, and Jay Gould considered him a "safe" man for the White House. Garfield won by only seven thousand popular votes strategically scattered among the states so as to give him a comfortable majority of the electoral votes. Four years later, the railroads wanted James G. Blaine (he also had been involved in stock scandals), but the Democratic candidate, Grover Cleveland, made such a strong campaign that the tycoons secretly gave huge contributions to both parties so that their interests would be protected no matter which candidate won.

With their control of local and national governments, the railroad owners operated their lines almost free of taxes, paying nothing at all on their unpatented land grants. The Western settlers who had to pay extremely high taxes gradually became aware of this unjust situation, but any public complaint was met with indifference by the *Grand Seigneurs* who ruled the West. If they responded at all to criticism they would bluster indignantly that without them and their railroads the West would still be inhabited only by "savage" Indians. They completely disregarded the fact that the railroads had been constructed with loans from the public, and that their fortunes were based upon millions of acres of public lands and forests given to them by prodigal representatives of the people. Their attitude was that the public had no rights, and the railroads, instead of being public utilities for the benefit of all, were private properties to be operated solely to earn profits for the owners.

This feudal treatment by the railroad corporations created among the Western settlers a disillusionment with the American political system. Switching from Republican to Democratic or Democratic to Republican candidates did not seem to change anything. They would elect a man who promised to defend their interests, and a few months later he would enrage them by riding back home on free railroad passes, or sometimes in a luxurious private car. Like the journalists who expected retainers from the railroads, congressmen and state legislators also expected favors from them. Such emoluments were generally understood by politicians to be one of the main reasons for seeking public office.

The Western settlers' first effort to break this ring of corruption was through a farmers' organization, the Patrons of Husbandry, popularly known as the National Grange, which was formed shortly after the Civil War. During the 1870s, thousands of Grange lodges in the West devoted much of their time to fighting the power of the railroads. "The history of the present railroad monopoly is a history of repeated injuries and oppressions," the members declared in a general assembly of 1873, "all having in direct object the establishment of a absolute tyranny over the people of these States unequalled in any monarchy of the Old World, and having its only parallel in the history of the mediaeval ages, when the strong hand was the only law, and the highways of commerce were taxed by the feudal barons, who, from their strongholds, surrounded by their armies of vassals, could lay such tribute upon the travellers as their own wills alone should dictate."

By voting in solid blocs, the Grangers elected enough of their members to legislatures of eleven Western states to gain the passage of laws to control their railroad enemies, whom they condemned in stirring speeches as "robber barons" and "bloated bondholders" and "money sharks." The laws varied from state to state, but they all established controls on freight rates, which were to be fixed by state railroad commissions.

To this surprising rebellion, the railroad kings responded vigorously. Collis Huntington railed out at these impudent "agrarians" who dared invade his sacred property rights. "Communists!" he shouted, and demanded that the federal courts halt their interference with interstate commerce and the charter rights of Western railroads. Through their controlled newspapers, the railroads launched a propaganda campaign against the "subversive" Grangers, and banded together to deliberately ignore the state laws regulating freight rates. When the state commissions insisted on enforcement, the railroads tried to "buy" enough members to influence the decisions, and no doubt were successful in some cases. In 1876, however, the magnates suffered a shock when the Supreme Court ruled that the state Granger laws were constitutional, and that a state had the right to impose restrictions "on public undertakings which were in the nature of monopolies."

The railroads now began a long campaign against the Grangers. They punished geographical areas where Grangers were strong by changing schedules so that trains no longer stopped to discharge or pick up passengers or freight, inconveniencing entire communities so that local resentment built up against the Grangers. They spent money freely to defeat Granger candidates for office, employed legions of lawyers to find loopholes in the Granger laws, and constantly whittled away at the laws until they secured the repeal of those they considered most restrictive. In 1886, ten years after its decision in favor of the Grangers, the Supreme Court reversed itself in another case brought by the railroads. This time the court declared that no state could regulate railroad commerce that passed beyond its limits. Before the mighty power of the railroad corporations, the Grange eventually collapsed as a political force. Although they were left in disarray, the resolute Western settlers would soon assemble again for another battle against the giants.

In its decision of 1886 forbidding regulation of railroads by the states, the Supreme Court suggested that there should be a federal agency to watch over these giant corporations. When a bill was introduced in Congress to establish the Interstate Commerce Commission, scores of railroad lobbyists descended upon Washington to block its passage. At the time, however, there was so much national resentment against the railroads that the will of the people miraculously prevailed, and after long and bitter hearings a five-man commission was created and the railroads became the first industry to be officially regulated by the federal government. In the beginning, the Interstate Commerce Commission was almost impotent, having the power only to prevent railroads from charging more for short hauls than for long hauls and to require them to publish their rates. Not until well into the twentieth century was the commission able to set maximum rates. Even so, the railroads tried to abolish the commission until they gradually came to the realization that it might prove to be a useful shield. "It satisfies the popular clamor for government supervision of railroads, at the same time that that supervision is almost entirely minimal," observed the legal counsel for the Burlington. "The part of wisdom is not to destroy the Commission, but to utilize it." And utilize it they did, until the I.C.C. became a dead hand upon the railroad system of America.

In the meantime, the temporarily disorganized settlers of the West, who still considered themselves pawns of the "grasping and domineering" railroads, were re-forming themselves into a multitude of alliances, unions, green-backers, argricultural wheels, and cooperatives—all openly political and determined to carry on the fight started by the Grangers.

During the 1870s and 1880s the colonizing efforts of the transcontinental railroads created almost two million farms in the West, and by the end of the 1880s local prices of their agricultural products suffered sharp declines. Although corn sold for a dollar a bushel in Chicago, a plains farmer received only ten cents a bushel. As this was cheaper than the price they had to pay for coal, Westerners began burning corn for fuel, and left their wheat rotting on the plains from Kansas and Colorado to the Dakotas. To a man, they viewed the situation as a rigged deal, blamed it on the railroads, and hastened to join one of the numerous splinter parties springing up across the West.

The great droughts that began in the late 1880s and worsened into the 1890s served to bring all these despairing and disenchanted Americans into one grand alliance, the People's party. For years these Populists had been attempting to elect—through the Republican and Democratic parties—representatives who would respond to their will, and time after time they had failed. Now they were launched upon a heroic adventure that would match those of the first explorers of the West. They would prove that the West was still a poor-man's country, that the old legends of Good conquering Evil were still valid, that people could still be free upon the Western land. "It was a religious revival," one of the participants recalled afterward, "a crusade, a Pentecost of politics in which a tongue of flame sat upon every man, and each spake as the spirit gave him utterance."

Although women had not then won the right to vote, except in Wyoming, they took a large part in the campaign across the West. One of the outstanding leaders of the People's party was Mary Elizabeth Lease of Kansas, whose slogan was "Raise less corn and more hell." Left an orphan in Pennsylvania when her father died in the Civil War, she came West to teach school, married a young man who tried to farm, and was caught in a life of drudgery. The Leases raised crops that made no profit because of high railroad shipping rates and they were unable to support their four children. Eventually their farm was taken from them in foreclosure, and they moved to Wichita, where Mary Lease worked as a laundress and began reading law. Soon after she won admittance to the bar, she helped organize the People's party, and during the first big campaign of 1890 she traveled widely, delivering 160 speeches. In her rich contralto voice she emphasized such points as: "Kansas suffers from two great robbers, the Santa Fe Railroad and the loan companies. The common people are robbed to enrich their masters. . . . We want money, land, and transportation. . . . The people are at bay, let the bloodhounds of money who have dogged us thus far beware."

Another Kansan, Jerry Simpson, was an equally effective orator. In a race for Congress, Simpson constantly charged that the railroads controlled the political power of the West, and he demanded that they be taken over by the government and run for the benefit of the people. He gloried in the nickname "Sockless Jerry" given him by his Republican opponent. Simpson pointed out that his rival rode in a private car supplied by the railroads, dubbed him "Prince Hal," and won the election.

In 1890 the Populist movement made deep inroads against the old parties, and in 1892, a presidential year, its members geared up for a national rebellion against "railroad oppression." Somewhat symbolically they assembled for a convention in Omaha, where scarcely more than a quarter of a century before the first transcontinental railway had begun driving westward. In the reading of their platform, the anti-railroad plank received a tumultuous ovation, and after nominating a former Union general, James Weaver, for President, and a former Confederate general, James Fields, for

Vice-President, the delegates returned to their states to do battle in the most intensive political campaign ever waged against the American establishment.

After the ballots were counted, the Populists were in control of governments in Colorado, Idaho, Kansas, Nevada, and North Dakota, and elected several governors, congressmen, legislators, and mayors in other Western states. The momentum continued four more years until William Jennings Bryan captured the movement and swept it into the Democratic party.

For all its weaknesses of sectionalism and primitive prejudices, the Populist party's war against the railroads had a remarkable effect upon the national consciousness of America. The party's ideals and images seeped into the popular literature, with scores of muckraking journalists prying into the sources of power that had gained control of government. Ignatius Donnelly of Minnesota, one of the golden-tongued orators of the movement, published a best-seller, *Caesar's Column*, in which his fictitious heroes fight the evil plutocrats of America down to the year 1988, are defeated, and flee to Africa to found a new democracy. It was Frank Norris, however, who created the antirailroad literary classic, *The Octopus*, published in 1901, which after seventy-five years is still in print in several editions. As a Californian, Norris witnessed the corrupting effects of railroad power upon human beings and their institutions in that state. Those who refused to "turn railroad" could be crushed by it; those who fought the corporation sometimes died by violence.

For Norris's hero, the Iron Horse was not the romantic breathing engine of the poets, the messenger who steamed through the nights of a thousand small towns of the West, singing with its musical whistle to dreaming youths and calling them to ride with it to find their fortunes by the Western or the Eastern Sea. For Norris, the Iron Horse of the West was "the galloping monster, the terror of steel and steam, with its single eye, Cyclopean, red, shooting from horizon to horizon . . . the symbol of a vast power, huge, terrible, flinging the echo of its thunder over the reaches of the valley, leaving blood and destruction in its path; the leviathan, with tentacles of steel clutching into the soil, the soulless Force, the iron-hearted Power, the monster, the Colossus, the Octopus."

In retrospect, the Iron Horse powered by steam may well have been the most efficient engine ever devised for a nation endowed with billions of tons of coal. After those giant international combines of oil and motors (which superseded the railroad corporations) conspired to kill off the electric locomotive in the East and the steam locomotive in the West, replacing them with the sullen diesel, the old Iron Horse became an object of charm and nostalgia. In comparison with that oil-gulping Afreet, the diesel, which inspires neither awe nor affection, the steam locomotive with its sounds and smells of life had become a symbol of a lost cause. A few survive now in the way that the wild buffalo of the lost West survive—in parks and zoos where people come to see them, riding for short distances behind the clanking engines in refurbished coaches, photographing the smoke pluming gloriously above them, recording the sounds of escaping steam, puffing stacks, ringing bells, and resonating whistles.

As for the tracks on which the Iron Horses ran across America in their days of grandeur, thousands of miles now lie rusting under sun and rain. A few true railroaders still survive, carrying on the traditions of service and promptitude, but their numbers decline year by year. Over the long transcontinental roads of the West millions of tons of freight are still hauled, but few human beings attempt that leisurely adventure anymore, knowing that the elegance and allurement have vanished.

After receiving a bad fright from the Populists in the 1890s, the railroads made a few pretenses of running a public utility. The old moguls died off or retired to their palaces to admire their collections of paintings and rare bindings, and were replaced by a new breed of faceless managerial and financial executives, who established public-relations departments to fool the public while they drained the railroads' profits off into oil, mining, real estate, and other ventures. By the time the nation entered World War I, the railroads and their equipment were in such dilapidated condition that the government had to put them under federal control, rebuilding and restocking at government expense in order to meet the transportation needs of the war. This was the second, third, or fourth time that the American people had paid for some of these railroads, but as soon as the war ended, the government handed the rebuilt system back to the owners, who then had the gall to demand more than a billion dollars from the Treasury for alleged losses during the war.

During the years that followed, the railroad owners reverted to their old ways, forming syndicates, manipulating stocks, diverting funds, until by World War II they were again approaching a state of collapse. The demands of war, with vast sums of the people's money being spent for transportation, revived the roads until the postwar period when one by one they began to decline, incapable of or uninterested in meeting the competition of trucks and airplanes. Now only a handful of efficiently operated freight railroads remain. Most of the passenger traffic has been subsidized by the people's money in a bureaucratic absurdity known as Amtrak, which attempts to run passenger trains over privately owned tracks so worn out that they would not have passed

(*Photograph by David Plowden © 1972*)

inspection during construction of the first transcontinental railways a century ago. In 1974, the people of the United States began paying for some of these bankrupt railroads again through an act of their Congress, called the Regional Rail Reorganization Act, a plan that was drafted by the railroad owners instead of by representatives of the people.

More than a hundred years ago, one of those pioneer travelers who made that romantic journey by rail to the Western Sea, and was affronted by the arrogance displayed by the railroad he traveled upon, paused to make a prophecy in his notebook. "Some day in this country," he wrote, "as it has been in England, it will be decided that railroads are to be run for the public, and for their benefit and accommodation. Corporations and monopolies, cliques and combinations, may, for a time, oppress and hinder the people; but there always comes a day when the public assert, and, asserting, maintain their rights."

The prophecy has not yet come to pass.

NOTES

1. THE IRON HORSE COMES TO THE WATERS
OF THE MIGHTY MISSISSIPPI

1   "Amid the acclamations . . ."   *Rock Island Advertiser,* March 1, 1854.

2–3   The speakers that . . .   *Chicago Tribune,* Feb. 24, 1854.

7   It was mainly . . .   Sandburg, *Abraham Lincoln, the Prairie Years,* p. 37.

8   Encouraged by this . . .   Zobrist, "Steamboat Men," p. 164.

8   "Swiftly we sped . . ."   *Rock Island Advertiser,* April 30, 1856.

8–9   In Davenport and . . .   *Rock Island Advertiser,* May 14, 1856.

11   As the trial . . .   *Chicago Democratic Press,* Sept. 25, 1857.

11–12   In his closing . . .   Starr, *Lincoln and the Railroads,* pp. 110–12.

12   The theme that . . .   *Rock Island Magazine,* vol. 21, Feb. 1926, p. 6.

12   Although the jurors . . .   Zobrist, p. 170; Parish, "The First Mississippi Bridge," p. 138.

14–15   While a large . . .   *Davenport Democrat,* Oct. 22, 1905.

16   On New Year's . . .   Agnew, "Iowa's First Railroad," p. 25.

17   "We advocate the . . ."   *Chicago Democratic Press,* April 1, 1856; Agnew, "The Mississippi & Missouri Railroad," pp. 211–12.

17   Although he did . . .   Farnam, *Memoir of Henry Farnam,* p. 55.

2. "WITH THE WINGS OF THE WIND"

19   "Less than a . . ."   Farnam, *Memoir of Henry Farnam,* p. 73.

20   Much impressed by . . .   Brown, *History of the First Locomotives,* pp. 16, 86–88.

21–22   "The impression was . . ."   Ibid., p. 91.

23   "The safety valve . . ."   Edwards, *Modern American Locomotive Engines,* pp. 93–94.

25   Before beginning work . . .   Kelly, *Matthias W. Baldwin,* p. 15.

26   It was no . . .   *Congressional Globe,* Feb. 6, 1846, p. 323.

27–28   Typical of the . . .   Johnson, "Plumbe's Railroad," p. 92; Fern and Kaplan, "John Plumbe, Jr.," pp. 2–20.

29   In 1845 Whitney . . .   *Senate Report 161,* pp. 6–10.

31–32   In the late . . .   Cotterill, "Early Agitation," p. 408.

33   Despite all the . . .   *Congressional Globe,* July 29, 1848, p. 1011.

33   In a last . . .   *London Athenaeum,* Dec. 1, 1849.

34   Meanwhile in its . . .   *Congressional Globe,* March 2, 1853, p. 841.

37   Soon after the . . .   Manypenny, *Our Indian Wards,* p. 117.

3. WAR SLOWS THE MARCH TO THE WESTERN SEA

41   In August 1859 . . .   Johnson, *Peter Anthony Dey*, p. 82.
41–42   Whether Lincoln was . . .   Farnham, "Grenville Dodge and the Union Pacific," pp. 635–37.
43   At about noon . . .   Smith, *Story of the Pony Express*, p. 75.
44–45   In the meantime . . .   Judah, *A Practical Plan*, p. 17.
47   In reporting this . . .   U.S. Office of Indian Affairs, *Report*, p. 328.
48   It was soon . . .   *Senate Misc. Doc. 108*, pp. 4–9.
50   "Everybody felt happy . . ."   *Sacramento Union,* Jan. 9, 1863.
51   Meanwhile in the . . .   *N.Y. Times*, Sept. 6, 1862.
51–52   Although Dr. Thomas . . .   *Chicago Tribune*, Oct. 7, 1863.
52–54   Train could not . . .   Nevins, *Frémont*, p. 570.
54   The impatient George . . .   Sorenson, *Early History of Omaha*, p. 235.

4. DRILL, YE TARRIERS, DRILL, WHILE THE OWNERS TAKE THE PLUNDER

57   As the honest . . .   *House of Rep. Report 78*, pp. 65, 240.
59–60   In November, Dey . . .   Johnson, *Peter Anthony Dey*, p. 124.
61   Sherman made no . . .   Sorenson, *Early History of Omaha*, pp. 239–40.
61   "With numerous plans . . ."   *N.Y. Times*, Oct. 23, 1865.
64   From the swarms . . .   Hirshson, *Grenville M. Dodge*, p. 117.
64–65   With the arrival . . .   Bailey, *Story of the First Transcontinental Railroad*, pp. 53–54.
65   It was at . . .   Ordway, "Reminiscences," p. 158.
65–66   Exactly when they . . .   *N.Y. Times*, June 19, 1867.
67   After the Casement . . .   Seymour, *Incidents of a Trip*, p. 73.
70   Late that evening . . .   Ibid., p. 109.
71   "The larger part . . ."   *N.Y. Times*, June 11, 1867; Parry, "Letters from the Frontier," p. 128.
71–72   When Henry Morton . . .   Stanley, *My Early Travels*, pp. 106–107.
74   After Strobridge had . . .   Kraus, *High Road to Promontory*, p. 111.
77   To mark the . . .   *Sacramento Union*, Dec. 31, 1866.

5. THE ERA OF THE COWBOY IS BORN

78   "From Leavenworth I . . ."   Richardson, *Beyond the Mississippi*, p. 550.
79–80   In 1866, Palmer's . . .   Leland, *The Union Pacific Railroad*, p. 11.

80   One of the reporters . . . Ibid., p. 63.

80–81   That General Palmer's . . . Stanley, *My Early Travels*, pp. 89–91.

85–86   A few hundred . . . Byers, "When Railroading Outdid the Wild West Stories," p. 343.

87   Although Hancock was . . . Keim, *Sheridan's Troopers*, p. 45.

88   On May 28 . . . Roenigk, "Railroad Grading Among the Indians," pp. 385–87.

90   "We were running . . ." Cruise, "Early Days on the Union Pacific," pp. 542–43.

90   "Putting spurs to . . ." Ibid., p. 545.

90–91   During the month . . . White, "Indian Raids," p. 384.

91   During the Hancock . . . Grinnell, *The Fighting Cheyennes*, pp. 265–66.

91–92   In the pursuit . . . Stanley, pp. 156–57.

92–93   Reprisals upon the . . . *N.Y. Times*, June 17, 1867.

93   One of the . . . Parry, "Letters from the Frontier," p. 135.

94–95   When Henry Stanley . . . Stanley, pp. 165–67.

95   On through the . . . Parry, p. 142.

96–97   It was Samuel . . . Bowles, *Our New West*, p. 56.

98   "We hauled locomotives . . ." U.S. Pacific Railway Commission, *Reports and Testimony*, p. 3646.

6. THE GREAT RACE

100   Early in the . . . Kraus, *High Road to Promontory*, pp. 196–98.

101   Strobridge and his . . . Sabin, *Building the Pacific Railway*, pp. 231–32.

101–102 On one occasion . . . Kraus, p. 201.

103   In September, after . . . Ibid., p. 210.

104–105 Although engineers for . . . Dodge, *How We Built the Union Pacific Railway*, p. 24.

106–107 At the same . . . Ordway, "Reminiscences," pp. 157–58.

107   During April an . . . Lewis, *The Big Four*, p. 64.

110   When Dodge arrived . . . Perkins, *Trails, Rails and War*, p. 219.

110–111 Grading and filling . . . Hirshson, *Grenville M. Dodge*, pp. 164–65.

111   During its Hell . . . Beadle, *The Undeveloped West*, pp. 87–90.

112   Before Benton died . . . Athearn, *Union Pacific Country*, pp. 66, 406–407.

114   Durant plunged immediately . . . Perkins, pp. 221–22.

114–15 If Durant or . . . Ibid.

115   As the summer . . . Sabin, p. 175.

117   They celebrated Christmas . . . Beadle, p. 139.

117–118 When Jack Casement . . . Athearn, p. 96.

119   Although Dillon of . . . Hirshson, p. 168.

121   As soon as . . .   Best, *Iron Horses to Promontory*, p. 196; Beadle,
            pp. 120–21.
121–22   Only fifty miles . . .   Miller, *The Golden Spike*, p. 35.
124   Although Dr. Durant . . .   Perkins, p. 238.
125–27   While these events . . .   Utley, "The Dash to Promontory," p.
            112.
128   None of those . . .   Dillon, "Historic Moments," p. 258.
128–29   To speed this . . .   Bowman, "Driving the Last Spike," p. 97;
            Dillon, p. 258.
129   Durant, his head . . .   Sabin, pp. 218–20.
133   Somewhat reluctantly, the . . .   *N.Y. Times*, May 11, 1869.
133–35   "What was it . . ."   Harte, *Poetical Works*, pp. 292–93.

7. FIRST TRAVELERS ON THE TRANSCONTINENTAL

137   "Seventy-five minutes . . ."   Rae, *Westward by Rail*, p. 34.
137–38   Until a bridge . . .   Ibid., pp. 66–67.
138   And then after . . .   Lester, *The Atlantic to the Pacific*, pp. 16,
            260, 281.
138   Early travelers on . . .   Rae, p. 69.
138–39   Except for a . . .   Lester, p. 19.
139   In springtime the . . .   Rae, p. 63.
140   Even in an . . .   Parson, *To San Francisco and Back*, p. 36.
141–42   British travelers were . . .   Robertson, *Our American Tour*, p.
            91; Parson, p. 52.
142   Judging from comments . . .   Robertson, p. 68; Coolidge, "A Few
            Hints on the California Journey," p. 27; Rice, "A Trip to Cali-
            fornia," p. 676.
142–43   According to William . . .   Humason, *From the Atlantic Surf to
            the Golden Gate*, pp. 15, 48, 53.
143–44   At most dining . . .   Lester, p. 260.
144   Because Cheyenne was . . .   Parson, pp. 46, 53; Coolidge, pp.
            27–28.
144–45   Prairie-dog villages . . .   Putnam, "A Trip to the End of the
            Union Pacific," p. 198.
145   Although only thinning . . .   Keim, *Sheridan's Troopers*, p. 38.
145   In its early . . .   Putnam, pp. 198–99.
145–46   So eager was . . .   Keim, pp. 62–63.
146   The buffalo and . . .   Humason, p. 12.
147–48   Along the way . . .   Lester, p. 60.
148   When there were . . .   Rice, pp. 675–76.
148   Winter travelers could . . .   Rae, p. 340.
150   "We were regaled . . ."   Rice, p. 678.
150   Lady Duffus Hardy . . .   Hardy, *Through Cities and Prairie
            Lands*, pp. 260–61.
150–51   Other travelers spent . . .   Humason, p. 51.

153–54   Not all train . . .   Ibid., p. 18.
156–57   Sophisticated travelers such . . .   Rae, pp. 89–90.
157   Bill Dadd, the . . .   Atwell, *Great Transcontinental Railroad Guide*, p. 32.
158   At times on . . .   Lester, pp. 21, 31, 242.
158–59   According to most . . .   Parson, p. 46; Hardy, p. 260.
159   There may have . . .   French, *Railroadman*, p. 93.
159–60   As in any . . .   Keim, p. 37.
160   At Sherman, some . . .   Lester, p. 26; Buss, *Wanderings in the West*, p. 127.
161   A group of . . .   Humason, pp. 19–20.
161–62   About fifty miles . . .   Rae, pp. 99–100; Hardy, p. 103.
162–63   Salt Lake City . . .   Rice, pp. 677–78.
163   At Ogden, passengers . . .   Hardy, p. 101.
165   As they rolled . . .   Humason, p. 39; Rae, p. 185.
166   By this time . . .   Putnam, p. 202
166   The bracing air . . .   Lester, p. 57.
166–67   From the summit . . .   Humason, p. 49; Rae, p. 126.
168   "A blarsted long . . ."   Parson, p. 64.
168   Although passage through . . .   Rae, p. 227.
169   American travelers on . . .   Rice, pp. 675–76.

8. RAILROADERS WEST

172   Veteran railroad man . . .   Reinhardt, *Workin' on the Railroad*, p. 98.
172–73   To find engineers . . .   Byers, "When Railroading Outdid the Wild West Stories," p. 345.
173   Nevertheless, to most . . .   "The Engineer," pp. 5–6.
174   Before Eli Janney . . .   Richardson, "Iron Horse Wrangler," p. 137.
175   The same reluctance . . .   Reinhardt, p. 96; Richardson, p. 136.
176   The railroad employee . . .   Holbrook, *The Story of American Railroads*, p. 408.
177   Not all travelers . . .   Shepherd, *Prairie Experiences*, p. 68.
177–78   Robert Louis Stevenson . . .   Stevenson, *Across the Plains*, pp. 37–39.
178   Many of the . . .   Husband, *The Story of the Pullman Car*, p. 30.
179   Like the black . . .   Holbrook, pp. 337–38.
179   Because of the . . .   Byers, p. 346.
179–80   All station agents . . .   Cruise, "Early Days on the Union Pacific," p. 547.
180   "An American conductor . . ."   Reinhardt, pp. 282–83.
181   Another British traveler . . .   Robinson, *Sinners and Saints*, p. 52.
181   Even so, most . . .   George, *Forty Years on the Rails*, p. 244.

9. EXIT THE LAND GRABBERS, ENTER THE STOCK MANIPULATORS

183   "The Pacific Railroad . . ." Adams, "Railroad Inflation," pp. 144–45.

184–85   A traveler in . . . Morris, *Condition of the Union Pacific Railroad*, pp. 9–11.

186   The greatest disillusionment . . . Trottman, *History of the Union Pacific*, p. 73.

186–87   Because publication of . . . Adams, pp. 147–48.

187–88   As Congress began . . . *N.Y. Herald,* Jan. 24, 1873.

189   As might have . . . *The Nation,* March 13, 1873, p. 174.

190–92   With less than . . . U.S. Pacific Railway Commission, *Reports and Testimony*, p. 447; Grodinsky, *Transcontinental Railway Strategy*, p. 71.

193   Gould was now . . . Josephson, *The Robber Barons*, p. 101.

194–95   Before construction could . . . U.S. Pacific Railway Commission, p. 3821.

196   "Young men without . . ." Storey, "William Jackson Palmer," p. 46.

196–97   Sixty miles south . . . Athearn, *Rebel of the Rockies*, p. 10.

200   As soon as . . . Grodinsky, p. 63.

200   In railroad building . . . Woodward, *Reunion and Reaction*, p. 256; Grodinsky, p. 65.

10. SITTING BULL AND THE NORTHERN ROUTE

205–206   This brought Sitting . . . U.S. Commissioner of Indian Affairs, *Report*, 1872, pp. 659, 840–41.

206   Commanding the expedition . . . Stanley, *Personal Memoirs*, p. 239; Merington, *The Custer Story*, pp. 251–52.

207   The conflict between . . . Custer, "Battling With the Sioux," pp. 92–93.

207–208   Litton Shields, a . . . Shields, "Reminiscences of a Railroad Builder," pp. 47–48.

212   In 1870, so . . . Larson, *Jay Cooke*, p. 275.

214   What motivated Cooke . . . Julian, "Railway Influence in the Land Office," pp. 241, 255–56.

215   Immediate conversion of . . . Smalley, *History of the Northern Pacific Railroad*, p. 196.

11. ELEGANCE ON THE WESTERN RAILS

218–19   During the Centennial . . . Brown, *The Year of the Century*, pp. 258–61.

221   For their tour . . . Leslie, *California, a Pleasure Trip*, p. 35.

221–22   At Cheyenne, the . . . Ibid., pp. 48–50.

224–25 The handsome waitresses . . . Henderson, *"Meals by Fred Harvey,"* p. 493; Marshall, *Santa Fe,* p. 101.

226–27 At Corinne, Utah . . . Lewis and Smith, *Oscar Wilde Discovers America,* p. 286.

227 Wilde's main complaint . . . Wilde, "Impressions of America," pp. 200, 217.

227 Rudyard Kipling, who . . . Kipling, *From Sea to Sea,* p. 19.

228 Like all Pullman . . . Ibid., p. 56.

228 Typical of American . . . Davis, *The West from a Car Window,* pp. 4, 27.

228–29 He regretted missing . . . Ibid. pp. 6, 226.

229 One of the . . . Gripenberg, *A Half Year in the New World,* p. 109.

229 From her car . . . Ibid., pp. 110–11.

229 Alexandra Gripenberg was . . . Ibid., p. 121.

229–30 The Pullman washroom . . . Hamer, *From Ocean to Ocean,* p. 63; Sala, *America Revisited,* vol. 2, p. 179.

230 On the whole . . . Vivian, *Notes of a Tour in America,* p. 98.

230 Several travelers who . . . Robinson, *Sinners and Saints,* p. 278.

230 It would be . . . Hamer, p. 61; Jackson, *Bits of Travel at Home,* p. 4.

230–31 Travel-writer Emily . . . Faithfull, *Three Visits to America,* pp. 46–47.

231 A French traveler . . . O'Rell, *Jonathan and His Continent,* p. 270.

232 One Briton commented . . . Robinson, p. 60.

232 American trainmen also . . . O'Rell, pp. 272–73.

232–33 The remarkable efficiency . . . Marshall, W. G., *Through America,* pp. 60–61, 69.

233 And some foreigners . . . Saunders, *Through the Light Continent,* pp. 123–25.

233 Until well into . . . Gripenberg, p. 113; Faithfull, p. 48.

233–34 Traveling Britons missed . . . Robinson, p. 53.

234 As early as . . . Sala, vol. 2, p. 155.

12. The Immigrant

235 "Every foreign labourer . . ." Bell, *New Tracks in North America,* p. 511.

235 Immigrants were needed . . . Overton, *Burlington West,* p. 349.

236 Almost every handbook . . . A.S.S.A., *Handbook for Emigrants,* pp. 2–3.

237–38 In 1879, a . . . Stevenson, *Across the Plains,* pp. 56, 58–61.

238 One of Stevenson's . . . Hardy, *Through Cities and Prairie Lands,* pp. 84–85.

241–42 Robert Louis Stevenson . . . Stevenson, pp. 2–3, 7.

243 Although passengers on . . . Hine, *William Andrew Spalding,* p. 4.

244   G. F. Byron . . .   Byron, "The Overland Emigrant," p. 639.

244–45   They overlooked no . . .   Buchanan, "The Great Railroad Mi-
           gration," p. 30.

245   During the 1870s . . .   Overton, p. 363.

245–46   Armies of agents . . .   Ibid., p. 360.

251   Bribery was another . . .   Hedges, "The Colonization Work of
           the Northern Pacific," p. 338.

252   In Scandinavia, where . . .   Overton, p. 368.

254   Sometimes entire groups . . .   Hedges, "Promotion of Immigra-
           tion," p. 195.

13. TRAMPLING THE FRONTIER

256   Villard's carefully staged . . .   Tilden, *Following the Frontier*, p.
           144.

258   Instead of using . . .   *St. Paul Pioneer Press*, Sept. 9, 1883.

259–60   Whenever the Northern . . .   *Senate Exec. Doc. 32*, pp. 13,
           23–24.

260   None of these . . .   Bryce, *The American Commonwealth*, vol. 2,
           p. 362.

260–61   Bryce also must . . .   Ibid.

261   On that late . . .   Fairweather, "The Northern Pacific Railroad,"
           p. 98.

261–62   Villard's rapid rise . . .   Grodinsky, *Transcontinental Railway
           Strategy*, pp. 183–84.

262   In 1875, Frederick . . .   Smalley, *History of the Northern Pacific
           Railroad*, pp. 236–37.

264   With the same . . .   *N.Y. Times*, Nov. 16, 1890.

271   So much of . . .   Bryce, vol. 2, p. 530.

14. THE IRON HORSE ASSUMES A DEVIL IMAGE

272   "We are so . . ."   George, "What the Railroad Will Bring Us," p.
           38.

273   As early as . . .   *Saline County* (Nebraska) *Post*, Dec. 15, 1871.

274   From the lowliest . . .   White, *Autobiography*, pp. 149–50.

274–75   As for national . . .   Larrabee, *The Railroad Question*, pp.
           224–25.

276   The Western settlers' . . .   Adams, *Railroads*, p. 129.

276   By voting in . . .   Ibid., p. 145.

277–78   In its decision . . .   Lyon, *To Hell in a Day Coach*, p. 107.

278   The great droughts . . .   Hicks, *The Populist Revolt*, p. 159.

278–79   Although women had . . .   Ibid., p. 160.

280–81   For Norris's hero . . .   Norris, *The Octopus*, p. 48.

282–83   During the years . . .   Hall, "Straightening Out the Rails,"
           p. 20.

283   More than a . . .   Lester, *The Atlantic to the Pacific*, p. 254.

BIBLIOGRAPHY

1. THE IRON HORSE COMES TO THE WATERS OF THE MIGHTY MISSISSIPPI

Agnew, Dwight L. "Iowa's First Railroad." *Iowa Journal of History,* vol. 48, 1950, pp. 1–26.

———"Jefferson Davis and the Rock Island Bridge." *Iowa Journal of History,* vol. 47, 1949, pp. 3–14.

———"The Mississippi & Missouri Railroad, 1856–1860." *Iowa Journal of History,* vol. 51, 1953, pp. 211–32.

Beveridge, Albert J. *Abraham Lincoln, 1809–1858,* vol. I. Boston, Houghton Mifflin, 1928.

Chicago and North Western Railway Company, *Reports,* 1865–68.

Chicago Democratic Press, April 1, 1856; Sept. 25, 1857.

Chicago Tribune, Feb. 24, 1854.

Davenport (Iowa) *Democrat,* Oct. 22, 1905.

Donovan, Frank P. "The Race to Council Bluffs." *Palimpsest,* vol. 43, 1962, pp. 545–56.

Farnam, Henry W. *Memoir of Henry Farnam,* New Haven, Conn., 1889.

Hayes, William E. *Iron Road to Empire, the History of 100 Years of the Progress and Achievements of the Rock Island Lines.* N.Y., Simmons-Boardman, 1953.

Parish, John C. "The First Mississippi Bridge." *Palimpsest,* vol. 3, 1922, pp. 133–41.

Rock Island (Ill.) *Advertiser,* March 1, 1854; April 30, 1856; May 14, 1856; Feb. 11, 1857.

Rock Island Magazine, vols. 21–23, 1926–28.

Sandburg, Carl. *Abraham Lincoln, the Prairie Years.* N.Y., Harcourt, Brace, 1926.

Starr, John W., Jr. *Lincoln and the Railroads.* N.Y., Dodd, Mead, 1927.

Zobrist, Benedict K. "Steamboat Men versus Railroad Men." *Missouri Historical Review,* vol. 59, 1965, pp. 159–72.

2. "WITH THE WINGS OF THE WIND"

Alexander, E. P. *Iron Horses, American Locomotives 1829–1900.* N.Y., Bonanza Books, 1941.

Brown, Margaret L. "Asa Whitney and His Pacific Railroad Publicity Campaign." *Mississippi Valley Historical Review,* vol. 20, 1933, pp. 209–24.

Brown, William H. *The History of the First Locomotives in America.* N.Y., Appleton, 1874.

Comstock, Henry B. *The Iron Horse*, N.Y., Galahad Books, 1971.

Congressional Globe, Feb. 6, 1846; July 29, 1848; March 2, 1853.

Cotterill, Robert S. "Early Agitation for a Pacific Railroad, 1845–1850." *Mississippi Valley Historical Review*, vol. 5, 1919, pp. 396–409.

――― "Memphis Railroad Convention, 1849." *Tennessee Historical Magazine*, vol. 4, 1918, pp 83–94.

――― "The National Railroad Convention in St. Louis, 1849." *Missouri Historical Review*, vol. 12, 1918, pp. 203–15.

Edwards, Emory. *Modern American Locomotive Engines*. Philadelphia, Henry Carey Baird & Co., 1883.

Farnam, Henry W. *Memoir of Henry Farnam*. New Haven, Conn., 1889.

Fern, Alan and Kaplan, Milton. "John Plumbe, Jr., and the First Architectural Photographs of the Nation's Capitol." *Quarterly Journal of the Library of Congress*, vol. 31, 1974, pp. 2–20.

Foreman, Grant. *The Last Trek of the Indians*. Chicago, University of Chicago Press, 1946.

Goetzmann, William H. *Army Exploration in the American West, 1803–1863*. New Haven, Yale University Press, 1959.

Johnson, Jack T. "Plumbe's Railroad to the Moon." *Palimpsest*, vol. 19, 1938, pp. 89–97.

Kelly, Ralph. *Matthias W. Baldwin*, N.Y., Newcomen Society, 1946.

Kinert, Reed. *Early American Steam Locomotives*. N.Y., Bonanza Books, 1962.

London Athenaeum, Dec. 1, 1849.

Manypenny, George W. *Our Indian Wards*. Cincinnati, Clarke, 1880.

U.S. Congress, 29th, 1st sess. *Senate Report 161* (Memorial of A. Whitney). Washington, Feb. 24, 1846.

Westing, Fred. *The Locomotives that Baldwin Built*. N.Y., Bonanza Books, 1956.

3. WAR SLOWS THE MARCH TO THE WESTERN SEA

Chicago Tribune, Oct. 7, 1863.

Clevenger, Homer. "The Building of the Hannibal and St. Joseph Railroad." *Missouri Historical Review*, vol. 36, 1941, pp. 32–47.

Cruise, John D. "Early Days on the Union Pacific." Kansas State Historical Society, *Collections*, vol. 11, 1909–10, pp. 529–47.

Farnham, Wallace D. "The Pacific Railroad Act of 1862." *Nebraska History*, vol. 43, 1962, pp. 141–67.

――― "Grenville Dodge and the Union Pacific: A Study of Historical Legends." *Journal of American History*, vol. 51, 1964–65, pp. 632–50.

Fitzsimmons, Margaret Louise. "Missouri Railroads During the Civil War and Reconstruction." *Missouri Historical Review*, vol. 35, 1941, pp. 188–206.

Johnson, Jack T. *Peter Anthony Dey*. Iowa City, State Historical Society of
    Iowa, 1939.
Judah, Theodore D. *A Practical Plan for Building the Pacific Railroad*.
    Washington, 1857.
Kraus, George. High Road to Promontory. N.Y., Castle Books, 1969.
Lewis, Oscar. *The Big Four*. N.Y., Knopf, 1938.
Nevins, Allan. *Frémont, Pathmarker of the West*. N.Y., Appleton-Century,
    1939.
New York Times, Sept. 6, 1862.
Overton, Richard C. *Burlington Route*. N.Y., Knopf, 1965.
Sacramento Union, Jan. 9, 1863.
Smith, Waddell F., ed. *The Story of the Pony Express*. San Rafael, Calif.,
    Pony Express History and Art Gallery, 1964.
Sorenson, Alfred. *Early History of Omaha*, 1889.
U.S. Congress, 37th, 2d sess. *Senate Miscellaneous Document 108* (An Act
    to Aid in the Construction of a Railroad and Telegraph Line from the
    Missouri River to the Pacific Ocean . . .). Washington, July 14,
    1862.
U.S. Office of Indian Affairs. *Report*. Washington, 1860.

4. Drill, Ye Tarriers, Drill, While the
Owners Take the Plunder

Bailey, W. F. *The Story of the First Transcontinental Railroad*. Pittsburgh,
    1906.
Bowles, Samuel. *Across the Continent*. Springfield, Mass., 1865.
Hirshson, Stanley P. *Grenville M. Dodge, Soldier, Politician, Railroad Pio-
    neer*. Bloomington, Indiana University Press, 1967.
History of the State of Nebraska. Chicago, Western Historical Co., 1882.
Howard, Robert West. *The Great Iron Trail*. N.Y., Bonanza Books, 1962.
Kraus, George. *High Road to Promontory*. N.Y., Castle Books, 1969.
New York Times, Oct. 23, 1865; June 11, 17, and 19, 1867.
O'Connor, Richard. *Iron Wheels and Broken Men*. N.Y., G. P. Putnam's
    Sons, 1973.
Ordway, Edward. "Reminiscences." *Annals of Wyoming*, vol. 5, 1927, pp.
    149–60.
Parry, Henry C. "Letters from the Frontier—1867." *Annals of Wyoming*,
    vol. 38, 1972, pp. 127–44.
Sacramento Union, Dec. 31, 1866.
Seymour, Silas. *Incidents of a Trip Through the Great Platte Valley to the
    Rocky Mountains* . . . N.Y., Van Nostrand, 1867.
Sorenson, Alfred. *Early History of Omaha*. Omaha, 1889.
Stanley, Henry Morton. *My Early Travels and Adventures*, vol. 1. N.Y.,
    Charles Scribner's Sons, 1895.

Trottman, Nelson. *History of the Union Pacific, a Financial and Economic Survey.* N.Y., Ronald Press, 1923.

U.S. Congress, 42d, 3d sess. *House of Representatives Report 78* (Select Committee on Credit Mobilier and the Union Pacific Railroad, Report). Washington, Government Printing Office, 1873.

U.S. Secretary of the Interior. *Report.* Washington, 1866.

5. THE ERA OF THE COWBOY IS BORN

Bowles, Samuel. *Our New West.* Hartford, Conn., Hartford Publishing Co., 1869.

Byers, O. P. "When Railroading Outdid the Wild West Stories." Kansas State Historical Society, *Transactions,* vol. 17, 1926–28, pp. 339–48.

Cheyenne Leader, Nov. 16, 1867.

Cruise, John D. "Early Days on the Union Pacific." Kansas State Historical Society, *Transactions,* vol. 11, 1909–10, pp. 529–47.

Grinnell, George B. *The Fighting Cheyennes.* Norman, University of Oklahoma Press, 1956.

Keim, De B. Randolph. *Sheridan's Troopers on the Border.* Philadelphia, 1885.

Leland, Charles G. *The Union Pacific Railroad, Eastern Division; or Three Thousand Miles in a Railway Car.* Philadelphia, Ringwalt and Brown, 1867.

McCague, James. *Moguls and Iron Men, the Story of the First Transcontinental Railroad.* N.Y., Harper & Row, 1964.

McCoy, Joseph G. *Historic Sketches of the Cattle Trade in the West and Southwest.* Kansas City, Mo., Ramsey, Millet & Hudson, 1874.

New York Times, June 17, 1867.

Parry, Henry C. "Letters from the Frontier—1867." *Annals of Wyoming,* vol. 38, 1972, pp. 127–44.

Richardson, Albert D. *Beyond the Mississippi.* Hartford, Conn., American Publishing Co., 1867.

Roenigk, Adolph. "Railroad Grading Among the Indians." Kansas State Historical Society, *Transactions,* vol. 8, 1903–04, pp. 384–89.

Stanley, Henry M. *My Early Travels and Adventures,* vol. 1. N.Y., Charles Scribner's Sons, 1895.

U.S. Pacific Railway Commission. *Reports and Testimony.* Washington, 1888.

White, Lonnie J. "Indian Raids on the Kansas Frontier, 1869," *Kansas Historical Quarterly,* vol. 38, 1972, pp. 369–88.

6. THE GREAT RACE

Athearn, Robert G. *Union Pacific Country.* Chicago, Rand McNally Co., 1971.

Beadle, John Hanson. *The Undeveloped West.* Philadelphia, National Publishing Co., 1873.

Best, Gerald M. *Iron Horses to Promontory.* San Marino, Calif., Golden West Books, 1969.

Bowman, J. N. "Driving the Last Spike at Promontory, 1869." *California Historical Society Quarterly,* vol. 36, 1957, pp. 97–106, 263–74.

Dillon, Sidney. "Historic Moments: Driving the Last Spike of the Union Pacific." *Scribner's Magazine,* vol. 12, 1892, pp. 255–59.

Dodge, Grenville M. *How We Built the Union Pacific Railway* (U.S. Congress, 2d sess., *Senate Document 447*). Washington, Government Printing Office, 1910.

Harte, Bret. *Poetical Works.* Boston, Houghton Mifflin, 1896.

Hirshson, Stanley P. *Grenville M. Dodge, Soldier, Politician, Railroad Pioneer.* Bloomington, Indiana University Press, 1967.

Kraus, George P. *High Road to Promontory,* N.Y., Castle Books, 1969.

Lewis, Oscar. *The Big Four.* N.Y., Alfred A. Knopf, 1938.

Miller, David E., ed. *The Golden Spike.* Salt Lake City, University of Utah Press, 1973.

New York Times, May 11, 1869.

Ordway, Edward. "Reminiscences." *Annals of Wyoming,* vol. 5, 1927, pp. 149–60.

Perkins, J. R. *Trails, Rails and War, the Life of General G. M. Dodge.* Indianapolis, Bobbs-Merrill, 1929.

Sabin, Edwin L. *Building the Pacific Railway.* Philadelphia, Lippincott, 1919.

Utley, Robert M. "The Dash to Promontory." *Utah Historical Quarterly,* vol. 29, 1961, pp. 99–117.

Utley, Robert M. and Ketterson, Francis A., Jr. *Golden Spike.* Washington, U.S. National Park Service, 1969.

7. FIRST TRAVELERS ON THE TRANSCONTINENTAL

Atwell, H. Wallace. *Great Transcontinental Railroad Guide.* Chicago, Geo. A. Crofutt & Co., 1869.

Buss, H. *Wanderings in the West During the Year 1870.* London, Thomas Danks, 1871.

Coolidge, Susan. "A Few Hints on the California Journey." *Scribner's Monthly,* vol. 6, 1873, pp. 25–31.

French, Chauncey D. *Railroadman.* N.Y., Macmillan, 1938.

Hardy, Lady Duffus. *Through Cities and Prairie Lands, Sketches of an American Tour.* N.Y., Worthington, 1890.

Humason, W. L. *From the Atlantic Surf to the Golden Gate.* Hartford, Conn., 1869.

Keim, De B. Randolph. *Sheridan's Troopers on the Border.* Philadelphia, 1885.

Lester, John E. *The Atlantic to the Pacific, What to See, and How to See It.* Boston, Shepard & Gill, 1873.

[A London Parson]. *To San Francisco and Back.* London, Society for Promoting Christian Knowledge, 1870.

Pattison, William D. "Westward by Rail with Professor Sedgwick: a Lantern Journey of 1873." *Historical Society of Southern California, Quarterly*, vol. 42, 1960, pp. 335–49.

Putnam, John H. "A Trip to the End of the Union Pacific in 1868." *Kansas Historical Quarterly*, vol. 13, 1944–45, pp. 196–203.

Rae, William F. *Westward by Rail: the New Route to the East.* N.Y., Appleton, 1871.

Rice, Harvey. "A Trip to California in 1869." *Magazine of Western History*, vols. 7–8, 1887–88, pp. 675–79, 1–7.

Robertson, William and W. F. *Our American Tour: Being a Run of Ten Thousand Miles from the Atlantic to the Golden Gate, in the Autumn of 1869.* Edinburgh, 1871.

Turner, Fitzhugh. "Railroad in a Barn." *American Heritage*, vol. 10, 1958, pp. 52–57, 107–09.

Williams, Henry T. *The Pacific Tourist.* N.Y., Williams, 1879.

8. RAILROADERS WEST

The American Railway, its Construction, Development, Management, and Appliances. N.Y., Charles Scribner's Sons, 1889.

Byers, O. P. "When Railroading Outdid the Wild West Stories." *Kansas State Historical Society, Transactions*, vol. 17, 1926–28, pp. 339–48.

Chambers, William. *Things as They Are in America.* London & Edinburgh, 1854.

Cruise, John D. "Early Days on the Union Pacific." *Kansas State Historical Society, Transactions*, vol. 11, 1909–10, pp. 529–47.

"The Engineer." *The Monthly Journal*, vol. 1, no. 11, pp. 5–6.

George, Charles. *Forty Years on the Rails.* Chicago, R. R. Donnelly & Sons, 1887.

Holbrook, Stewart H. *The Story of American Railroads.* N.Y., Crown Publishers, 1947.

Husband, Joseph. *The Story of the Pullman Car.* Chicago, A. C. McClurg & Co., 1917.

Reinhardt, Richard, ed. *Workin' on the Railroad.* Palo Alto, Calif., American West Publishing Co., 1971.

Richardson, Ernest M. "Iron Horse Wrangler." *Annals of Wyoming*, vol. 31, 1959, pp. 127–37.

Robinson, Phil. *Sinners and Saints, A Tour Across the States, and Round Them.* London, 1883.

Shepherd, William. *Prairie Experiences*, N.Y., Orange Judd, 1885.

Stevenson, Robert Louis. *Across the Plains.* London, Chatto & Windus, 1892.

9. EXIT THE LAND GRABBERS, ENTER THE STOCK MANIPULATORS

Adams, Charles F., Jr. "Railroad Inflation." *North American Review*, vol. 109, 1869, pp. 130–64.

Athearn, Robert G. *Rebel of the Rockies, a History of the Denver and Rio Grande Western Railroad.* New Haven, Yale University Press, 1962.

Bowers, Claude G. *The Tragic Era.* Cambridge, Mass., Houghton Mifflin Co., 1929.

Crawford, J. B. *The Credit Mobilier of America.* Boston, C. W. Calkins Co., 1880.

Green, Philip J. "Railroad Building from 1865 to 1885." North Dakota University, *Quarterly Journal,* vol. 19, 1928–29, pp. 59–75.

Greene, Thomas L. "Railroad Stock-Watering." *Political Science Quarterly,* vol. 6, 1891, pp. 474–92.

Grodinsky, Julius. *Transcontinental Railway Strategy, 1869–1893: a Study of Businessmen.* Philadelphia, University of Pennsylvania Press, 1962.

Henry, Robert S. "The Railroad Land Grant Legend in American History Texts." *Mississippi Valley Historical Review,* vol. 32, 1945–46, pp. 171–94.

Hochschild, Harold K. *Doctor Durant and His Iron Horse.* Blue Mountain Lake, N.Y., Adirondack Museum, 1961.

Josephson, Matthew. *The Robber Barons.* N.Y., Harcourt, Brace & World, 1962.

Morris, Isaac. *Condition of the Union Pacific Railroad* (U.S. Congress, 44th, 1st sess. *House of Representatives Executive Document 180*). Washington, 1876.

The Nation, vol. XVI, January–June 1873.

New York Herald, January–February 1873.

O'Connor, Richard. *Gould's Millions.* Garden City, N.Y., Doubleday, 1962.

Storey, Brit Allan. "William Jackson Palmer, Promoter." *Colorado Magazine,* vol. 43, 1966, pp. 44–55.

Trottman, Nelson. *History of the Union Pacific, a Financial and Economic Survey.* N.Y., Ronald Press, 1923.

U.S. Pacific Railway Commission. *Reports and Testimony.* Washington, 1888.

Waters, L. L. *Steel Trails to Santa Fe.* Lawrence, University of Kansas Press, 1950.

Woodward, C. Vann. *Reunion and Reaction.* Garden City, N.Y., Doubleday Anchor Books, 1956.

10. SITTING BULL AND THE NORTHERN ROUTE

Adams, Alexander B. *Sitting Bull, an Epic of the Plains.* N.Y., G.P. Putman's Sons, 1973.

Custer, George A. "Battling with the Sioux on the Yellowstone." *Galaxy Magazine,* vol. 22, 1876, pp. 91–102.

Fairweather, Hanford. "The Northern Pacific Railroad and Some of its History." *Washington Historical Quarterly,* vol. X, 1919, pp. 95–101.

Julian, George W. "Railway Influence in the Land Office." *North American Review,* vol. 136, 1883, pp. 237–56.

Larson, Henrietta M. *Jay Cooke, Private Banker*. Cambridge, Mass., Harvard University Press, 1936.

Merington, Marguerite, ed. *The Custer Story, the Life and Intimate Letters of General George A. Custer and His Wife Elizabeth*. N.Y., Devin-Adair, 1950.

Oberholtzer, E. P. *Jay Cooke, Financier of the Civil War*. Philadelphia, Jacobs, 1907. 2 vols.

Power, James B. "Bits of History Connected with the Early Days of the Northern Pacific Railway and the Organization of Its Land Department." North Dakota State Historical Society, *Collections*, vol. 13, 1910, pp. 337–49.

Shields, L. R. "Reminiscences of a Railroad Builder." *North Dakota Historical Quarterly*, vol. 1, no. 3, 1926–27, pp. 46–59.

Smalley, Eugene V. *History of the Northern Pacific Railroad*, N.Y., G. P. Putnam's Sons, 1883.

Stanley, Major-General D. S. *Personal Memoirs*. Cambridge, Mass., Harvard University Press, 1917.

U.S. Commissioner of Indian Affairs. *Reports*. Washington, D.C., 1872, 1873.

Vestal, Stanley. *Sitting Bull, Champion of the Sioux*. Norman, University of Oklahoma Press, 1957.

Wood, Charles R. *The Northern Pacific, Main Street of the Northwest*. N.Y., Bonanza Books, 1968.

11. Elegance on the Western Rails

Brown, Dee. *The Year of the Century: 1876*. N.Y., Charles Scribner's Sons, 1966.

Brown, Joseph G. "My Recollections of Eugene Field." *Colorado Magazine*, vol. 4, 1927, pp. 46–47.

Davis, Richard Harding. *The West from a Car Window*. N.Y., Harper & Bros., 1892.

Easterwood, Thomas Jefferson. *In Pursuit of the Sun*. Dundee, Oregon, 1880.

Faithfull, Emily. *Three Visits to America*. Edinburgh, David Douglas, 1884.

Gripenberg, Alexandra. *A Half Year in the New World*, translated and edited by Ernest J. Moyne. Newark (Del.), University of Delaware Press, 1954.

Hamer, P. W. *From Ocean to Ocean*. London, 1871.

Henderson, James David. *"Meals by Fred Harvey," a Phenomenon of the American West*. Fort Worth, Texas Christian University Press, 1969.

Jackson, Helen Hunt. *Bits of Travel at Home*. Boston, Roberts Brothers, 1878.

Kipling, Rudyard. *From Sea to Sea; Letters of Travel*. N.Y., Doubleday & McClure Co., 1899.

Leslie, Mrs. Frank. *California, a Pleasure Trip from Gotham to the Golden Gate.* N.Y., 1877.

Lewis, Lloyd and Smith, Henry Justin. *Oscar Wilde Discovers America.* N.Y., Harcourt, Brace and Co., 1946.

Marshall, James. *Santa Fe, the Railroad that Built an Empire.* N.Y., Random House, 1945.

Marshall, Walter G. *Through America, or Nine Months in the United States.* London, Sampson, Low, 1881.

O'Rell, Max. *Jonathan and His Continent (Rambles Through American Society).* N.Y., Cassell & Co., 1889.

Prout, H. G. "Railroad Travel in England and America." *Scribner's Magazine,* vol. 16, 1894, pp. 399–419.

Robinson, Phil. *Sinners and Saints, a Tour Across the States and Round Them.* Boston, Roberts Brothers, 1883.

Sala, George Augustus. *America Revisited.* 2 vols. London, Vizetelly & Co., 1883.

Saunders, William. *Through the Light Continent; or, the United States in 1877–78.* London, Cassell, Petter, and Galpin, 1879.

Vivian, H. Hussey. *Notes of a Tour in America.* London, Edward Stanford, 1878.

Waters, L. L. *Steel Trails to Santa Fe.* Lawrence, University of Kansas Press, 1950.

Wilde, Oscar. "Impressions of America," in *Works,* vol. 14, N.Y., G.P. Putnam's Sons, 1915.

12. THE IMMIGRANT

American Social Science Association. *Handbook for Immigrants to the United States.* Cambridge, Mass., Riverside Press, 1871.

Bell, William A. *New Tracks in North America.* London, Chapman and Hall, 1870.

Buchanan, J. R. "The Great Railroad Migration Into Northern Nebraska." Nebraska State Historical Society, *Proceedings and Collections,* vol. 15, 1907, pp. 25–34.

Byron, G. F. "The Overland Emigrant." *Cornhill Magazine,* vol. 65, 1892, pp. 637–45.

Fulton, Robert Lardon. *Epic of the Overland.* San Francisco, A. M. Robertson, 1924.

Hardy, Lady Duffus. *Through Cities and Prairie Lands, Sketches of an American Tour.* N.Y., Worthington, 1890.

Hedges, James B. "The Colonization Work of the Northern Pacific Railroad." *Mississippi Valley Historical Review,* vol. 13, 1926–27, pp. 311–42.

———"Promotion of Immigration to the Pacific Northwest by the Railroads." *Mississippi Valley Historical Review,* vol. 15, 1928–29, pp. 183–203.

Hine, Robert V., ed. *William Andrew Spalding, Los Angeles Newspaper-man*. San Marino, Calif., Huntington Library, 1961.

Overton, Richard C. *Burlington West, a Colonization History of the Burlington Railroad*. Cambridge, Harvard University Press, 1941.

Peterson, Harold F. "Some Colonization Projects of the Northern Pacific Railroad." *Minnesota History*, vol. 10, 1929, pp. 127–44.

Stevenson, Robert Louis. *Across the Plains*. Freeport, N.Y., Books For Libraries Press, 1972.

13. TRAMPLING THE FRONTIER

Bryce, James. *The American Commonwealth*. London, Macmillan and Co., 1891. 2 vols.

Fairweather, Hanford W. "The Northern Pacific Railroad and Some of Its History." *Washington Historical Quarterly*, vol. 10, 1919, pp. 95–101.

Grodinsky, Julius. *Transcontinental Railway Strategy, 1869–1893*. Philadelphia, University of Pennsylvania Press, 1962.

Hedges, James B. *Henry Villard and the Railways of the Northwest*. New Haven, Yale University Press, 1930.

Kemble, John H. "The Transpacific Railroads, 1869–1915." *Pacific Historical Review*, vol. 18, 1949, pp. 331–43.

New York Times, November 16, 1890.

Poor, Henry V. *Manual of Railroads of the United States for 1883*. N.Y., 1883.

Pyle, Joseph G. *The Life of James J. Hill*. Gloucester, Mass., Peter Smith, 1968. 2 vols.

Russell, Charles Edward. *Stories of the Great Railroads*. Chicago, Charles H. Kerr & Co., 1914.

St. Paul Pioneer Press, September 9, 1883.

Smalley, Eugene V. *History of the Northern Pacific Railroad*. N.Y., G. P. Putnam's Sons, 1883.

Tilden, Freeman. *Following the Frontier with F. Jay Haynes*. N.Y., Knopf, 1964.

U.S. Congress, 48th, 1st sess. *House of Representatives Executive Document 11*. Washington, 1883.

U.S. Congress, 52d, 1st sess. *Senate Executive Document 32*. Washington, 1892.

Villard, Henry. *Memoirs*. Boston, Houghton Mifflin, 1904. 2 vols.

14. THE IRON HORSE ASSUMES A DEVIL IMAGE

Adams, Charles Francis. *Railroads: Their Origin and Problems*, N.Y., G. P. Putnam's Sons, 1886.

Barr, Elizabeth N. "The Populist Uprising." *A Standard History of Kansas*, edited by William E. Connelly. Chicago, 1918, vol. 2, pp. 1115–95.

BIBLIOGRAPHY303

Buck, Solon Justus. *The Granger Movement.* Cambridge, Harvard University Press, 1913.

George, Henry. "What the Railroad Will Bring Us." *Overland Monthly,* vol. 1, no. 4, October 1868.

Hall, Ridgway M., Jr. "Straightening Out the Rails." *Environment,* vol. 17, no. 6, September 1975, pp. 16–20.

Hicks, John D. *The Populist Revolt.* Minneapolis, University of Minnesota Press, 1931.

Larrabee, William. *The Railroad Question.* Chicago, 1893.

Lester, John E. *The Atlantic to the Pacific.* Boston, Shepard and Gill, 1873.

Lyon, Peter. *To Hell in a Day Coach.* Philadelphia, Lippincott, 1968.

Martin, Edward Winslow. *History of the Grange Movement.* Chicago, 1874.

Miller, George H. *Railroads and the Granger Laws.* Madison, University of Wisconsin, 1971.

Norris, Frank. *The Octopus.* Garden City, N.Y., Doubleday & Co., Inc., 1952.

Saline County (Nebraska) *Post,* December 15, 1871.

White, William Allen. *The Autobiography of William Allen White.* N.Y., Macmillan, 1946.